A Brotherhood of Liberty

AMERICA IN THE NINETEENTH CENTURY

Series editors:
Brian DeLay, Steven Hahn, Amy Dru Stanley

America in the Nineteenth Century proposes a rigorous
rethinking of this most formative period in U.S. history. Books
in the series will be wide-ranging and eclectic, with an interest
in politics at all levels, culture and capitalism, race and slavery,
law, gender, and the environment, and regional and transnational
history. The series aims to expand the scope of nineteenth-century
historiography by bringing classic questions into dialogue with
innovative perspectives, approaches, and methodologies.

A BROTHERHOOD *of* LIBERTY

Black Reconstruction and Its Legacies in Baltimore, 1865–1920

Dennis Patrick Halpin

PENN

UNIVERSITY OF PENNSYLVANIA PRESS

PHILADELPHIA

Published by
University of Pennsylvania Press
Philadelphia, Pennsylvania 19104-4112
www.upenn.edu/pennpress

Printed in the United States of America
on acid-free paper
1 3 5 7 9 10 8 6 4 2

Library of Congress Cataloging-in-Publication Data

Names: Halpin, Dennis Patrick, author.
Title: A Brotherhood of Liberty : black Reconstruction and its legacies in
    Baltimore, 1865–1920 / Dennis Patrick Halpin.
Other titles: America in the nineteenth century.
Description: 1st edition. | Philadelphia : University of Pennsylvania Press, [2019] |
    Series: America in the nineteenth century | Includes bibliographical references
    and index.
Identifiers: LCCN 2018054711 | ISBN 9780812251395 (hardcover)
Subjects: LCSH: African Americans—Civil rights—Maryland—Baltimore—
    History. | Civil rights movements—Maryland—Baltimore—History. |
    Brotherhood of Liberty. | Baltimore (Md.)—Race relations—History.
Classification: LCC E185.93.M2 H35 2019 | DDC 323.1196/07307526—dc23
LC record available at https://lccn.loc.gov/2018054711

In memory of Ward A. Stavig

CONTENTS

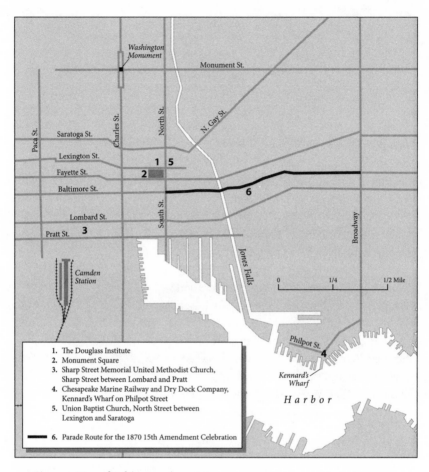

Figure 1. Map of Baltimore, circa 1870.

Introduction

In 1870 most Baltimoreans did not need reminders of how much their city had changed. Over the course of the previous decade, residents had experienced the end of slavery and witnessed the Confederacy's final days. Nonetheless, on 19 May African Americans powerfully demonstrated just how different life was going to be following Emancipation. On "one of the brightest day[s] of the season," black Baltimoreans organized an "imposing procession" to celebrate the ratification of the Fifteenth Amendment. The demonstrators marched through the heart of downtown along Baltimore Street, laying symbolic claim to the city their labor helped construct. All along the parade route, observers and participants filled city streets while women and children crowded into doors and windows to view the spectacle. In total, an estimated twenty thousand participated in and witnessed the procession. The parade included laborers, bands, community leaders, and beneficial associations. Many hoisted banners, some with blunt political messages reflecting the dawning of a new era. One marcher carried a portrait of Thaddeus Stevens, the face of Radical Republicanism, with a caption that read, "No government can be free that does not allow all its citizens to participate in the formation and the execution of her laws." A wagon transported a printing press that reproduced handbills of the Fifteenth Amendment, advertised the Freedman's Savings Bank, and promised that black Baltimoreans would cast their first ballots "for the radical ticket."[1]

Frederick Douglass, Maryland's native son, abolitionist, and a hero to many black Americans, capped the day's festivities. Douglass delivered a speech in Monument Square, in the shadow of the "Lady Baltimore" statue, which commemorated those who died defending the city in the War of 1812.[2] He began by acknowledging the tremendous changes that had transpired during his lifetime. "When we remember how slavery was interlinked with all our institutions," Douglass remarked, "it is amazing that today we witness this demonstration. When toiling on the plantation we

Figure 2. Stereoview of the 19 May 1870 Fifteenth Amendment Celebration in Baltimore. Courtesy of the Maryland Historical Society.

slaves desired to talk of emancipation," he recalled, "but there stood the overseer and a word would ensure a flogging. To talk about emancipation without being discovered we invented a vocabulary," he continued, "and when the overseer thought we were talking of the most simple thing we were really speaking of emancipation but in a way that was Greek to him." Now Douglass stood in the city of his youth, flanked by thousands of African Americans, some proudly brandishing firearms and openly discussing ways to shape the future that freedom promised. Subterfuge was no longer necessary; times had changed indeed.[3]

That afternoon, Douglass promised that African Americans would continue to strive for full equality. Blending history and prognostication, he told the crowd that African Americans first received the "cartridge box" shortly followed by the "ballot box." "Next we want the jury box," Douglass exclaimed. "While the negro hating element sits in the jury box the colored man's welfare is insecure and we demand that he be represented in the halls of justice." Douglass challenged African Americans to ensure that future generations prospered. "Educate your sons and daughters," he advised his audience. "Send them to school and show that besides the cartridge box, the ballot box and the jury box you have also the knowledge box."[4] Douglass proved to be prescient. For the next fifty years, African Americans in Baltimore and throughout the country would battle to obtain equal access to Douglass's boxes.

A Brotherhood of Liberty documents a crucial chapter in the history of the long black freedom struggle: African American activism in Baltimore in the half century following Douglass's impassioned speech at Monument Square. With the end of the Civil War, Baltimore became the epicenter of civil rights activism in the United States as black Baltimoreans built on the work of antebellum-era activists to forge the contours of their freedom. Throughout the Reconstruction era, black Baltimoreans initiated lawsuits to battle segregation, fought for labor rights, and pressured politicians to live up to the country's founding ideals. Activists pushed the city and state to offer equal access to public education, and when they refused, black Baltimoreans built their own network of schools. Barred from participating in state and local politics until the early 1870s, black Baltimoreans also built connections with African Americans outside of the state, forming some of the earliest civil rights groups in the nation.

During the 1880s, black Baltimoreans refused to allow the country to retreat from Reconstruction's promises of racial equality. Led by Rev. Harvey Johnson, a dynamic, uncompromising leader, a new group of activists sustained the fight for civil rights. This time, however, they did so with greater sophistication and organization. Johnson formed the Mutual United Brotherhood of Liberty, the first civil rights organization in Baltimore and one of the first in the country, to direct an unceasing battle against racial inequality. The organization used the courts and coordinated community protests to challenge Supreme Court decisions that hastened the advent of Jim Crow, expanded educational opportunities to black children, opened the bar to black attorneys, and defended laborers re-enslaved on a Caribbean island by a US-based company.

Although short-lived, the Brotherhood of Liberty placed Baltimore's activists at the forefront of the fight for racial equality and left behind important legacies. Locally, the men and women who participated in its campaigns blunted the impact of Baltimore's and Maryland's most egregious forms of racial discrimination. Throughout these years, hundreds, if not thousands, of black Baltimoreans supported and participated in the Brotherhood's rallies and protests. The Brotherhood, despite its name, welcomed women as participants and supporters. It engaged in coordinated acts of civil disobedience and articulated an expansive program that included labor and education rights as central components of its vision for racial equality.

Unfortunately, extant records present an incomplete picture of the Brotherhood's rank and file as well as its motivations. Although black Baltimoreans published many newspapers in the 1880s, none has survived the passage of time. White-owned newspapers reported on black activism but often did not provide names or attempt to explain how African Americans understood events in the city. The white press also filtered their perceptions of black activism through their own racism and prejudices. The surviving sources, therefore, present a limited but rich history. Newspaper articles (including coverage from the emerging black press) published tracts and books, and court transcripts demonstrate the ways that the Brotherhood pushed civil rights activism in new directions. These sources provide insights into the Brotherhood's goals, but they often only hint at the rank and file's motivations and the extent of the group's planning.

Better records exist for the Brotherhood's leadership. In addition to Harvey Johnson, the other leaders of the group became well known in activist circles. The Brotherhood trained some of the city's most important activists. Rev. William M. Alexander, one of the group's founding members, led local campaigns that defeated disfranchisement efforts in Maryland on three separate occasions in the early twentieth century. Others had an impact locally and nationally. Joseph S. Davis, one of the group's lawyers, fought for education rights and defended re-enslaved laborers on Navassa. He also used his experience with the Brotherhood to push T. Thomas Fortune's Afro-American League, one of the earliest national civil rights organizations, to pursue a legal path to combat inequality. W. Ashbie Hawkins managed numerous legal efforts to secure greater civil rights. Although largely forgotten today, he served as one of the Niagara Movement's attorneys and became one of the first to work for the National Association for the Advancement of Colored People (NAACP). Black Baltimoreans' triumphs stopped the advance of Jim Crow at Maryland's border and demonstrated to the nation the efficacy of legal challenges to racial inequality.

The accomplishments of Baltimore's activist community are even more impressive when considering the obstacles they faced. The tensions that collided in Baltimore, the largest city in the Border States, reflected the strains felt by the country following the Civil War. Located on the precipice between the North and South, Baltimore existed as an urban borderland that offered African Americans both promise and peril. Baltimore emerged from the Civil War as an industrial city with a diverse economy, a government dominated by a Democratic machine, and a rapidly expanding population. Between 1860 and 1880 the total number of Baltimore's residents grew from 212,418 to 332,313. Fueling these changes in demography were the many African Americans who migrated to the city. In 1860 Baltimore's black population stood at 27,898, but by 1880 it had nearly doubled to 53,715, making the city home to the second-largest black population in the country, trailing only New Orleans.[5]

While Baltimore seemed northern in some respects, it also exhibited marked southern traits. Baltimore was a place that had exploited slave labor until Emancipation. The city's slave population was small by the 1860s, accounting for approximately 1 percent of its total population, but the institution's legal status exerted a disproportionate influence. For Alfred J. Pairpoint, a Londoner who visited the United States in the mid-1850s, arriving in Baltimore from Boston made him feel as if he had been "transported to some unknown land." "In fact," Pairpoint remarked, "there is a very great contrast between this city and New York, Boston, and other towns in the Northern States, where the heavy labour is chiefly performed by the Irish." Not surprisingly, many residents and government officials held strong sympathies with the Confederacy, which continued to influence politics well after the Civil War ended.[6]

The collision of these circumstances in the borderland pushes us to reconsider the stories that focus on Reconstruction's rise and fall in the Deep South.[7] It is tempting to envision the Border States as the moderate middle ground between the Union and the Confederacy. The reality, however, was that many of the divisions and political conflicts tearing apart the United States existed in concentrated form in the Border States. Because the Border States had not seceded, the federal government did not oversee Reconstruction in Maryland, Missouri, Kentucky, and Delaware as it did in the former Confederacy.[8]

Without the presence of federal troops, African Americans were even more vulnerable to the depredation of southern redeemers intent on limiting the prospects of racial equality. This discrepancy of circumstance was not lost on contemporaries who felt that conditions in the Border States were worse than in the former Confederacy. A reporter for the *Christian Recorder,* an African American newspaper published in Philadelphia, observed in 1866 that "it is now, as it was during the war—the Border States are a hindrance. . . . South Carolina is, today, ahead of Maryland, as she has repealed her black laws; but Maryland has not yet done so."[9] These tensions persisted in the Border States throughout the Reconstruction era. On the eve of the Fifteenth Amendment's ratification in 1870, the *New York Times* reported that "in no part of the Union has society been more convulsed, or has it taken longer for the turbulent elements to become tranquil. As they were the main campaigning grounds in war," the *Times* continued, "so in peace the political cauldron has in them seethed with greatest fury."[10]

In Maryland, Reconstruction faltered years before the federal government abandoned it. The lack of federal oversight allowed Confederate sympathizers in Maryland to effectively end any attempts at Reconstruction less than two years after the Confederacy's defeat. The state's white political leaders engaged in a protracted struggle that culminated in 1866 when Democrats seized power through a bloodless coup. With little opposition remaining, Democrats essentially returned Maryland to its prewar status quo, with the notable exception that all African Americans were free.[11] Unlike states farther south, Maryland did not experience an extended period of Republican rule, nor did black Marylanders obtain political office immediately following the Civil War. Hugh Lennox Bond, a judge and Radical Republican from Baltimore, lamented at the time that "in Maryland [African Americans'] only safeguard is the sense of justice and of religious obligation of the people."[12] This proved to be an insufficient defense. Maryland's political leaders refused to enfranchise black men and did not ratify the Thirteenth, Fourteenth, and Fifteenth Amendments to the Constitution.

At the turn of the twentieth century, Princeton historian William Starr Myers contended that Maryland "Self-Reconstructed." For Myers, Maryland's immediate post–Civil War years were a triumphant story of southern redemption that arrived years before other areas of the South violently overthrew Reconstruction. His account largely excluded African Americans, who only appeared as problems that white Marylanders needed to solve. His erasure of African Americans, while typical of histories written in the period, still lingers in our collective amnesia of black Baltimoreans' struggle for equality.[13]

In many respects, the lack of federal oversight limited the possibilities open to black Baltimoreans. Without the benefit of federal protection, black Baltimoreans forged their own future in a politically turbulent state as hostile to civil rights as those in the Deep South. Nevertheless, African Americans fought prolonged battles with the state to fashion a black self-reconstruction of Maryland that sought to obtain the boxes Douglass outlined in his speech celebrating the Fifteenth Amendment. Their efforts shaped Maryland's post–Civil War society in profound ways. Black Baltimoreans chipped away at the state's remaining black laws and fought segregation. They organized themselves, created strategies, and implemented them piece by piece. In many cases, this occurred at the same historical moment when national leaders, including T. Thomas Fortune, Booker T. Washington, and W. E. B. DuBois, were formulating their own strategies to fight racial inequality. This was not the much-discussed "nadir" or "Age of Accommodation" for African Americans in Baltimore. Instead, it was a period of intense and protracted activism. The work that black Baltimoreans accomplished inspired national African American civil rights organizations including the Afro-American League, the Niagara Movement, and the NAACP, which were founded on the heels and the blueprints of black Baltimoreans' successes.

Chapter 1 examines how black Baltimoreans created their own "self-reconstruction" of Maryland in the face of racial oppression. Black Baltimoreans were determined to protect themselves and secure their newly promised rights. With the political process still closed to them, they built on the protest tradition of African Americans in the antebellum era but refashioned these tactics to fit Maryland's post-Emancipation reality. Black Baltimoreans used changes in federal law to challenge the state's black codes in courts, expanded the network of community schools established during the antebellum era, and organized labor unions. Others built community-based businesses, such as the Chesapeake Marine Railway and Dry Dock Company, a black-owned shipyard that ensured African Americans could obtain employment in a racially stratified market. African American activists also looked beyond state lines to shape their freedom. They helped organize groups such as the Border States Convention, one of the first post-Emancipation black political meetings, which drew together representatives from various states to appeal to the federal government for support.

Activists left a legacy that subsequent generations used as a foundation to continue the push for racial equality. Chapters 2 and 3 analyze the intense debates conducted by black Baltimoreans over the direction of civil rights initiatives in the 1880s and early 1890s. This period is crucial in the history of African American reform movements as communities across the United States clashed over the scope, direction, and strategies for addressing racial inequalities following Reconstruction's formal demise in 1877.[14] In Baltimore, these heated debates precipitated a leadership shift that had profound repercussions in the city for the next forty years. By 1885, a younger generation wrested control from community leaders who had come to prominence at the end of the Civil War. This ascendant group of activists was the Mutual United Brotherhood of Liberty. A forerunner to the Niagara Movement and the NAACP, the Brotherhood pursued equality through the courts, broadened the city's activist community, and included women in the fight against racial injustice and inequality.

While activists scored impressive victories over racial injustice, the early successes of the black freedom struggle in Baltimore hit substantial road-blocks by the mid-1890s. Scholars have documented how formal Jim Crow restrictions fit comfortably into progressive ideas that viewed interracial contact as dangerous.[15] They have paid comparatively less attention to how Progressive Era concerns with public order and political corruption changed understandings of race in the late nineteenth and early twentieth centuries. In Baltimore, efforts to instill public order and end political cor-ruption, touted as progressive reforms, paved the way for institutionalizing racism in policing, government, and real estate.

The advent of the racialized carceral state became the lynchpin of Pro-gressive Era segregation that restructured race relations both north and south of the Mason-Dixon Line long into the twentieth century. In the late nineteenth century, segregationists across the United States connected concerns over crime, political corruption, and public order with race to criminalize African Americans. Citizens, politicians, justices, and the press called for the systematic surveillance and arrest of African Americans. As a result, African Americans congregating on the streets, in leisure spaces, and on public transportation came under intensive scrutiny. Interacting with whites (especially white women) posed an increased possibility of police harassment, arrest, and imprisonment.[16] The rhetorical linkage of race and criminality became so widely disseminated by the 1910s that segregationists no longer had to explicitly draw these connections.

The triumph of these ideas in the public's imagination changed the trajectory of the black freedom struggle in Baltimore. The book's fourth chapter analyzes the public debates between African Americans and segre-gationists over the issue of crime, a turning point in the history of race relations in the city. Beginning in the mid-1890s, police, citizens, politicians, magistrates, and the press blamed African Americans for rising crime rates in the city. By connecting race and crime, segregationists discredited Afri-can Americans as citizens, restricted their mobility, left them vulnerable to police harassment, and subjected them to longer prison sentences. Politicians across the state used the fear of "negro disorder" and "rowdyism" to change the course of politics in Maryland. In 1899 Democrats cited the alleged increase in black criminality in their campaign to reclaim power in Maryland during the waning years of the nineteenth century. Their campaign to make Baltimore a "white man's city" traded in stock images of African American criminals who threatened public order and benefited from political favors. This strategy paid dividends as Democrats connected race, crime, and political corruption to regain power across the state. Once in office, they wasted little time inaugurating the Jim Crow era in the Old Line State. African American activists fought these characterizations throughout the period. Although they had ample evidence to contradict these specious claims, black Baltimoreans could not match the exposure that the city's white press and politicians provided segregationists.

The book's final chapters analyze two of the immediate fallouts of Baltimore's Democratic redemption and the widespread public acceptance of connections between race and crime. Chapter 5 examines African Americans' fight to defeat multiple disfranchisement efforts in the early twentieth century, which Democrats attempted to sell as a corrective to rising crime rates and political malfeasance. Using a combination of political agitation, educational initiatives, boycotts, and voter registration drives, black Baltimoreans led a statewide effort to retain the franchise. In doing so, African Americans across the state became part of a coalition, including immigrants, Republicans, and disaffected Democrats, who defeated racially based voting restrictions in 1904, 1909, and 1911.

The book's concluding chapter analyzes African Americans' struggle against Baltimore's segregation ordinances, the first attempt to legalize residential segregation in the United States. The chapter focuses on the streets of Baltimore's racial frontiers and the black-led courtroom challenges to the law. The movement to impose residential segregation was both promulgated and opposed at the grass roots. An examination of street-level battles in Baltimore illuminates the violence and racism that were central to the push for legalized segregation. It also reveals a fuller picture of black resistance in the period. Black Baltimoreans contested segregation by continuously defying the law and moving into blocks that the city categorized as "white." Others built on the legacy of black reformers in the 1880s and 1890s. Activists, led by W. Ashbie Hawkins, successfully challenged the legislation on multiple occasions in the nation's courts, before the Supreme Court ultimately ruled residential segregation unconstitutional.

While this book focuses on African American activism, it also reveals important insights into the resilience of white supremacy and segregation, as well as its connection to reform initiatives. As recent scholars have illustrated, Jim Crow was in constant flux due to African American activism and resistance. Throughout the late nineteenth and twentieth centuries, segregationists constantly shifted strategies to counter black claims of equality. Maryland segregationists repeatedly resorted to undemocratic measures to curtail African Americans' ability to vote and challenge laws in the courts. Segregationists used Progressive Era concerns with crime and order to connect African Americans with political corruption. Politicians passed laws that limited black Baltimoreans' ability to move and live in sections of the city without risking violence and police harassment. As the case of Baltimore demonstrates, Jim Crow's power did not reside solely in its ability to codify racial separation or restrict the franchise. Each effort to institute Jim Crow—whether through voting restrictions or housing segregation—taught residents lessons about race and validated racial fears. Even with a strong, active, and successful community of civil rights activists, Baltimore became a city wracked by racial violence, marked by segregation, and burdened with an inequitable criminal justice system.

While scholars have found much to celebrate in the Progressive Era's push to democratize the country, segregationists used some of their concerns toward undemocratic ends. If we are to celebrate the Progressive Era's democratic initiatives, we must include the voices of African Americans. Despite considerable perils, Baltimore's black community battled on the front lines to define Reconstruction's legacy and achieve full racial equality during a profoundly dangerous period. Their efforts not only saved their own rights but also preserved democracy for all Marylanders. *A Brotherhood of Liberty* demonstrates that what was radical about the decades following the Civil War was not the white middle-class reform agenda but rather the audacity of African American activists.

CHAPTER 1

African Americans' Struggle to Define
Freedom on the Border

On 29 September 1865, Baltimoreans gathered at the old Newton University building amid much fanfare and celebration. The night marked a notable achievement. Just over four months after the Civil War ended, and less than a year after Maryland abolished slavery, a group of thirty to forty African Americans pooled their money to purchase the building for $16,000. The new owners spent an additional $5,000 to transform the structure into a multipurpose community center, which they named the Douglass Institute in honor of Frederick Douglass. The building's new owners hoped that the institute would serve as the preeminent center of black political, social, and educational activities. Located on Lexington Avenue in the heart of the city's downtown, the renovated building, according to the *Baltimore Sun*, had a "fine hall for lectures or exhibitions, a library, musical department, school rooms, &c."[1]

Approximately eight hundred Baltimoreans (including two hundred white residents) attended the Douglass Institute's dedication to hear its namesake deliver the keynote address. "The establishment of an Institute bearing my name by the colored people in the city of my boyhood, so soon after the act of emancipation in this state," Douglass remarked, "looms before me as a first grand indication of progress." Douglass recognized the importance and potential of the space. "Here we can assemble," he proudly proclaimed, "and have our minds enlightened upon the whole circle of social, moral, political and education duties." But the building's value, as Douglass recognized, extended beyond its physical presence. It held symbolic importance. "The building," Douglass observed, "is an indication of the rise of a people long oppressed, enslaved and bound in the chains of ignorance, to a freer and higher plane of life, manhood, usefulness and civilization." Even the institute's name was emblematic of a new era. Douglass's life story represented the journey from slavery to freedom, a road down which many black Baltimoreans were now traveling. His achievements signified the new possibilities open to black Americans in the realms of education, politics, and society as the nation rebuilt itself following the Civil War.[2]

The founding of the Douglass Institute came at an important moment. In 1865 African Americans living in a free Baltimore saw tremendous opportunity and encountered great uncertainty. Black Baltimoreans sought to define their newly gained freedom by transforming struggles that reached back generations to fit the new realities of life following Emancipation. They organized labor unions, defied segregation, and challenged discriminatory laws in the city's courtrooms. They played vital roles in establishing a statewide public education system for African American students. They also helped organize, and participated in, some of the first post-Emancipation civil rights meetings. Their resolve and dedication created, in the words of historian Charles M. Payne, an "organizing tradition" that made Baltimore the epicenter for movements that challenged Jim Crow as it emerged in response to black claims of equality in the late nineteenth century.[3]

Maryland's antebellum era cast a long shadow over the rest of the nineteenth century. At the beginning of the century, free blacks looked to Baltimore as a sanctuary. Even though it was a slave city in a slave state, Baltimore offered comparatively relaxed race relations and a large black community. In the 1830s, however, the tenor of race relations began to change in marked ways. As slavery's importance declined in Maryland, Baltimore became home to the largest population of free blacks residing in a slave state. Slaveholders viewed this population as a threat. At the same moment, Irish and German immigration swelled Baltimore's population. These recent arrivals competed with African Americans for jobs during a period when the city's economy was particularly turbulent. Racial antagonism grew as Marylanders resorted to a number of schemes to maintain white supremacy, including colonization, violence, and an effort in the late 1850s to re-enslave African Americans.[4]

Black Baltimoreans did not allow rising racial hostility to go unchallenged and fought restrictions on their freedoms with increasing sophistication. In the antebellum era, black Baltimoreans targeted the institution of slavery as well as colonization schemes. Ministers condemned slavery from the pulpit and rallied community support. In response to slavers kidnapping black city residents and selling them into slavery, African Americans organized neighborhood watch patrols. Teacher and activist William Watkins became the leading voice against colonization. Throughout the 1830s, Watkins—assuming the pen name "A Colored Baltimorean"—wrote a series of letters to William Lloyd Garrison's *Liberator*. In one letter, he denounced the Maryland State Colonization Society's plan as a "cruel alternative" and "pseudo-philanthropy." These protests continued into the 1850s when, for instance, African Americans gathered to voice their ardent opposition at an 1852 colonization convention in Baltimore called by a group of black community leaders.[5]

Black Baltimoreans also built a long tradition of fighting for educational rights during the antebellum era. Prior to 1826, Baltimore did not operate public schools. When it did open its first public schools in the late 1820s, it barred black students from attending. Nevertheless, the city taxed white and black residents to fund the schools. Beginning in the 1830s, black Baltimoreans demanded the city reform its public education system. Initially, black residents petitioned the city to exempt them from the tax before expanding their demands. On at least two other occasions, black Baltimoreans petitioned Baltimore's government to fund African American schools. In the 1850s, they once again pushed the city to open public education to black students. Their efforts ultimately failed to move the recalcitrant city and state governments before the Civil War, but African Americans would continue to fight for educational rights.[6]

Unable to attend public schools, African Americans provided for their own education. Black Baltimoreans (at times with the help of white individuals or philanthropic institutions) had operated several schools or sent their children to private instructors. In the early nineteenth century, a group of black Methodists established a church and school on Sharp Street. Activist and community leader Daniel Coker ran the school that came to be known as the African Academy. As an adolescent, Coker fled to New York to escape his enslavement before returning to the state of his birth. Throughout its existence, the African Academy provided black Baltimoreans an opportunity to educate their children. By the early 1820s, it boasted an enrollment of 150 students, including some who traveled from Washington, DC, to attend.[7]

Following in the footsteps of the African Academy, black churches across the city began to offer classes. Saint James Episcopal Church, Waters

AME, and the Saratoga Street Church all operated schools. Rev. W. Livingston conducted a school in his church on Saratoga and North Streets. The Oblate Sisters of Providence, an order of black nuns who had migrated from San Domingo in the 1820s, ran a school for African American girls that boasted an enrollment of 150 students prior to the Civil War. Other individuals augmented these efforts. William Watkins administered one of the city's longest-running schools. In his youth, Watkins attended Coker's school. In 1819 Coker accepted the American Colonization Society's invitation to move to Liberia, and Watkins assumed his position. For the next twenty-five years, Watkins, his wife, and his son operated what came to be known as the Watkins Academy. Finally, African Methodist Episcopal (AME) minster Daniel Payne conducted classes from Bethel Church.[8]

By the end of the antebellum era, black Baltimoreans operated and maintained approximately fifteen schools. Many employed black teachers who worked diligently to overcome a lack of resources and white indifference. African Americans valued this loose network of institutions and charitable initiatives. Free blacks needed an education to help them navigate the antebellum job market where basic literacy proved a valuable commodity. Antebellum schools nurtured a sense of racial pride and promoted abolitionism. In addition, they established a culture that valued education. Youth literacy rates in the city attested to the success of these endeavors. At the start of the Civil War, nearly 70 percent of black Baltimoreans between the ages of thirteen and twenty-nine possessed some degree of literacy, a feat made all the more remarkable by the complete lack of state support.[9]

African Americans also sustained a tradition of organizing to protect their employment options and status. Unlike Charleston and New Orleans, free black Baltimoreans were largely excluded from skilled or semiskilled occupations. Ship caulking proved to be one notable exception. Throughout the early nineteenth century, African Americans dominated the ship-caulking trade and accumulated a remarkable amount of power over their working lives. In 1838 black caulkers formed a Caulkers' Association, a union that provided benefits and served as a literary society. Through the Caulkers' Association, workers collectively bargained and exercised control over their working conditions throughout the 1830s and 1840s.[10] In the next decade, Baltimore's waterfront labor market underwent important shifts. As the city's African American population declined, European immigration, especially from Germany and Ireland, accelerated. In 1850 the foreign-born population of Baltimore stood at 35,492. Ten years later it had grown to

52,497 residents. Many of these immigrants sought employment as caulkers, often working at lower rates than their black counterparts.[11]

As more immigrants arrived, job competition and racial tensions intensified. Beginning in 1858, white workers rioted against their black counterparts across Baltimore's workplaces. In May, white workers attacked African Americans at a Federal Hill brickyard. The next month, the violence spilled onto the waterfront. Over a two-year period, white laborers periodically assaulted black workers in an effort to force them off the job. White attacks on African American caulkers struck at the heart of black organization, employment, and status. The occupation was a point of pride for African Americans, a source of decent income, and one of the few semi-skilled trades where they could find employment. The occupation also held historical resonance for black Baltimoreans: Frederick Douglass had worked as a caulker.[12]

African Americans reacted to white violence in numerous ways. The *Baltimore Sun* reported that some African Americans left the city, but others continued to organize for mutual protection. White workers complained that black caulkers zealously guarded their employment. One white worker contended, "When the proprietor of any yard employed a white Caulker the negroes would not work for that employer till he discharged the white man." Despite the violence and recriminations, black Baltimoreans maintained a strong presence in the shipyards during the war years. The years of racial strife, however, left the city's docks and labor organizations segregated along racial lines.[13]

In the late 1850s, black Baltimoreans put the organizational experience they had gained over the previous decades to good use when they rallied against the Jacobs Bill. Passed in 1859, the Jacobs Bill sought to prohibit manumissions and re-enslave free blacks in Maryland. In response, African Americans gathered signatures to petition the state, held protest meetings, and formed organizations to fight the bill. Their efforts paid off as public opinion turned against the measure and the state legislature passed two compromise bills in its stead. Voters across the state later rejected these measures by an overwhelming margin.[14]

During the Civil War years, black Baltimoreans continued to organize. As the loyalist Union Party hammered out the details of a new state constitution in 1864, African Americans conducted meetings to draw attention to issues of unequal pay and treatment accorded to black soldiers. When racial tensions flared up along the waterfront shortly after the state abolished slavery, black labor organizations wrote to the *Baltimore American* to complain about the "indefinable apprehension of an antagonism on the part of the white working men." Then at the end of 1865, black Baltimoreans demanded a voice in the state's affairs by convening a multiday "State Convention of Colored Men" at the Douglass Institute. In addition to agitating for the franchise, the group demanded that black teachers teach in African American schools, that the state end discriminatory apprenticeship laws that extended the life of slavery, and that the government protect laborers regardless of race. Attendees also authored an address to the "colored people of Maryland," which advised African Americans to focus on becoming self-supporting, "virtuous," and "industrious." These guidelines, the group explained, were political. "We advise you to use every exertion to contradict the predictions of your enemies," the writers proclaimed, "which were uttered previous to the emancipation of the State—that if the slaves were freed they would become a pest to society, and paupers dependent on public charities."[15]

With the end of the Civil War, the city would experience even more change. Following the South's surrender, former slaves in the Virginia and Maryland countryside streamed into Baltimore, already the largest city in the Border States. During the 1860s, Baltimore's African American population grew approximately 40 percent, from 27,898 to 39,558. During the next decade, it reached 53,716.[16] Together, black Baltimoreans—longtime residents and new arrivals, recently emancipated and those who spent their lives free—would define the contours of their own freedom. They would do so, however, in an increasingly volatile and inhospitable political context, at both the state and national levels.

In 1865 Maryland's fragile post–Civil War society already hung in the balance just months after hostilities ended. The schisms in the Union Party between its radical and conservative wings became more pronounced against the backdrop of national debates over Reconstruction policy. The Unconditional Unionists supported Radical Republicans' efforts to pass the Fourteenth Amendment while conservatives backed President Andrew Johnson's more lenient version of Reconstruction. As the relationship between Johnson and Congress unraveled on the national stage, Conservative Unionists increasingly allied with Democrats in Maryland.[17]

Throughout 1865, the Union Party teetered on the brink of collapse. Local political machinations hastened their demise. The party's tenuous grasp on power rested on Maryland's enforcement of the registry law and loyalty oath that barred many ex-Confederates from voting. Following the war, Democrats campaigned to end these laws that stymied their chances for electoral success in the state. They found their solution in Thomas Swann, Maryland's former Know-Nothing mayor and current Conservative Union governor. Swann, whom the *Chicago Tribune* described as a "shrewd, tricky and ambitious politician," coveted a seat in the US Senate. Democrats offered him a deal. In exchange for the Senate seat he desired, Swann abolished the registry law and loyalty oath, paving the way for the restoration of full white male suffrage ahead of the 1866 election.[18]

In Baltimore, citizens stood at the center of a political maelstrom. The *Philadelphia Press* reported, "For Maryland to fall into the hands of what are denominated 'Conservatives,' would be in fact to put the Government of the State into the hands of the enemies of both the State and the United States." The *Chicago Tribune* stated that some observers feared the outbreak of a new civil war.[19] The direst predictions failed to materialize, but Democrats' ascendancy marked the demise of the Union Party. It also foreclosed the possibility of the state administering anything approximating federal Reconstruction.[20]

At the same moment when Radical Reconstruction became the law of the land in the former Confederacy, black Baltimoreans faced an uncertain future in a city careening back toward its antebellum past.[21] Although some Marylanders implored the federal government to intervene, their appeals fell on deaf ears. Congress and the courts were content to let white Marylanders figure out the state's postwar future with minimal interference.[22] Black Baltimoreans had different ideas. By the mid-1860s, they had built an activist community and had gained experience fighting for equality that they would put to use in the years to come.

Although Democrats quickly regained power in the state, they could not stop developments at the national level. In particular, the passage of the Civil Rights Act of 1866 gave African Americans a valuable tool to begin a new era of political and social protest in Maryland. One of the legislation's chief benefits was that it opened a pathway for activists to challenge prejudicial laws in the courts by guaranteeing "full and equal benefit of all laws and proceedings for the security of person and property" regardless of race.[23]

Black Marylanders first targeted restrictions on their mobility, an issue that had deep roots in the slave past. In the decades prior to the Civil War, free African Americans envisioned unfettered mobility as essential to their claims of citizenship. Across the country, they made steamboats, trains, stagecoaches, and ocean liners contested terrain. Segregationists, who denied that African Americans could make any such assertion, restricted the mobility of people of color in numerous ways, including through the issuance of passes and free papers. By the 1830s and 1840s, restrictions on black mobility extended to public conveyances where operators barred African Americans from first-class accommodations or segregated them in Jim Crow cars.[24]

In Maryland, railroad officials continued to enforce segregation after the Civil War. Just a month after the Civil Rights Act became law, black Baltimoreans sought to use it to expand their rights and better define their freedom. In May 1866 two teachers, Mary J. C. Anderson and Ellen G. Jackson, opened a new chapter in the fight for respect and equality on mass transportation in postwar Baltimore. The women claimed that Adam Smyzer (an employee for the Philadelphia, Wilmington, and Baltimore Railroad Company) "forcibly" removed them from a "white ladies' parlor" in Baltimore's President Street rail station. The women, according to the *Baltimore Sun*, pursued the case "mainly for the purpose of testing whether, under the late act of Congress known as the 'civil rights bill,' colored persons are entitled to the same privileges of travel and accommodation on railroad routes as white persons." Although their original intent is not reflected in the historic record, it is clear that once arrested, Anderson and Jackson recognized the legal opportunity opened by the Civil Rights Acts of 1866. Smyzer requested a jury trial and thereafter the case disappeared from the local newspapers. Most likely, Anderson and Jackson realized that they stood little chance of winning their case before an all-white jury.[25]

Anderson and Jackson were not alone in pressing such charges or testing the efficacy of the new law. African American attorney Aaron A. Bradley orchestrated two additional challenges that same month. A former slave who had self-emancipated and fled north before the Civil War, Bradley spent time in Boston, a hotbed of abolition, before returning south to challenge racial inequalities.[26] In May 1866 Bradley filed two suits challenging segregation. He filed the first suit in Maryland's state court after an employee for the Baltimore and Ohio Railroad (B&O) expelled him for violating a segregation ordinance. The same day, Bradley filed a second suit in a separate matter. This time he represented Baltimoreans Mary G. Hutt (a teacher) and Jas. H. Davis (a shoemaker), who sought an injunction in the US District Court against Baltimore's City Passenger Railway Company.[27]

These initial challenges ended in disappointment. In the first suit, the B&O countered that their treatment of Bradley on account of his race was no different than barring a man from entering a "ladies' car." This was a common legal justification in the nineteenth century. During the period between 1865 and 1890, the regulations governing common carriers—trains, steamboats, streetcars, and so on—were in flux. Prior to Jim Crow, carriers governed themselves by using a set of common laws to ostensibly protect the sanctity of respectable white women. Toward this end, carriers segregated passengers by sex and class as early as the 1830s, a practice that formed the legal analog for racial segregation in the post-Emancipation United States. Although carriers could not refuse admittance to someone based on race, the courts gave them wide latitude to institute common-law regulations to segregate passengers as long as they were "reasonable," consistently enforced, and known. The judge in this case apparently found that the B&O met these benchmarks. According to the *Baltimore Sun,* he rendered a *non pros* judgment because "there was no cause of action."[28] The US District Court dismissed Bradley's second suit on a technicality. The plaintiffs had violated a city ordinance that prohibited African Americans from riding in a car's interior. Bradley filed his suit in US District Court, but since the plaintiffs were city residents, the Baltimore Criminal Court held jurisdiction. Undeterred, Bradley (as a resident of Massachusetts) amended his petition, named himself as the plaintiff, and claimed that railway employees "committed the crime of assault and battery" by "dragging him out of his seat in said city passenger railway car." The judge hearing this case ruled that Bradley should seek remedy before a jury, and the attorney declined to pursue the case further.[29]

African Americans continued to challenge segregation following these initial cases. In July 1866 Annie A. Jakes pursued assault charges against conductor Francis Lawn after he ejected her from a city passenger car. Annie Jakes was the wife of Henry Jakes, a "well-known colored barber and waiter of this city" who had been involved with the abolitionist movement. Building from an antebellum engagement with politics, Annie Jakes used her plight as a test case. She employed the services of Archibald Stirling, Jr., a prominent lawyer and Republican Party supporter. In the coming years, Stirling would serve as counsel in other civil rights cases. According to the *Baltimore Sun,* he intended to use the Jakes case to "contest before the court and jury the right of colored persons to all the privileges of travel on the city passenger railway." After Lawn requested a jury trial, however, the papers stopped reporting on the suit.[30]

Even though African Americans did not win these early challenges, black Baltimoreans continued to seek redress because others had found success in civil rights suits across Maryland. Black Marylanders used the 1866 Civil Rights Act to overturn a law that prohibited them from testifying against whites in court.[31] African Americans also successfully petitioned courts to end the odious practice of "involuntary apprenticeship." Following Emancipation, white landowners forced black children into indefinite "apprenticeships" that extended the life of slavery beyond 1864 in a system that mirrored the antebellum era's gradual abolition in states such as New Jersey.[32] In 1867 the Freedmen's Bureau's Henry S. Stockbridge, who played a leading role in pushing Maryland to abolish slavery a few years earlier, represented Elizabeth Turner in US District Court. Just two days after the state abolished slavery, Turner's mother bound her underage daughter to their former master, Philemon T. Hamilton. Under state law, Hamilton was not required to educate his black apprentices, a right that was guaranteed to white apprentices. Stockbridge filed a petition that argued that the system of involuntary apprenticeship violated the US Constitution since it had differing requirements for black and white apprentices. The Supreme Court's chief justice, Salmon P. Chase, who presided over the case, concurred.[33] Despite their frustrations with the initial public transportation rulings, African Americans surely realized that the courts were siding with them on civil rights issues.

Conditions on the city's passenger rails remained contentious throughout the 1860s. On October 30, 1869, the Baltimore Passenger Railway ousted Andrew Thompson, who was visiting from New York. Thompson hired lawyers Archibald Stirling, Jr., and George C. Maund and filed suit. The railway cited the 1859 city ordinance that permitted segregation. Judge William Fells Giles, a Quaker who had opposed slavery prior to the Civil War, dismissed this justification. He noted that it was a relic of slavery and no longer held relevance. Yet Giles objected to the accommodations being unequal, not to segregation itself, and the rest of his ruling tempered Thompson's initial victory.[34] To comply with Giles's ruling, the Baltimore Passenger Railway designated separate, but ostensibly equal, cars for African Americans.

Black Baltimoreans immediately challenged Giles's ruling. On the first day of operations, two black males pushed their way ahead of a group of white women, after which one of the men (identified only as Gillard) blocked the women's entrance. The conductor demanded that the men move to the front platform, where African Americans could still ride even if the car was designated for "whites only." Gillard initially resisted before acquiescing, threatening to sue the railway as he exited. Then in July, a stevedore named William Weaver attempted to sue the City Passenger Railway Company after he was thrown off a whites-only car. The *Baltimore Sun* reported that Weaver employed the services of Henry S. Stockbridge with the intention of challenging segregation.[35]

All of these challenges served as a prelude to John W. Fields's legal challenge. In early 1871, Fields boarded a railway car on the South Baltimore line. When the conductor noticed that Fields was black, he ordered him to move to the "front platform" of the car. Fields refused and the conductor threw him from the vehicle.[36] Fields filed suit in the US Circuit Court, appearing before judges Hugh Lennox Bond and Giles. Judge Bond, an outspoken opponent of slavery and a Republican, made certain that the verdict in the Fields case would settle the question of whether the railway could segregate passengers by race. While Judge Giles reaffirmed the concept of "separate but equal" in the Thompson case a year earlier, Bond instructed the jury to only consider if Fields was denied service because of his color. The jury sided with Fields. The case served as the culmination of protest and legal challenges around the issue of equal access and mobility stretching back at least a half decade in Baltimore and longer in other parts of the United States. The next morning, employees of the City Passenger Railway removed the signs that mandated racial separation.[37]

When Congress passed the Civil Rights Act of 1866, the *Baltimore Sun* assured its white readership that "the bill does not execute itself." Although the paper contended that the bill "demand[s] the active agency of the executive department, and the sanction of judicial authority," in actuality it was black Baltimoreans who used the law to shape Baltimore's post-Emancipation society. Even though Democrats quickly closed the political process to black Marylanders, African Americans found in federal legislation the means to directly challenge inequality. Black men and women violated segregation ordinances, challenged the laws in court, and refused to accept compromises. After five years of protest, African Americans used the Civil Rights Act of 1866 to defeat segregation in the courts. Black Marylanders similarly used the law to gain the right to testify against whites in court and end the system of involuntary apprenticeships. The use of the courts and direct protest pushed black Baltimoreans' activism in new directions. It also proved to have a lasting impact. In the years that followed, African

Americans would continue to use the judicial system to expand their freedom and attack inequalities.

Even though the judicial system offered black Baltimoreans tangible gains,
the city became progressively more segregated during the 1860s. Nowhere
was this more evident than on the waterfront, where the struggles of the
antebellum era assumed new urgency following Emancipation. On 25 September 1865 white caulkers marched to Henderson's Wharf demanding that
African Americans quit their jobs. White carpenters and other maritime
workers joined in solidarity, refusing to work until black caulkers were
"driven off." By the end of the week, the white Journeymen Carpenters'
Association of East Baltimore locked out the docks, threatening to fine
offenders twenty dollars if they disobeyed the edict.[38] Black caulkers recognized that race was the central issue in the strike. In a letter published in
the *Baltimore Sun*, the caulkers wrote, "And now, whilst quietly and diligently trying to make an honest livelihood—having the good will of our
employers—an inhuman and unjust cry is raised: Away with negro caulkers! Extermination! Annihilation!—and for what? Because God chose to
make our skins dark."[39]

    Initially, Baltimore's shipbuilders resisted white working-class appeals
to racial solidarity. Shortly after the strike commenced, seven shipbuilders
agreed to cease operating until the white caulkers returned to work and
abandoned their lockout. In response, white workers escalated their challenge. The Association of Journeymen Shipwrights leased a shipyard in the
nearby neighborhood of Canton to employ white workers. The move
directly challenged recalcitrant employers whose yards remained idle due
to the lockout. The gambit worked. A mere three days later, employers
agreed to gradually hire white workers and only hire African Americans "as
needed." Black Baltimoreans had lost a major battle. They continued to
work in reduced numbers until November, when they walked off the job
en masse never to regain their positions.[40] The caulkers' strike was just one
of many setbacks for black workers on the city's docks. White workers also
assaulted black stevedores and oyster shuckers on two separate instances in
1865 before threatening a general strike against black laborers. By the end
of 1866, nearly a thousand black workers (including two to three hundred
caulkers) lost their jobs.[41]

    The racial strife and increasingly segregated job market that plagued
Baltimore must have hit Isaac Myers, a pioneering black labor organizer

and civil rights activist, particularly hard. Born in Baltimore in 1835, Myers spent the early part of his adulthood working as a caulker before gaining employment with a grocer during the Civil War. In 1865 Myers returned to the waterfront, working as a caulker in the months before white workers forced African Americans from the job. Throughout his life, Myers witnessed firsthand the racial hostilities that bred violence and constricted job opportunities for African Americans. The racism that Myers experienced, however, could not shake his faith that the path to racial equality laid within unionization, self-improvement, and the Republican Party.[42]

Myers and other community leaders were determined to mitigate the effects of the caulkers' strike and the racially constricted job market. In 1866 a group of black Baltimoreans banded together to fund a cooperative shipyard. The group of fifteen included some of Baltimore's most prominent and successful black businessmen, including Myers; George A. Hackett, who operated a livery stable; and John H. Smith, who worked as a hack operator. In one of their initial advertisements, the founders noted that they hoped to "establish Mechanical and other branches of business, to give employment to colored men throughout the state." The group initially raised $40,000, and African American churches pitched in another $10,000. When they began to search for a shipyard, white owners refused to deal with African Americans. Instead, the men subleased two pieces of property on Philpot Street in Fells Point from William Applegarth, who had established a reputation as a trustworthy white ally for black Baltimoreans. The group established the John H. Smith Company, which they later renamed the Chesapeake Marine Railway and Dry Dock Company.[43]

The establishment of the Chesapeake Marine Railway and Dry Dock Company stood as a remarkable achievement. Founded just two years after Maryland abolished slavery, it put into practice Myers's vision for racial uplift. Like the Douglass Institute, the venture also had symbolic importance. The *Christian Recorder,* an early black newspaper published by the African Methodist Episcopal Church, proclaimed it "a vindication of our race against the untruthful and wicked charge of indolence and incompetency, which our enemies bring against us." The company had practical importance as well. At the end of its first year of operations, the company employed between 150 and 250 men, paying them between $3.00 and $3.50 per day. At its peak, it employed three hundred black workers along with a few white employees. It also did substantial business. In its first year, the cooperative claimed to have handled $65,000; in its second year that number jumped to $89,000. By its fifth year of operations, the cooperative managed to pay off the debts it had incurred.[44]

By the mid-1870s, however, the shipyard, like much of the nation, had fallen on hard financial times. Some black Baltimoreans charged the company with financial malfeasance. In an 1879 lawsuit, the company admitted that it had failed to make dividend payments, although it denied squandering its financial resources. In addition, the original terms of the company's formation became increasingly controversial. The precise details remain unclear, but African Americans may have believed, or been led to believe by Applegarth and Smith, that they were purchasing, not leasing, the shipyard's property. Although the presiding judge dismissed the case, the cooperative never recovered. It managed to hang on until it folded in 1884. Despite its hardships, the company employed hundreds (if not thousands) of workers in the course of its nearly twenty-year existence.[45]

For the majority of black Baltimoreans, however, prejudice and increased immigration in the 1870s and 1880s eroded job opportunities. Jeffrey R. Brackett, a social worker at Johns Hopkins University, reported, "Whites are, with a few exceptions, the skilled workmen, the artisans, of the community." Not only did white workers push African Americans out of skilled trades; they also formed racially exclusive unions to guard the color line. Other factors curtailed the job prospects for black Baltimoreans. Most white Baltimoreans did not shop in black-owned stores, and those who did often required that merchants and entrepreneurs refuse to serve African American customers.[46]

Black Baltimoreans struggled to overcome racial obstacles but managed to carve out an economic niche in the city. Black entrepreneurs opened small shops, sometimes in markets, that sold "china and glass-ware, groceries, produce, oysters, 'notions,' &c." Others dealt in coal, and black business owners also dominated the "junk business." Many former slaves also worked as waiters, caterers, cooks, and day laborers. Others found employment as clerks, porters, or messengers; in the printing business; as dressmakers; or in the carpentry trade. Black women mainly found employment "keeping house," as servants, and as washerwomen. Isaac Myers continued working to create employment options for African Americans. In 1879 he opened up a wood and coal yard, seemingly modeled after the Chesapeake Marine Railway and Dry Dock Company, which "carrie[d] on a large business, besides giving employment to a number of men."[47]

African Americans continued to unionize to stretch financial resources and to protect themselves against further white encroachment. Throughout the 1870s and 1880s, black Baltimoreans joined and founded a number of unions. One of the strongest black labor organizations in the city was the hod carriers' union, which managed to keep their trade exclusively African American. In addition, the group extended death benefits and paid members a dividend. In the 1880s the caulkers initially looked to the Knights of Labor before starting a new union that functioned in much the same way as the hod carriers' union. There was also at least one instance of a biracial union in Baltimore. During the 1880s, black and white brickmakers organized a union that grew to more than three thousand members by the end of the decade.[48]

Myers championed unionization as the central component of larger reform effort. In the late 1860s and throughout the 1870s, the labor organizer expanded the purview of unions to marry the worlds of electoral politics, reform, work, and education. In July 1869 Myers helped organize a meeting of African American mechanics at the Douglass Institute. Myers believed that suffrage meant little to African Americans if they could not also gain labor rights. The organizers contended that employment would "prepare [black laborers] to support their families, educate their children and more intelligently discharge the responsible duties of American citizenship." The men resolved to help African Americans navigate the job market or undertake "cooperative or joint stock associations" to create jobs. The next week, the group made plans to send a delegation (including Myers) to the national labor convention in Philadelphia and issued a call for a national labor meeting of black unionists in Washington, DC.[49]

Black Baltimoreans were instrumental in organizing the five-day Colored National Labor Convention in December 1869. Attendees from across the nation converged on Washington, DC, to push for employment rights and racial equality. At the convention, attendees formed the National Colored Labor Union (NCLU), an auxiliary to the white National Labor Union (NLU), and they elected Myers to serve as president. The convention's opening statement set the tone for the proceedings. While acknowledging Republicans' roles in abolishing slavery, the group chided the party for its failures during Reconstruction. Republicans "should have been with us in the wilderness," the statement read. "It should have fed us during our pilgrimage; . . . it should have given us quails and manna, homes, and the letter." Delegates further demanded the right to vote and for the government to redistribute land in the South to former slaves. The convention's platform included calls to support education and equal rights.[50]

Ultimately, the NCLU proved short-lived. By 1871, racial tensions drove a wedge between many African American and white members. In addition, many black participants refused to abandon the Republican Party for the Labor Reform Party championed by the NLU's white constituents. Following the 1872 presidential election, both the NCLU and the NLU collapsed. Nevertheless, the NCLU stands as one of the earliest national post-Emancipation civil rights organizations in the United States. The group pushed black Baltimoreans, as well as leaders throughout the country, to think expansively about the connections between work, politics, racial equality, and education. The *New National Era*, an African American newspaper edited by Frederick Douglass, wrote, "It was a movement in the right direction, and one which may prove the beginning of an important movement for the improvement and advantage of our suffering class."[51]

A few years after the NCLU's demise, Myers attempted to replicate its ideals on the local level when he formed the Colored Men's Progressive and Cooperative Union in 1875. The organization resolved to "secure a full and complete recognition of our civil rights, and to defend by all proper means any abridgement of the same." It also identified obtaining equal educational opportunities, the "moral and social elevation of our people," and mechanical training for young children among its goals. Although the group was most likely short-lived, as very little documentation concerning them has survived, Myers's idea was ahead of its time. Like the NCLU, Myers envisioned the union as a vehicle to connect political, social, educational, and labor concerns under the purview of one organization. In the years ahead, the battles black Baltimoreans fought over this terrain increasingly defined their activism, but the lack of an organizing body would continue to hamper their prospects for success.[52]

For black Baltimoreans, the worlds of politics, labor, and reform most forcefully collided over the issue of education. Following the war, Maryland made incremental steps toward updating their antiquated public education system. The Union Party's State Constitution of 1864 created, and funded, public schools that were required to operate at least half the year.[53] Still, many white Marylanders did not support black schooling and conservatives effectively blocked the state from extending public education to black citizens. Instead, the new constitution neither prohibited nor mandated black education but left the door open for future reform efforts. The following January, the state took another tentative step toward supporting black education by making taxes paid by African Americans available for the construction of segregated schools. They did not, however, mandate that localities use these funds, and many left the monies on the table.[54]

In Baltimore, philanthropists did not want to wait on the state government. During the years surrounding the Civil War, two groups promoted black education. Maryland Unionists organized the first, known as the Gailbraith Lyceum, to help build schools throughout Maryland and states farther south. William E. Matthews, a black Baltimorean who served as the organization's agent, traveled throughout Maryland to establish schools and engage in moral uplift work. The group was most likely biracial, but little documentation of their work survives in the historical record.[55]

The second philanthropic group proved to have a more lasting impact in Maryland. In 1864 a group of white politicians, businessmen, church officials, and lawyers formed the Baltimore Association for the Moral and Educational Improvement of the Colored People. The organization coordinated numerous educational initiatives. Women (most likely white) affiliated with the group founded the Industrial Colored Schools of Baltimore "for the improvement of the Colored People in industry, morality and the comfort of home-life." The managers also created a "Monthly Meeting" for students and their mothers that brought in a number of guest speakers, including representatives from the Freedmen's Bureau as well as black and white city ministers.[56] The organization immediately attracted national attention for its efforts, including funding from the Pennsylvania Freedmen's Relief Association, various churches throughout New York State, and international aid from the Society of Friends of England and Central Committee of the Society of Friends of England for the Relief of Emancipated Negroes. On the local level, however, the group's efforts proved less successful. They managed to secure $10,000 from the city but little else from white Marylanders with the exception of the local Freedmen's Bureau, which contributed "many thousands of dollars worth of Lumber, sufficient to build over fifty school houses throughout the State."[57]

Given the hostility, apathy, and/or inability of the Maryland public to aid the group, the Baltimore Association experienced surprising initial success. In its first year of operation, the association operated eighteen schools throughout Maryland; that number increased to seventy-three by 1868. In

Baltimore, where the group spent the vast majority of its budget, they oversaw sixteen schools (including its Normal School for teacher education)
that enrolled 1,206 students and employed sixteen teachers. By the end of
their first year the schools were functioning at capacity. "These Schools are
now crowded to their utmost capacity, and could be made much larger,
could rooms be obtained for the accommodation of the increase," the association reported. During the organization's second year, the number of
attendees in Baltimore grew to 2,420, and the number of schools mush-
roomed to twenty-two. In its third year of existence, they were educating
2,800 students in Baltimore alone.[58]

In the span of three years, the Baltimore Association significantly
expanded the educational infrastructure that black Baltimoreans had established before the war. Their efforts, however, would not have succeeded
were it not for African Americans. Black Marylanders built on the tradition
of education they established during the antebellum era and made enormous sacrifices to obtain it. The association's schools were in such demand
that the organization operated them day and night. In at least some cases,
black students attended school after putting in a day's work. "Note this,
and remember that all the night scholars have hard work to do all day," the
association reported, "that many of the day scholars have to aid in the
support of their families; and then reflect how strong must be the desire
for knowledge to induce people, who have grown up in ignorance, to make
such exertions to obtain it, even leading them to spend at school their only
season of relaxation and amusement."[59]

African Americans gave time, labor, and crucial resources to the Baltimore Association's efforts. As they did during the antebellum era, churches
led the way in fostering black educational opportunities. Sharp Street Memorial United Methodist Church and Orchard Street Colored Church hosted
classrooms sponsored by the association. Labor organizations pitched in as
well. The Caulkers' Association volunteered their meeting hall for use as a
classroom. During the association's first year, three black teachers worked in
Baltimore while fourteen others taught in the counties. During the second
year, the organization employed four African American teachers in the city
and another forty-three in the counties. Black Marylanders also donated
financially to the organization. In its first year of existence, African Americans contributed $2,000 to the Baltimore Association. The level of support
ballooned the next year to $9,821.19 in donations and book sales. At the
association's third annual meeting in December 1867, black Marylanders had

contributed a total of $23,371.14 toward the Baltimore Association, which represented the group's single largest source of financial support.[60]

African Americans expanded the antebellum practice of conducting private schools to augment the association's efforts. A teacher named William H. Woods oversaw a classroom in the Douglass Institute with the help of an assistant and an academic department. Rev. William T. Carr operated a classroom with his wife and another teacher named William H. Francis. The three educators taught approximately two hundred students in his Old School Presbyterian Church. Rev. Harrison Holmes Webb continued to use his church, Saint James First African, as a classroom, a practice he had begun before the Civil War. One account proclaimed that "many of the older Marylanders, still alive, received their education in his school." In total, the *Baltimore City Directory of 1867* listed twenty-six black schoolteachers residing in the city.[61] Whether through private initiatives or the Baltimore Association, black teachers sacrificed to support education. After watching Reverend Carr, the *Christian Recorder* found "it very hard work [for Carr to] teach all the week, in addition to the duties of his church. We do not see how both can be attended to *properly*." The paper also observed that William H. Woods devoted "his whole time to his work in the school, which is necessary in order to succeed."[62]

Ultimately, the Baltimore Association turned out to be a mixed blessing for African Americans. On the one hand, the group established schools and hired qualified teachers—including African American educators—when the state refused to fund black education. On the other hand, the association did not include any African Americans on its board of managers. There were also indications of internal racial tensions. The *Christian Recorder* reported that the Baltimore Association used race to determine teaching assignments. When the New England Freedmen's Association sent "several finely educated young colored ladies" to teach in Baltimore, the association directed them to the counties, a more dangerous assignment, where teachers faced physical assaults and intimidation. The association reserved the safer city jobs for white teachers. The paper also observed that some in the organization refused to address African Americans as "Miss," referring to them instead by first name only.[63]

Financial shortfalls eventually doomed the association. At its second anniversary meeting, the managers reported a debt of over $10,000. Looking ahead, they noted that they would need slightly more than $52,000 to continue to operate but had thus far only been able to raise $27,800. The next year, the association built fifty new schoolhouses throughout the state but lamented that many remained vacant due to a lack of funds. Struggling to make ends meet, the association's managers implored city officials to absorb the schools. In 1868 the city council responded.[64] After an investigation, the School Board of Commissioners established ten schools for black students, limited to primary grades, where population demanded. They also terminated the jobs of the current teachers employed by the association, including many African Americans, replacing them with exclusively white instructors.[65]

When city officials assumed control of the schools, they established the foundation for Jim Crow. Throughout the late nineteenth century, black public education in Baltimore lagged well behind white education by design. The city not only limited African Americans to primary grades but also provided less support. An 1871 school board hearing reported that "scarcely any of the [African American] schools are in buildings suited for the purpose." This was not surprising since black schools in Baltimore operated on a $60,000 budget while white schools received $540,000 by the end of the 1870s. Furthermore, the city refused to hire African American teachers, a policy that robbed black Baltimoreans of needed job opportunities.[66]

African Americans responded by continuing to operate private schools. In some cases, black educators administered these schools in their homes. The Berry sisters, Elizabeth, Martha, and Mary, conducted one of the more popular schools. Although little is known about the sisters, according to the 1860 census, Mary worked as a schoolteacher, Elizabeth as a nurse, and Martha as an "Assistant in School." From that moment, the sisters appeared periodically in the pages of Baltimore's city directories. In 1866 Martha worked as a teacher while Elizabeth (no occupation given) lived on 97 North Pine. According to John R. Slattery, the white reverend of Baltimore's Saint Joseph's Seminary, the sisters "dropped off one by one, the school still holding on, till the last, known to every one of her race as 'Cousin Lizzie,' died some years ago." "Cousin Lizzie" was almost certainly Elizabeth, who conducted the school on North Pine until at least 1881, the last time she appeared in the city directory.[67] Charles C. Quin ran another school from a house on West Biddle for three years prior to becoming the superintendent of Saint Mary the Virgin's school. Hutchens Chew Bishop succeeded Quin and continued his work for an indeterminate period thereafter.[68]

Black Baltimoreans also continued to send their children to schools administered by churches. The quality of these schools varied greatly in terms of facilities and level of instruction. The Oblate Sisters of Providence continued to operate the Saint Francis Academy for African American girls. In 1871 the order moved to a new building north of the city's downtown, which according to the *Baltimore Sun* contained "spacious school-rooms." The Oblate Sisters also maintained a separate free public school for African American children.[69] Calbreath B. Perry, the white reverend of Baltimore's Saint Mary the Virgin (a black church), visited a number of Sabbath schools during the 1870s. He found one in a small church that he described as a "shanty." There a husband and wife—whom Perry dismissed as "faithful, devout but ignorant"—taught classes. Perry then visited a "stately building" where a Methodist chaplain instructed "several hundred scholars" in classics, geometry, and literature. Perry's church also maintained schools for African American students, including one that taught primary grades and a boys' academy.[70] These private and religious schools mitigated some of the problems stemming from unequal education but lacked the resources to fully replace public schools.

African Americans protested Baltimore's unequal education system throughout the late 1860s and 1870s to little avail. In 1869 a group of black Baltimoreans petitioned the city's Board of Commissioners of Public Schools to improve conditions in the city's black facilities, extend education beyond the primary schools, and hire African American teachers. The commissioners agreed to expand black access to grammar schools but refused to hire African American teachers.[71] Throughout the decade problems persisted. In 1879 African Americans reported, "The condition of those schools in sanitary and other respects was very bad." Another report claimed that the only black grammar school in the city "was in very bad condition, and there was evident need of new buildings for some of the other schools." The city's policy of only hiring white teachers further degraded the educational experience for African Americans. "They call them niggers, not negroes," one observer complained, "and teach them to speak ungrammatically that they may remain ignorant."[72]

The declining state of public education for African Americans was matched by the dwindling hopes for a viable democracy. Throughout the 1860s, black Marylanders remained disfranchised. Without the right to vote, black Baltimoreans looked beyond Maryland's borders. Activists sought to make common cause with African Americans in other Border States and farther south. They also hoped to pressure the federal government to intercede on their behalf.

On 5 August 1868 African Americans, including activist Henry Jerome (H. J.) Brown and William Howard Day (the Freedmen's Bureau's inspector of schools for Maryland), hosted a two-day Colored Men's Border State Convention at the Douglass Institute. The group—which included representatives from Delaware, Maryland, Virginia, Tennessee, Missouri, New York, New Jersey, and Pennsylvania—followed in the tradition of the Colored Convention movement. Beginning in the 1830s, state, regional, and national groups periodically met to discuss a variety of social and political issues. While most of the meetings took place in northern locations, free African Americans in Maryland organized a state convention in 1852. This tradition continued after the war, where the conventions served as one of the primary venues for black political organizing prior to the 1880s.[73]

At the Colored Men's Border State Convention, attendees focused much of their attention on the Border States where the pace of civil rights lagged behind the former Confederacy. The men pointed out that while more than three million African Americans were able to vote in the United States, more than one million remained disfranchised. "The wrong which must be apparent to you, is that *All* these men, the represented and the unrepresented, are Citizens," the group declared. "Citizens not only according to our reading of the Constitution as originally framed," they continued, "but declared to be so 1st, by the highest law officer of the Government; 2d by Acts of Congress; and 3d by an Amendment to the Constitution of the United States." The attendees urged the federal government to safeguard black voting rights and insisted on women's suffrage.[74]

The Colored Border State Convention left important legacies. The gathering provided H. J. Brown with a local and national platform. Educated in the antebellum North, Brown worked as a "lecturer" and physician. At the convention, he delivered one of the evening's most impassioned speeches. Brown urged African Americans in the former Confederacy to use their ballot to vote Republican in order to aid disfranchised blacks in the Border States and the North. In the years following the Civil War, the federal government sent troops to the former Confederacy as part of Reconstruction to ensure black voting rights, even as states farther north still did not allow African American men the franchise. "We look to you to relieve us and yourselves from the perilous situation in which we find ourselves," Brown counseled, "and which awaits you, unless you marshal your mighty hosts, and like a well-disciplined legion march to the ballot-box, and there put the enemy to fight who would oppress and tyrannize you."[75] More radical than his frequent rival Myers, Brown demanded full racial equality and emerged as one of the city's foremost activists after the Civil War.

The Colored Border State Convention also served as a springboard for the planning of other civil rights meetings. During the gathering, attendees agreed to convene a National Convention of Colored Men the next year. On 13 January 1869 African Americans from twenty states, including Maryland, met in Washington, DC, to demand racial equality. Despite the passage of the Fourteenth Amendment, the convention attendees knew that universal manhood suffrage remained an empty promise for many African Americans. "The partial or total exclusion of colored citizens from the exercise of the elective franchise and other citizen rights," the convention's opening statement remarked, "in so many States of the Union, especially demand and ought to receive the continued consideration of every colored man, and of the Congress of the nation." The convention organizers issued a call to "earnest action, by petition, by personal appeal, by protest, and by what votes we have, until justice be done."[76]

Despite their pioneering roles in national and regional civil rights efforts, black Baltimoreans continued to struggle to find their footing in local politics during the 1870s. With the passage of the Fifteenth Amendment—which Maryland did not ratify—black Marylanders finally secured the right to vote.[77] Throughout the rest of the decade, black Baltimoreans fiercely debated the best course of action, and black-led Republican meetings often became flash points for disagreements. On one side, Isaac Myers and many black Baltimoreans championed loyalty to the Republican Party. At a Republican meeting in 1870, Myers told African Americans that they "owed a debt of gratitude to the republican party for the rights and privileges they enjoyed, and it was the duty of every colored man to deposit his vote for that party." In part, Myers personally benefited from his stance. State Republican officials rewarded Myers's support with a string of patronage positions in the custom house, the post office, and on the Republican State Central Committee. Yet Myers's personal beliefs also aligned with the Republican Party. Myers emphasized economic opportunities for African Americans. He also valued the Republican Party's previous defense of black voting rights and its immediate post–Civil War record of fighting for racial equality.[78]

A vocal minority frequently clashed with Isaac Myers and his supporters. At one meeting, a group of dissatisfied black Baltimoreans labeled

Myers a "conservative negro, a traitor to the best interests of his race, and unworthy of the confidence and respect of that class to which he professes to belong."[79] Some black Baltimoreans had grown frustrated with the slow pace of civil rights and the Republican Party's record. Dissatisfaction with Republicans reached its peak in 1872 and 1873 as African Americans openly discussed alternatives. Some supported Horace Greeley's Liberal Republican ticket in the 1872 election. The next year, African Americans continued to lodge numerous complaints against the Republican Party and its spotty record in handing out patronage positions. At one meeting in June 1873, an unnamed African American advocated that black voters vote for any candidate they felt qualified, regardless of party affiliation. A group of black Baltimoreans held at least one rally to form a separate party. At the time, the radical voices lost out to Myers's more cautious approach. By all appearances, most African Americans, even more forthright activists such as H. J. Brown, remained Republican throughout the decade.[80]

As the 1870s wore on, however, it became more and more apparent that electoral politics offered African Americans little hope of achieving equality. Maryland's Republican Party was moribund. Frank Richardson Kent, a political reporter for the *Baltimore Sun,* described them as "disorganized, disheartened, without able leaders." This exposed one of the major flaws in Myers's advocacy of the Republican Party: African Americans stood little chance of gaining office. Even if the Republican Party was organized and viable, they had shown little interest in advancing civil rights. Throughout the 1870s, the party excluded all but a small number of African Americans from the State Central Committee and from patronage positions. Nor did they support black aspirants to public office. Democrats also had no interest in attracting African American voters. In fact, they countered the black franchise with fraud and violence.[81]

Elections during the 1870s further underscored how little electoral politics offered black Baltimoreans. In 1871 Democrats paid African Americans to abstain from voting and engaged in other frauds to suppress the black vote. Then, in 1875, Maryland state delegate Arthur Pue Gorman and Baltimore's Democratic Party leader I. Freeman Raisin, who together ran the state's political machine known as the Ring, used violence to thwart a revolt by reform Democrats and Republicans. After Gorman and Raisin's candidate, John Lee Carroll, prevailed over William T. Hamilton, disaffected supporters of the latter bolted the party. Less than six weeks later, the dissenters and Republicans nominated Henry Warfield on the Citizen's Reform ticket.

For African Americans, the advent of the Citizen's Reform movement offered little practical benefits.[82] The new party did not champion racial equality, nor did they nominate African Americans for office. Yet with no Republicans to vote for, African Americans threw their lot in with the new coalition that threatened to topple Maryland's nascent political machine. In Democrats' eyes, black voters became a threat.

The 1875 citywide election, which preceded the statewide contests by a week, amplified the stakes and ratcheted up the tension. Despite little violence, the *New York Times* reported that Democrats "carried the city, but only by the employment of audacious fraud." The Democratic mayoral candidate won the contest by 2,500 votes. The election, however, drew approximately ten thousand more voters to the polls than the previous presidential contest. For Democrats, alarm bells rang when their returns shrank by nearly fifteen thousand votes and the Reform ticket prevailed in half of the races for city council.[83] The Ring was not going to idly watch their prospects of controlling the state slip by the wayside.

Election night for the statewide races played out like a scene from Baltimore's tumultuous "Mob-Town" past. The city was in a state of open war. The *New York Times* described the evening as a "saturnalia of bloodshed." Across the city, police made 209 arrests, mostly for disorderly conduct and rioting. At least two hundred reform voters had been "shot, stabbed or beaten to-day." The *Chicago Tribune* described the scene as "a dark and bloody day in the history of Baltimore. Justice vacated her seat, law was thrown aside and for twelve hours ruffianism ruled the city, the legally constituted authorities making no resistance." In the Third Ward, Democratic mobs roamed the streets attacking voters; in the south end of the city mobs killed several "inoffensive citizens." The next day, the *New York Times* headline declared, "The Republican and Reform Ticket Defeated by Fraud and Terrorism in Baltimore."[84]

For African Americans, the 1875 Election Day was an especially harrowing experience. According to the *New York Times*, "An organized onslaught was made on the colored voters early in the morning. The wards in which they principally live were taken possession of by the Ring ruffians and as they appeared at the polls they were knocked down and shot. A reign of terror," the *Times* continued, "prevailed from dawn until sunset."[85] The *Chicago Daily Tribune* reported that in the First Ward, African Americans were forced to "flee for their lives" from polling stations. Ruffians attacked African Americans in the Fifth Ward while the police reportedly laughed.

After an African American man knifed a would-be assailant, white men roamed the streets "knocking down every colored man who dared show his face."[86] James W. Jackson, a city resident, later recalled seeing African American oyster shuckers—with hammers and lunch pails in hand—lined up outside the Chestnut Street polling station ten minutes prior to their opening at 5:00 A.M. Bob Hayes, a justice of the peace and a Democratic Party official, approached the line with a group of men at his side. Hayes and his men opened fire, chasing the would-be voters from the polls, and African Americans responded in kind, pursuing their attackers down the street. Jackson recalled that whites used firearms to terrorize voters in nearly every ward. H. J. Brown remembered "armed and organized bands of men" who resorted to "numerous and well-laid plans to intimidate and terrorize over colored voters, by which wholesale bloodshed, assassination and demoralization thousands of republican voters were disfranchised and driven from the polls at every precinct, without that protection to which they were entitled under the law."[87]

The election of 1875 in Baltimore foreshadowed Reconstruction's national demise by two years. While Maryland's politicians had excluded African Americans from the political process since the end of the Civil War, 1875 marked the first time since Emancipation that Democrats resorted to systematic violence to assure their political ascendancy. It was the moment when the prejudice and racism that guided the city's politics manifested itself in physical form on the streets. And it was only a preview of things to come. Throughout the rest of the decade, Democrats used a combination of violence, intimidation, and fraud to disfranchise black voters. In 1876 the *New York Times* claimed that "throngs of roughs and strikers made pandemonium of day and night." The "roughs" and "strikers" belted Confederate songs while assaulting would-be Republican voters.[88] In 1879 African Americans and Republicans claimed they were "wrongfully stricken from the poll-list, and that a great many frauds were practiced by Democrats during the municipal election." They got off easy. In the statewide election, "Democratic ward rounders" from Baltimore traveled to towns around the state and attacked Republican voters.[89] While African American voters were one of the primary targets, these eyewitness accounts also make it clear that the violence was aimed at undermining democracy.

By 1879 H. J. Brown had seen enough. "In 1875 the colored voters were roughed out of their ballots," Brown recalled, "and last Wednesday they were defrauded out of their votes by false registration and tricks on names.

The great question for colored republicans is," Brown rhetorically asked, "will the constitutional amendments in their favor be carried out?"[90] At the time there was no clear answer, nor was a clear path forward evident. African Americans were growing increasingly dissatisfied with the political state of affairs in the city and the state. The promises of equality carved out during Reconstruction remained largely unfulfilled.

African Americans, however, learned some important lessons from these tumultuous decades. Without the benefit of federal protection, black Baltimoreans knew that the prospects of political reform were slim. An editorial in the *New National Era* captured African Americans' predicament. "The Government, in giving the negro his freedom, has given him the freedom to starve, and in giving him the ballot-box has given him a coffin," the editorialist observed. "It meant well enough to the negro but the result has been terrible indeed. It attempted to make men free," the editorial continued, "but withheld the only condition which they can be so. It has attempted to make men independent voters, but left them prey to conditions which, in many cases, makes such voting impossible."[91] Because the federal government did not reconstruct Maryland, the promise of political change in the state evaporated before black Baltimoreans had even caught their breath after Emancipation.

The political dead end in Maryland pushed African American activists to consider other avenues of redress. Black Baltimoreans realized that if they were to attain the promises offered by freedom, they would need to forge movements that connected labor, economics, and social equality. Thus black Baltimoreans organized immediately after the war ended. This first generation of African Americans to live in a free Baltimore built on the activism of their predecessors in the antebellum era but with new weapons. Although Maryland was not federally reconstructed, legislation—principally the Thirteenth, Fourteenth, and Fifteenth Amendments along with the 1866 Civil Rights Act—provided activists with advantages their forebears did not possess. Black Baltimoreans used these tools to define what freedom meant when they won courtroom battles that overturned segregation on public transportation, organized for labor rights, founded a public education system, and built lasting institutions such as the Douglass Institute. Black Baltimoreans' self-reconstruction of Maryland created an organizing tradition that connected the tradition of activism in the antebellum era to the new possibilities offered by Emancipation.

CHAPTER 2

Rebuilding a Radical African American
Activist Foundation

On 30 September 1885, members of the Colored Advisory Council crowded into Baltimore's Douglass Institute following the Republican Party primaries. Black Baltimoreans had formed the Colored Advisory Council in 1878 to promote "the political interests of colored people in the city and the State." Throughout the years, the group met frequently to protest, rally support for political causes, and help African Americans register to vote. Although officially nonpartisan, the Council, like African American voters throughout the country, had largely supported the party of Lincoln. Nevertheless, black Baltimoreans' repeated attempts to gain political office and recognition in the party had produced meager results. More importantly, the fight for racial equality, which had scored significant victories in the previous two decades, had effectively stalled by the early 1880s. Joseph E. Briscoe, the council's president, had seen enough of Republican apathy. For years the activist, newspaperman, and aspiring politician had persistently criticized the Republican Party for their poor civil rights record. The veteran activist Dr. H. J. Brown, who attended many of the council's meetings, echoed these sentiments. Yet, for the most part, the two men had stood in the minority. This was no longer true by 1885. "We intend to use our ballots as best serves the interests of our race in this community, according to our own judgment," Briscoe remarked, "without regard to any party, because it is not a question of parties, as far as we are concerned we have no party."[1]

The events that occurred during the 1885 primaries triggered the council's break with the Republican Party. After a black man, Calvin Wright, defeated W. E. Myers to serve as a precinct delegate to the legislative convention in Baltimore's downtown Ninth Ward, Myers (who was white) quickly renominated himself in a different precinct to challenge another

African American hopeful, Robert Squirrel. Although the *Baltimore Sun* played coy, the paper intimated that white primary attendees intimidated Squirrel into withdrawing from the contest. In the Sixteenth Ward, African American voters had to scrape tooth and nail for representation. When one black attendee declared equality with whites and then demanded representation on the Maryland Republican Party's Central Committee, he triggered a verbal altercation. After much debate, the Republican leadership finally assented. Their decision, however, proved costly. Many whites promptly left rather than pledge their support to candidates that would allow blacks to serve on the Central Committee. Others employed a bit of subterfuge to maintain their grip on the party. In the city's Fifth Ward, party operatives shifted the primary's location to an "obscure corner of the Seventh Ward," in an effort to limit black participation.[2]

At the Colored Advisory Council meeting, Briscoe railed against a Republican Party that had consistently failed black Baltimoreans. In the late 1870s and early 1880s, the Maryland Republican Party had at first limited African Americans from serving on the State Central Committee before barring them altogether in 1880. Republicans similarly limited black Baltimoreans from serving on the city's executive committee. "Our political condition has grown from bad to worse," Briscoe exclaimed, "until the treatment of the colored people by the so-called republican party of Maryland has become a byword and a reproach which can no longer be tolerated by any intelligent or self-respecting colored man." For Briscoe the time had come to look beyond existing political parties. "In the republican party the ostracism and discrimination has been practiced against an entire race, by a minority against a majority," Briscoe proclaimed, "and against which we meet here to utter our solemn protest and to hoist our standard of political freedom." Briscoe closed his speech by telling his audience, "I am, as I have always been, for my race against all political parties." It was not surprising that Briscoe, who had been frustrated with the Republican Party for years, reached a breaking point. This time, however, he was not alone. Isaac Myers, the city's leading black political activist, had always been a loyal Republican, but he sided with Briscoe. "The colored voters are justified in the course they are taking," Myers noted. "It is a new departure, and one very far-reaching in its results. Injustice in the recent primaries by white Republicans makes us the victims of treachery in our brother's house."[3]

Beginning in the mid-1870s, most black Baltimoreans looked toward electoral politics as the primary vehicle to achieve racial equality. Led by

Myers, black Baltimoreans steadfastly supported the Republican Party. By the mid-1880s, however, many had grown frustrated with the lack of results. The 1885 Colored Advisory Council meeting was representative of this mounting frustration, but it was only one manifestation of this anger. At the start of the decade, a new generation of more radical activists, who were generally younger and had moved to the city after experiencing the horrors of slavery in their youth, emerged to push the black freedom struggle in new directions. They disavowed a gradual approach to reform and questioned the wisdom of relying exclusively on partisan politics. Instead, they revived an earlier generation's style of protest that hinged on acts of civil disobedience and legal challenges to discrimination.[4]

Rev. Harvey Johnson stood at the center of this movement. In 1884 and 1885, Johnson spearheaded court challenges to discrimination. In the first case, six of Johnson's parishioners purposefully violated a steamboat's segregation rules. When they returned home, they filed a lawsuit that challenged their treatment as a violation of the Fourteenth Amendment. In the second case, Johnson orchestrated a challenge that overturned Baltimore's prohibition on black attorneys. In the wake of Johnson's success, Maryland's segregationists struck back. In early 1885 authorities arrested a black Marylander, Howard Cooper, for allegedly raping a white woman. Cooper's case galvanized Baltimore's black community. Johnson, along with other black Marylanders, saw in Cooper's legal plight an opportunity to mount a Supreme Court challenge to Maryland's prejudicial jury selection system. Their efforts demonstrated the problems with Maryland's prejudicial legal system but also revealed the lengths to which white Marylanders would go to maintain white supremacy. Faced with a possible Supreme Court appeal, a mob lynched Cooper. The lynching hit black Baltimoreans hard, but it only furthered their resolve to initiate more test cases to challenge racial inequality.

Black Baltimoreans' activism placed them at the forefront of the early African American freedom struggle. Scholars once dismissed the period between the 1880s and early 1900s as the era of accommodation. Recent studies, however, have demonstrated that this period was a crucial moment in the post-Emancipation struggle for racial equality across the United States. Activists with national profiles, such as John Mercer Langston and T. Thomas Fortune, articulated a vision of equality that held equal access to accommodations, transportation, and education as fundamental civil rights. They also insisted that African Americans challenge violations of these rights in the courts. In Maryland, Harvey Johnson and his associates put these ideas into action. Their work not only expanded civil rights in the state but also demonstrated to the nation that independent, nonpartisan organization and legal challenges could defeat the emerging Jim Crow system. Far from an era of accommodation, the work of Baltimore's activists pushed the long black freedom struggle in new direction.[5]

On the evening of 24 April 1882, Martin R. Delaney—the only African American major to serve in the Union Army during the Civil War, an abolitionist, author, and politician—arrived in Baltimore to speak in front of a packed house at Ebenezer AME Church. In 1874 Delaney had run for lieutenant governor in South Carolina on a "fusion ticket" supported by disgruntled Republicans and Democrats.[6] That night, Delaney spoke of these experiences but also, according to the *Baltimore Sun*, on "the fundamental principles of government and the formation of political parties." The *Sun* reported that Delaney advised his audience to "cut loose from both parties and to organize for self-protection." According to the paper, Delaney remarked that Democrats "were [African Americans'] enemies and republicans their friends when the colored people were freed, but now it is impossible to tell friend from foe."[7]

Delaney's message surely left an impression on Rev. Harvey Johnson. The minister was born into slavery in Fauquier County, Virginia, in 1843. It is unclear when he gained his freedom, and he rarely spoke of his time as a slave. On one of the rare occasions when he did so, he told a biographer, "I can only think of it with a righteous indignation." In 1868 the twenty-five-year-old Johnson found his calling in the Baptist church and moved to Washington, DC, to enroll in Wayland Seminary. Founded in 1865 by the white-led American Baptist Home Mission Society, with additional support from the Freedmen's Bureau, the school sought to train black ministers and educators after slavery's demise. On graduating in 1872, Johnson accepted a pastorate at the small Union Baptist Church in Baltimore, which only had 250 members. Initially, Johnson focused on expanding his new congregation. Under his watch, Union blossomed. By 1875 the church's membership had nearly quadrupled to 928 congregants. Having outgrown their small building, Johnson and his parishioners spent four years raising $20,000 to erect a new building on North Street. By 1885 Union Baptist had more than 2,200 parishioners, which made it the largest and most influential black church in Baltimore.[8]

Figure 3. Union Baptist Church's Rev. Harvey Johnson, a pioneering civil rights leader and founder of the Mutual United Brotherhood of Liberty. (Photograph date unknown.) Courtesy of Philip J. Merrill Nanny Jack & Co. Archives.

Johnson built his congregation at a time when African Americans were slowly losing the rights that the country promised them following the Civil War. By the early 1880s, Johnson had grown frustrated with the city and nation's politics. Johnson attended Delaney's visit at Ebenezer AME Church and had the difficult task of following Delaney's speech. Johnson did not disappoint. He assailed the state's recent record on civil rights. The *Baltimore Sun* reported that Johnson "said that the condition of the colored people of Maryland was worse than in any other State, that the laws relative to them were enacted before the war were still in force." The minister listed myriad wrongs including the state's prohibition on black attorneys, its bastardy law that punished African American women, and its jury selection system that excluded black Marylanders. For Johnson, the moment had come to act. He ended his speech by predicting that "the day was dawning when the power of the colored people in Maryland would be seen and felt."[9] That night, Johnson formulated an agenda that activists in Baltimore pursued throughout the rest of the decade.

Delaney's visit and Johnson's speech came at a particularly opportune moment in Baltimore's history. Many black Baltimoreans, like Johnson, had grown frustrated with the glacial pace of civil rights reforms and began searching for alternatives to the Republican Party. During this period, African Americans in other parts of the nation increasingly looked beyond the Republican Party as well. During the early 1880s, black Virginians supported the biracial Readjuster Movement, while black Floridians joined forces with whites to form the Independent Party.[10] In Baltimore, African Americans ran for elected office for the first time in the city's history. Defying Republican officials, three African Americans ran for city council as independents in 1880; more black candidates ran as independents in 1882, 1885, and 1886. In 1883 Joseph E. Briscoe made plans to form a "colored people's party," although his plans never materialized. Although African American candidates failed to win office, their actions demonstrated widespread dissatisfaction with the Republican Party.[11]

Black Baltimoreans further exhibited their displeasure with the state of race relations by forming independent organizations. Immediately following Delaney's visit, black Baltimoreans, including Harvey Johnson, organized the Order of Regulators to coordinate their efforts. Little is known about the organization, but Johnson, who presided over its formation, sought to capitalize on the momentum produced by years of political frustration and Delaney's visit. At the group's founding meeting, Rev. P. S. Henry of Baltimore's Methodist Protestant church echoed Johnson's demands to fight Maryland's prohibition on black attorneys and defeat the state's bastardy law. He further insisted that the city hire black teachers to work in the public schools. The Order of Regulators also worked to register black voters.[12]

Activists continued to meet under the auspices of the Colored Advisory Council as well. One of the more frequent and vocal attendees was H. J.

Brown, who served as a living link to Baltimore's previous generation of civil rights activism. Throughout the 1860s and 1870s Brown had been one of the most ardent, forceful activists in the city. Brown remained consistently critical of the Republican Party and the state's record on civil rights reform. Briscoe joined Brown's call for an uncompromising vision of civil rights and frequently amplified his colleagues' critiques of the Republican Party. Under Briscoe's leadership, the group met on multiple occasions to discuss politics, demand that the Republican Party nominate black candidates, and promote efforts to see African Americans elected to office.[13]

In 1882 clergymen and political activists sought to build on the city's independent political organizing to remake the city's highest court, the Supreme Bench. That year Baltimoreans needed to fill vacancies for four of the five seats on the Supreme Bench. The Democrats renominated Robert Gilmor, Jr., Henry F. Garey, and Campbell W. Pinkey. The fourth justice, George W. Dobbin, retired, and Democrats selected William A. Fisher to run as his replacement. Republicans and some Democrats objected to all of the nominees except Fisher. Instead, they coalesced around a "Citizens Independent Judiciary" ticket, which nominated William A. Stewart (Democrat), Charles E. Phelps (Republican), and Edward Duffy (Republican).[14] Black activists joined hands with white Republicans and Democrats to support the independent judiciary movement.

African Americans viewed the judicial election as pivotal. Justices on the Supreme Bench served fifteen-year terms. The election of 1882 was the first opportunity to replace the Democratic judges elected when that party seized power in 1867 and effectively ended Reconstruction in Maryland. In subsequent years, the city's judicial system played a key role in enforcing white supremacy. Assessing the system, Briscoe contended, "We have not been able to obtain justice in the present courts of the city, for when a person enters these courts as an alleged criminal his very color has more than once sealed his doom."[15]

African Americans also maintained that prejudicial courts enabled lynching. John H. Murphy, who would later publish the *Afro-American*, one of the nation's earliest large black newspapers, cited three recent lynchings in which the perpetrators went unpunished. "We do not ask for any special laws," Murphy proclaimed, "simply the self-same justice which will send a colored man and a white man to the House of Corrections for similar offenses; not the law which gives a negro five years in the penitentiary for snatching a lady's pocketbook and tells the white men to continue killing negroes."[16] Although the courts represented only one aspect of a system that maintained white supremacy, activists recognized that replacing the Democratic justices could be the first step toward achieving greater equality.

As Election Day approached, African American community leaders urged black Baltimoreans to vote the independent ticket. Numerous ministers, including Johnson, John Calvin Allen (First Colored Baptist), Ananias Brown (Leadenhall Baptist), and John A. Holmes (Sharp Street Memorial United Methodist Church), spoke in favor of the independent judges. Rev. William H. Hargrave of Knox Presbyterian Church remarked, according to the *Baltimore Sun*, that he "would vote for [the independent ticket] as the only means by which the colored men could obtain justice." Briscoe and Brown similarly threw their public support behind the independent movement. The Colored Advisory Council endorsed the independent movement as a "guarantee to the whole people that impartial justice which has been years denied the fifty-five thousand colored inhabitants of this city" will be done. Even Isaac Myers urged black voters to support the independent judiciary. The movement succeeded. The biracial coalition of African Americans, white Republicans, and disaffected Democrats remade the Supreme Bench, although the coalition failed to last beyond the election.[17]

By 1882, black Baltimoreans had shown an increasing willingness to move beyond the Republican Party. African Americans did not abandon the political process. Indeed, the Order of Regulators, the independent judiciary movement, and the Colored Advisory Council all sought change through the electoral process and often supported Republicans running for office. Nevertheless, by forming independent organizations, black Baltimoreans took a crucial step toward establishing new pathways to fight inequality. Black Baltimoreans demanded stronger representation and ran for political office themselves; they also made it known that they would withdraw their support from Republicans if necessary. Through word and deed, they demonstrated that they would no longer blindly support Republicans out of gratitude for the changes the party instituted during Reconstruction.

The increased political activism of the early 1880s culminated during Baltimore's judicial election. When black Baltimoreans joined a coalition of white Republicans and Democrats to elect the independent judiciary ticket, they scored their most notable victory since the fight against railway segregation in the early 1870s. In the days before the election, Briscoe published an open letter in the *Baltimore Sun*. Briscoe pointedly asked black

Baltimoreans, "Have we had our rights in this city? Have we good govern-ment? Most certainly we have not," he answered. "Good government, if it means anything," Briscoe continued, "means that impartial justice should be meted out to all citizens alike. This is not at present the state of affairs."[18]

While the new justices stopped short of protecting African Americans' full civil rights, they were a marked improvement over the Democratic Party's judges who had openly discriminated against and repressed black Baltimoreans. Whether anyone knew so at the time, by supporting the inde-pendent judiciary movement, black Baltimoreans once again made the courts a viable venue in which to fight discrimination. Within a few years, Harvey Johnson made sure to take advantage of this opportunity by open-ing a new chapter in Baltimore's fight for equality.

On 15 August 1884 a group of four black Baltimoreans purchased first-class tickets to board the steamer *Sue*, which plied the waters between Maryland and Virginia. The four sisters, Martha Stewart, Winnie Stewart, Mary M. Johnson, and Lucy Jones, were traveling with their aunt, Pauline Braxton, Mary's husband James, and Lucy's husband Charles to visit family. The women placed their belongings in their reserved cabin before heading to the ship's saloon. About an hour into the journey, the ship's chambermaid approached the travelers with their bedding in hand. The chambermaid informed them that, on the captain's orders, they would not be allowed back in their first-class cabin on account of their race. Martha defiantly shot back, "The captain must know very well he can't prevent us from going in that cabin. We got the first-class ticket." She proceeded back down the stairs to her quarters but found that the door to the first-class section had been locked. The five women remained in the saloon for the night. On their return trip, the captain again refused to honor their first-class ticket on account of their race. When the women arrived in Baltimore, their minister, Harvey Johnson, helped them file a lawsuit against the Baltimore, Chesapeake and Richmond Steamboat Company, which operated the steamer *Sue*.[19]

Historians have been mostly content to note the *Steamer Sue*'s forerun-ner status to later civil rights cases, especially *Plessy v. Ferguson*.[20] But the complexity of the case illuminates the motivations of the libellants and, more broadly, the shrewdness of Baltimore's black activist community. Black Baltimoreans' lawsuit against the steamer *Sue* was born out of both local and national contexts. Locally, Harvey Johnson and a number of his associates had begun to look to the courts to spearhead a civil rights campaign. Johnson's determination to use the courts was one of his enduring legacies as it altered the course of civil rights activism in the city. Over the next three decades, black Baltimoreans, including Johnson, initiated numerous legal challenges to discrimination and the emerging Jim Crow system. His friend and fellow activist W. Ashbie Hawkins celebrated Johnson's resort to the courts: "Due likely to Dr. Johnson's inquisitive mind, not satisfied alone with an investigation of the truths of religion and theology, he made excursions into the fields of jurisprudence, the result of which was that he early discovered, what so many of us refuse to see now, that courts of law are the final arbiters of our rights, and that to these same courts we must resort when justice is denied us."[21] Baltimoreans' determination to challenge segregation in the courts put them at the vanguard of the emerging national civil rights movement that was beginning to find its footing in the early 1880s. Black Baltimoreans, as well as national figures including John Mercer Langston and T. Thomas Fortune, were convinced that the Constitution had enshrined civil rights.[22]

Activists kept their faith in the legal system despite recent Supreme Court decisions that curtailed the gains of the Reconstruction era.[23] In 1872, for instance, a steamboat company operating in Louisiana and Mississippi denied an African American woman, Josephine DeCuir, the right to sit in a "white dining hall." In *Hall v. DeCuir,* the high court ruled that Louisiana's law, which ensured equal accommodations, was unconstitutional because it attempted to regulate travel across state borders.[24] The ruling dealt two blows to civil rights. First, it overturned state laws that prohibited racial segregation on interstate carriers. Second, and more damaging, was Justice Nathan Clifford's concurrence. Clifford ruled that carriers could not deny service to passengers based on race, but they could, and indeed should, segregate passengers as long as the policy was "reasonable." The decision limited the Fourteenth Amendment's Equal Protection Clause and set the stage for future attempts at racial segregation. Then in 1883, the Supreme Court, in a series of cases collectively referred to as the Civil Rights Cases, ruled that the 1875 Civil Rights Act violated the Constitution. This decision erased federal protections against racial discrimination on public transportation systems, inns, and schools.[25]

These Supreme Court decisions infuriated Baltimore's activists. The city's first civil rights organization, the Mutual United Brotherhood of Liberty (discussed at length in the next chapter), which Harvey Johnson founded, did not mince words. They termed the *Hall v. DeCuir* decision

"an overruling of this sacred provision of the Fourteenth Amendment."
The group was particularly bothered by the way that the ruling effectively
granted transportation companies and their employees the power to determine what constituted "reasonable" when they separated their passengers.
In the eyes of Baltimore's activists, the decision, along with those in the
1883 Civil Rights Cases, was nothing more than "new patches upon the
garment of Dred Scott."[26]

Black travelers across the United States refused to acquiesce to segregation in the wake of the Supreme Court's rulings. Some, like the Stewart
sisters, filed lawsuits against carriers that discriminated against them.[27] The
extant sources are silent on exactly how the sisters planned their act of civil
disobedience. Circumstantial evidence, however, points to the involvement
of Harvey and Amelia Johnson. "While his name is not mentioned in the
record," W. Ashbie Hawkins remembered, "it is history that to Harvey
Johnson is due the honor for the successful prosecution of this notable
case." It is also likely that Amelia, Harvey's wife, was involved. Johnson met
Amelia Etta Hall in the mid-1870s. Although she was born in Toronto in
1858, her family had roots in Baltimore. Her parents, Levi Hall and Eleanora
Doy Hall, lived in that city before moving to Canada, possibly due to the
passage of the 1850 Fugitive Slave Act. The family remained in Canada for
the first sixteen years of Amelia's life. Amelia and her mother (Levi Hall
died in 1872) moved back to Baltimore in 1874, just a few years after Harvey
arrived in the city.[28]

It is evident that Amelia, an accomplished writer in her own right, was
an active reader and editor of her husband's writings. Although her activism became more visible in the twentieth century, she was probably
involved in the 1880s, even if it was behind the scenes. Surviving records
only offer a glimpse. Yet the Johnson household served as an important
spot for local activists to meet and coordinate political action. Hawkins
remembered that Amelia "contributed much to her noted husband's
career."[29] In fact, her family history may have inspired the *Steamer Sue*
protests. In 1866 Annie A. Jakes, a member of Amelia's extended family,
filed a lawsuit to challenge segregation on public transportation after
employees of the City Passenger Railway ejected her from a Baltimore
streetcar. The lawsuit was part of the wave of court actions and acts of civil
disobedience that black Baltimoreans initiated following the passage of the
1866 Civil Rights Act. While it is impossible to confirm if Amelia knew of
Jakes's protest or of the city's activist tradition, it remains an intriguing

Figure 4. Amelia Johnson, Rev. Harvey Johnson's wife. She was an activist and author. (Photograph date unknown.) Courtesy of Philip J. Merrill Nanny Jack & Co. Archives.

possibility that the *Steamer Sue* test case took its cues from these earlier protests.[30]

While the amount of planning is unclear, it is evident that the plaintiffs and Johnson coordinated their efforts to challenge inequality. Johnson probably intended the lawsuit as a barometer to gauge the potential efficacy of legal challenges. He clearly viewed the case as important: he paid a stenographer to record the trial's testimony. Johnson also secured the services of Archibald Stirling, Jr., and Alexander W. Hobbs. Both attorneys had supported civil rights cases in the past. In fact, Stirling had represented Annie Jakes in her 1866 lawsuit. The defense, perhaps with Johnson's aid, lined up a series of witnesses to support the women's cases. At least three of the witnesses were Johnson's allies. The first, Dennis Johnson (no apparent relation), was a coachman who bought a first-class ticket on a previous journey. As happened in the Stewart case, the steamship's employees barred Johnson from accessing the first-class cabin on account of his race. The second was Andrew J. Reed, who had worked as a barber on the steamer in the 1870s. Reed offered corroborating details concerning the conditions found in the second-class cabin in his testimony. In the coming years, both men would join the Brotherhood of Liberty. In the late 1880s, Reed became the organization's president. The final known Johnson associate was a waiter named Dennis Gaskins. According to his testimony, he traveled frequently on the steamer *Sue* for the previous twenty years. Like Dennis Johnson and the Stewarts, the steamship had refused to honor Gaskins's first-class ticket. A host of black Baltimoreans also testified to the second-class cabin's inferior conditions or spoke about their own experiences with discrimination on the ship.[31]

Prior to Johnson's intervention, the Stewarts had engaged in their own protests. The women had previously taken the same journey and knew from past experience that the steamboat operators would likely prohibit them from staying in the first-class cabin. Although the women bought first-class tickets, employees offered to house them in the second-class cabins instead. The cabins on the steamer *Sue* were not explicitly race specific. Whites and blacks occupied the ship's second-class section. While both races slept in the second-class cabins, the crew barred African Americans from entering the first-class cabin, effectively making it a whites-only section. In one of their previous trips, Martha Stewart told the court that ship personnel had forced the women out of their first-class cabin. The women did not tolerate this overt discrimination. In her testimony, Winnie Stewart recalled that in the summer of 1882, two of her sisters refused to leave their quarters after employees for the steamboat ordered them out. Pauline Braxton, the women's aunt, also had refused to follow the captain's orders during an earlier trip. "Summer before last when I went down there I had undressed and gone to bed," Braxton testified, "and Lizzie [the chambermaid] came down and said the clerk said every colored person must come out of there. I told her I had undressed and gone to bed," Braxton continued, "and wasn't coming out by any means."[32]

The women objected to the second-class cabins for good reason. Not only did they buy the more expensive first-class tickets, but the second-class cabin offered substandard accommodations. Winnie described the second-class cabins as "not fitten for a dog to stay in." The sisters claimed they were dirty and lacking the comforts provided in the first-class cabins. Lucy Jones recalled, "The floor was dirty, and if there was any carpet on there it was so dirty you couldn't tell what it was. The mattresses was dirty. There was no bowl and pitcher in there that I saw." The women all noted that cattle, which the ship housed nearby, obstructed access to the second-class area. The conditions the women reported were not trivial points retold to dramatize their plight. Rather, they formed the foundation of their lawsuit by documenting problems where the categories of race, class, and gender overlapped.[33]

In some ways, the *Steamer Sue* case conformed to the pattern of other lawsuits initiated by African Americans in this period. Black women undertook a majority of the court challenges to segregation on common carriers in the late nineteenth and early twentieth century. This is because common carriers, before the solidification of Jim Crow legislation in the late 1880s and 1890s, segregated passengers along gender lines to ostensibly protect white female passengers. Carriers created the "ladies' car" to offer white women shelter from the rough, often dangerous conditions found in the masculine "smoker" car. State and federal courts permitted racial segregation, but only if carriers offered equal accommodations. Rather than incur the extra costs of maintaining equal, racially exclusive first-class cars, carriers often required all black travelers to stay in the smoker. When carriers directed all African Americans—men and women—to the smoker car because of their race, black women protested. Rather than base their claims on racial discrimination, they instead claimed that they deserved the gendered protections of the ladies' car.[34]

Throughout their testimony, the sisters repeatedly highlighted their respectability to highlight the discrimination they faced when forced to stay in the second-class cabins. The sisters' testimony revealed a middle-class standing. Martha worked as an assistant cook at a boardinghouse while Mary's husband, James, apparently made enough money as a private driver to allow her to stay at home. It is unclear if Winnie and Lucy worked, but their testimony hinted that their material conditions had improved in recent years. In 1881 they could not afford a first-class ticket and had to travel second class. Winnie resolved then that "if money will ever prevent me from staying in that hole [second class] I will never go in there again." As respectable, middle-class women, the sisters recognized that the presence of men denied them protections accorded to white women. Martha claimed that both men and women entered the second-class cabins through the same unlocked entrance. In any event, she maintained that the door was "thrown open all the time, and the windows sit open all the time." Men surrounded the entire area. Her sisters and aunt confirmed the details of Martha's testimony. All of the women, along with their witnesses, either noted men's unfettered access to the second-class cabin area or made mention of the unlocked door that nominally separated the men's and women's sections.[35]

While the women made claims to nineteenth-century gender and class protections, their lawsuit highlighted racial inequalities on the ship. The Stewart sisters detailed the conditions of the separate cabins to prove that the Sue's regulations were not "reasonable" because the accommodations for African Americans were not equal. This claim made their case somewhat unusual. When women sued carriers in the late nineteenth and early twentieth centuries, they usually focused on the particulars of their personal experience rather than challenging the system of segregation. The Sue case contested both the personal affront that the women endured by being assigned to inferior accommodations and, in the words of presiding judge C. J. Morris, "the legal right of the owners of the steam-boat to separate passengers for any purpose, because of race or color."[36]

For Judge Morris, the Steamer Sue case boiled down to two factors. First, it concerned a simple question of "fact": whether or not the ship's operators provided accommodations to the women equal to those enjoyed by whites. The second, and thornier, issue concerned the question of jurisdiction. At this point the case became more muddled. Since, as Morris noted, the steamer plied waters between two states, the jurisdiction in the case defaulted to Congress. However, Congress had not passed legislation to replace the Civil Rights Act of 1875. This inaction left ship operators free to impose their own restrictions. For their part, activists argued that Congress did not need to act since the Fourteenth Amendment barred discrimination based on race. "How can a regulation, which denies that *substantial equality* (upon which the Fourteenth Amendment so strong insists) on account of color, race or previous condition," the Brotherhood later asked, "be said to be a reasonable rule and regulation, when such rule overturns, repeals, and defeats the spirit, purpose and intent of the national legislation?"[37]

In early 1885 Judge Morris rendered his decision. Morris concurred with Justice Clifford's ruling in *Hall v. DeCuir* by maintaining that Congress, not the courts, could determine whether racial segregation was a "reasonable regulation." Morris therefore limited his ruling to the question of whether the steamboat provided the women with equal accommodations. Judge Morris reaffirmed the right of the steamboat operators to provide separate accommodations but only if they were equal. "The separation of the colored from the white passengers," the judge wrote, "goes to the verge of the carrier's legal right, and such a regulation cannot be upheld unless bona fide and diligently the officers of the ship see to it that the separation is free from any actual discrimination in comfort, attention, or appearance of inferiority." The plaintiffs' only salvation was that the judge found the *Sue* failed this test. Citing Judge William Fells Giles's decision in Andrew Thompson's 1870 lawsuit against the Baltimore Passenger Railway that desegregated Baltimore's rail system, Morris ruled that the steamboat operators discriminated against their black passengers and awarded each plaintiff one hundred dollars.[38]

African American activists hoped that the *Steamer Sue* case would restore the full reach of the Fourteenth Amendment. Instead, the judge issued a narrow ruling that applied only to the women's experience on board the ship. Nevertheless, the verdict provided African Americans with a legal victory and demonstrated that the courts at least offered the possibility of challenging discrimination. Johnson was encouraged by the outcome. He decided to take the next step in his plan to challenge segregation in the courts: defeat the law that prohibited African American lawyers from practicing in Maryland. "This [the *Steamer Sue* verdict] was a great legal

victory for us," Hawkins later remembered. "The successful termination of
this litigation . . . probably gave zest to Dr. Johnson's efforts, already begun,
to seek the admission of colored lawyers to the bar of this State."[39]

Johnson and his associates quickly began to plan their challenge to Maryland's prohibition on black attorneys. Although African Americans had
found able representation in white attorneys (such as Stirling) following
Emancipation, they recognized that opening the bar to black attorneys
would provide multiple benefits. The opening of the bar promised high-
profile jobs to black litigators. Hawkins observed, "The lawyer, as no other
professional man among us, tries conclusions every day, not only with the
best men of his own race, but with the best brains of the Caucasian race,
and it is no rare occurrence for him to win out in the contest." They could
also attract bright legal minds, dedicated to fighting racial inequality, to the
city. If Johnson hoped to initiate a civil rights campaign through the courts,
it was crucial to defeat Maryland's prohibition of black attorneys. Johnson
and his associates wrote Alexander H. Hobbs to ask if he would take on the
case, noting that the prohibition was "a barrier to our progress morally,
financially and intellectually." The case was so important to Johnson that
he paid Hobbs the ninety-five dollars' worth of fees from his own funds.[40]

In early 1885 Johnson contacted a thirty-year-old nonpracticing attorney
named Charles S. Wilson. It is unclear how Johnson knew Wilson. Before
Wilson moved to Maryland, he had earned a degree from Amherst College
in Massachusetts. After obtaining his license to practice law, Wilson worked
as an attorney in Boston before he moved to teach in Sunnybrook, Maryland. It seems certain that Wilson did not intend to practice law in Maryland, but he allowed Johnson to use his name and credentials to challenge
the state's prohibition of black attorneys before Baltimore's Supreme
Bench. It does not appear that Wilson even attended the hearings. Instead,
Hobbs argued in his stead that Maryland's law violated the Fourteenth
Amendment's Equal Protection Clause.[41]

Maryland's prohibition on black attorneys had roots reaching back to
the Reconstruction era. In 1872 the Maryland General Assembly had limited
admission to the bar to "any white citizen of Maryland, above the age of
twenty-one years old." They reaffirmed the decision in 1876. That same
year, African Americans James H. Wolff and Charles S. Taylor attempted to
open a practice at the Douglass Institute. For reasons that remain unclear,
Wolff would disappear from the case. Taylor, who had previously practiced

law in Massachusetts, persisted in his effort. In June 1877 he appeared in US District Court in Baltimore. Archibald Stirling, then a district attorney, made a motion to admit Taylor to the bar of the US Circuit and District Courts. That afternoon, Taylor was sworn in and became the first black Marylander to be admitted to practice law.[42]

Taylor, however, hoped to practice in the Maryland Court of Appeals and would have to apply separately for admission to the state's bar. His desire presented a quandary for state officials. Maryland law required a lawyer to be "white" but recognized attorneys licensed to practice in other states. Taylor had already been admitted to Massachusetts's bar. Nevertheless, Maryland prohibited him from practicing. Taylor appealed, arguing that Maryland's exclusion of African Americans was a violation of the Fourteenth Amendment. In one of his first acts of political activism, Harvey Johnson raised funds to secure the appeal, but the effort ended in disappointment. The court of appeals denied Taylor's application, citing the Supreme Court's decision in the case of Myra Bradwell. In 1872 Bradwell sought admittance to the Illinois bar and challenged her exclusion as a violation of the Fourteenth Amendment. In an 8–1 ruling, the Supreme Court decided that the amendment did not protect Bradwell's ability to practice law and that states, not the federal government, had the right to regulate professions. Taylor left Maryland following the decision, and afterward the issue lay dormant.[43]

In 1884 African Americans once again set their sights on Maryland's exclusionary law. An African American attorney named Richard E. King unsuccessfully tried to convince the Maryland House of Delegates to overturn the legislation. Not much is known about King's background, although one report noted that he came to Maryland from Massachusetts. The legislature's failure to pass the bill angered Hawkins, who was serving as the local correspondent to T. Thomas Fortune's *New York Globe*. "The bill allowing colored lawyers to practice in the courts of the State was left, as was expected, on the files. So far as the law is concerned," Hawkins continued, "the colored people of this State are practically little better off than they were in *ante-bellum* days."[44]

After King failed to win support in the state, he petitioned the US Senate to intercede on his behalf. King's efforts failed, but he reopened public discussion of racial inequality in the state's judicial system. The *New York Globe* updated their readers on the progress of the case. Locally, King gained an important ally in the *Baltimore Sun*. The newspaper came out in strong support of admitting African Americans to the Maryland bar. The *Sun* stated, "The law has no right to keep a colored man from earning his bread in any honest way he may see fit, provided that he shows himself able to meet the requirements imposed on all other classes of citizens." The *Sun* added, "The law as it stands formed only one part of a system that has passed away, and which no one wishes to bring back."[45]

Despite the *Sun*'s optimism, the "system that has passed away" had hardly vanished in 1885 when Wilson challenged the law. This time, however, activists had a key advantage that their predecessors did not possess.[46] Three years earlier, African Americans helped reshape the city's Supreme Bench by supporting the independent judiciary movement. The justices that African Americans had helped elect heard Wilson's case. On 19 March 1885 the city's Supreme Bench overturned Maryland's 1872 exclusionary law. The decision read, in part, "To deter any class of citizens from its membership is not only to prevent their engaging in a lawful calling, but, in the language of the Supreme Court, tends to degrade and stigmatize the whole class by depriving them of a privilege which all other citizens possess and of the equal protection of the law."[47]

The decision was an important, but initially limited, victory. The ruling only applied in Baltimore, and African Americans did not practice law in the rest of the state until 1888.[48] Still, the successful conclusion of Wilson's test case validated activists' existing strategy of attacking inequalities through the legal system. Rather than appealing to white politicians who could brush aside their concerns, disregard the black community, or simply pander to African Americans for votes, black activists could now spearhead their own efforts. Hawkins captured how important the victory was for activists and the larger community. "If Dr. Johnson ha[d] done nothing else in his public career he has laid aside his activities upon the attainment of this end, he would still be entitled to, and should have without stint, the everlasting gratitude of all people."[49]

The decision also held potentially wider implications. Like the *Sue* case, Wilson's suit sought to restore the reach of the Fourteenth Amendment. When the Supreme Bench decided that state laws, such as Maryland's prohibition on black attorneys, could not discriminate against blacks because of the protections laid forth in the Fourteenth Amendment, activists could then begin to chip away at other social injustices. Maryland still had plenty of laws on its books to target, including a discriminatory bastardy law and a jury selection system that excluded African Americans. Black Baltimoreans had long relished the chance to challenge these laws. However, they would have to wait. Although he won his challenge, Wilson did not apply to the bar. In the meantime, activists began a search to find a qualified black attorney.[50]

As activists searched for a qualified applicant to the bar, they confronted a new challenge. The plight of Howard Cooper, whom police arrested in April 1885 for allegedly raping a white woman, underscored the urgency of finding legal counsel committed to civil rights and defending black suspects. The case also demonstrated the deadly consequences of the state's jury selection system, which effectively excluded African Americans.

In April 1885 twenty-two-year-old Catherine Gray was walking home after seeing her sister off at a train station in rural Baltimore County. On her journey she passed the twenty-four-year-old Cooper. Cooper, who may have been mentally disabled, followed the young woman into "the thickest part of the woods," attacked her with a piece of wood, and allegedly raped her. Cooper's crime infuriated local whites and made national news.[51]

The case against Cooper was problematic from the outset. The only eyewitness was Gray. In the initial reporting, and in her testimony in court, Gray claimed that Cooper assaulted her but never accused him of rape. Cooper's testimony concurred. He admitted attacking Gray but repeatedly denied raping her, telling the *Baltimore Sun* that he "did not assault her after she was helpless." The only support for the rape charge came from Gray's doctor, H. Louis Naylor, who had examined her on the day after the assault. Not surprisingly, the all-white grand jury still charged Cooper with one count of rape and one count of assault with intent to murder. The rape charge was crucial; Cooper faced the death penalty because of the alleged sexual assault.[52]

The case's notoriety made it difficult for Cooper to secure an adequate defense. Cooper's first lawyer recused himself for unspecified reasons, prompting the judge to issue an open request to the Maryland bar. At first, he could find no takers.[53] The judge finally found two men, George Weld and A. Robinson White, who were willing to defend Cooper. The inexperienced Weld and White were the least appealing options in the case. According to a history of Baltimore published in 1898, White "was called to the bar of Baltimore in March 1878" but had never tried a criminal case. In fact, this would be the only criminal trial of his career. Weld had even less experience. Twenty-nine years old at the time of Cooper's trial, he had been admitted to Maryland's bar in 1884.[54] By all accounts the two men worked hard for their client. Still, in a high-profile capital case, the inexperienced Weld and White were less than ideal choices.

Despite their inexperience, Weld and White made a pair of shrewd legal moves during pretrial hearings. The attorneys filed a motion to move the case to the US Circuit Court, since black Marylanders were effectively "excluded from jury service, in violation of the equal rights secured to them by the fourteenth amendment." Although not officially prohibited from serving, African Americans rarely appeared on juries in Maryland's courts. Since 1867, counties ostensibly selected jurors from two separate lists: "white male taxables" and the poll books. Since the poll books contained the names of African Americans, county officials exclusively used the former list to populate jury pools. Judge William A. Stewart overruled the motion. Weld and White then filed a second motion to change Cooper's "not guilty" plea to a "plea in abatement," a legal maneuver designed to contest the court's proceedings since Cooper had pled before securing counsel. The court rejected this motion as well, but Weld and White now had grounds to file an appeal.[55]

Because of the animosity against Cooper in Baltimore County, the judge moved his trial to the city where the problems with Maryland's prejudicial jury selection system became immediately evident. According to the *Baltimore Sun*, "nearly every man called as a juror had formed an opinion, but all except a few said that it would not interfere with the rendering of an impartial verdict exclusively upon the evidence." One juror, John Eckstine, informed the court before the trial began that "he would hang Cooper if he was on the jury." The court excused Eckstine from service but kept the others. By design, the remaining jurors were all white males. Later that afternoon, the jury took less than a minute to find Cooper guilty of rape.[56]

Cooper's defense filed a procedural appeal that challenged not the verdict but the way in which it was reached. Weld and White contended before the State Court of Appeals that Baltimore County's grand jury selection system violated the Fourteenth Amendment. "It is well known in Baltimore county, with 11,000 colored people," Weld argued, "no colored man has ever been allowed to sit on the jury." The justices rejected the defense's arguments when they unanimously upheld the lower court's judgment.[57] As far as the state of Maryland was concerned, Cooper's fate was sealed.

Governor Henry Lloyd signed Cooper's death warrant and fixed the date of his execution as 31 July.[58]

Although the state felt satisfied that justice had been served in Cooper's case, Weld and White had other plans. The attorneys announced their intention to continue their pursuit of the procedural appeal before the US Supreme Court. Cooper needed to furnish an $800 bond and secure an additional $100–$300 to pay for court expenses. The *Baltimore Sun* reported that "Cooper's mother and several colored societies have talked about raising it, but nothing has been done, and unless they do it, an appeal will be impossible." The editors of the *Baltimore County Union* felt confident in stating that it was "very doubtful" that African Americans could secure the funds.[59]

Both newspapers underestimated African Americans' resolve to challenge Maryland's racist criminal justice system. In bringing the appeal before the Supreme Court, African Americans saw an opportunity to possibly overturn Maryland's de facto exclusion of black jurors. A group of black waiters in Baltimore organized the Progressive Association to solicit funds in Cooper's name. Not much is known of the group's efforts with no extant records documenting their activities. Yet throughout the early part of July they rallied support and raised funds for Cooper's appeal. Some of Baltimore's most prominent ministers, including Johnson, Robert Steele, P. G. Walker, and W. Charles Lawson, allowed the Progressive Association to use their names to solicit funds.[60]

Throughout early July, the *Baltimore Sun* kept its readership abreast of the fund-raising effort's progress. The paper reported on 9 July that the movement was "taking definite shape" and that Judge Richard H. Alvey set the bond at $250, considerably less than the $800 the *Sun* had reported earlier. Two days later, the newspaper reprinted the circular used by the Progressive Association to solicit donations. The circular read, in part, that their efforts were to "protect the colored people in their civil and constitutional rights, which have been flagrantly violated in the trial of Cooper. If we permit encroachments to stand in this case," the circular continued, "it will not be long before the safeguards of civil and religious liberty will be swept away." As the Progressive Association's efforts gathered momentum, Harvey Johnson and his parishioners donated the rest of the necessary funds for Cooper's appeal.[61]

On the same evening when Johnson secured the money to pay for Cooper's appeal, white Marylanders in Towson organized a lynch mob. On

12 July, rumors had circulated throughout Baltimore County that African Americans had raised the funds for Cooper's defense.[62] With a Supreme Court hearing now a distinct possibility, white Marylanders decided to act. Just before midnight "little squads of men" wearing masks and disguises descended on Towson, where Cooper awaited his appeal. A group of approximately seventy-five men set out for the jail. After forcing their way in, the vigilantes found Cooper hiding in his cell. With the assistance of a crowbar, they broke in, tied a rope around Cooper's neck, and led him to the nearest tree. Cooper reportedly told them, "Well, you have got Cooper haven't you? Good bye." With that, the lynch mob pulled the rope and hoisted Cooper to his death.[63]

Historians who study lynching have identified a striking pattern in this extralegal violence. Lynch mobs frequently claimed that they acted to defend the honor of white women against black rapists.[64] Indeed, many Marylanders claimed that their desire to protect Gray from testifying in a retrial compelled them to act. The *Baltimore Sun* reported, "One of the main reasons given for anticipating the processes of the law, as stated by citizens of the county, was that a new trial would subject Miss Gray to the painful ordeal of facing a jury with her wrongs a second time, and they thought she had been outraged enough." Many others, including Gray's father, justified the lynching using this same reasoning.[65]

Cooper's lynching conforms to this pattern. Yet both its timing and its explanation reveal that white Marylanders acted with other motivations as well, primarily to stop the case from reaching the Supreme Court. They had reason to fear this possibility. Just months before Cooper's murder, Johnson won two legal victories in Baltimore. These successes demonstrated the efficacy of legal challenges to discrimination. They also heightened segregationists' anxiety. Black Marylanders (including Johnson) and Cooper's defense team made it clear that they intended to challenge the state's jury selection process as a violation of the Fourteenth Amendment. The Cooper lynching, therefore, needs to be understood in the context of the *Steamer Sue* case and the effort to see African Americans admitted to the state bar. Activists intended all three cases to compel Maryland to enforce the Fourteenth Amendment. But the Cooper appeal posed an especially acute threat since it endangered the monopoly that whites had on the jury system.

Throughout the summer, the press closely followed African Americans' efforts to raise money for Cooper's appeal and frequently commented on the activists' motivations. White Marylanders understood the appeal as a civil rights challenge that threatened one of the pillars of white supremacy in Maryland. One snippet of evidence, left out of local reports but printed in the *Chicago Daily Tribune*, indicated that the mob had the potential civil rights challenge on their minds. As Cooper's body swung beneath a sycamore tree next to the Towson courthouse, a man climbed up on a barrel. "Boys, the fruit of that tree shows that the men of Baltimore County will protect their wives and daughters," the man announced. "I wish we had those lawyers swinging up there too."[66] The lyncher's statement cited the defense of white womanhood but coupled it with a verbal denunciation and threat aimed at a defense team that facilitated African Americans' challenge to white supremacy and claims to equality under the law. Even days after the lynching, the *Baltimore County Union* felt compelled to remind its angry readership that the attorneys were only performing the duties required of them.[67]

The trajectory of Cooper's legal journey makes it clear that white Marylanders were determined to keep the case in state. White Marylanders supported their own courts where a favorable outcome was assured. It was only when activists succeeded in raising the necessary funds to bring the trial before the Supreme Court that they objected to the legal proceedings. During Cooper's pretrial hearing, Judge Stewart articulated the dangers that the appeal posed to white supremacy in the state. When he ruled against the defense's motion to move the trial, he did so because he "would not undertake to pronounce the whole jury system of Maryland unconstitutional." Given the stakes, it is not surprising that the *Baltimore Sun* vehemently opposed the defense's plan to challenge what they termed a technicality. "The setting up anew of a technical plea, after it has been passed upon by the Court of Appeals and rejected as not valid," the editors argued, "is simply, under such circumstances, a retarding of justice."[68]

In this context, Cooper's lynching communicated to African Americans that the judicial process would maintain white supremacy or it would not be allowed to function at all. Because whites could not stop activists' use of legal channels, they resorted to extralegal violence that disrupted and interfered with the courts. This was a deliberate tactic to frighten African Americans and deter further civil rights activism. The rejection of the Supreme Court's authority and affront to African American legal activism was not a tacit message. Instead, editorialists overtly and repeatedly expressed it in the state's newspapers. The *Baltimore Sun*'s editorial boasted that white

Marylanders had allowed the law to take its course. "No more righteous
verdict was ever rendered. Nevertheless," the editors continued, "the right
of Cooper's counsel to take the case to the Court of Appeals on two points
ruled against them in the lower court admitted of no dispute, and there
was a quiet acquiescence in their course." Yet in the *Sun*'s retelling, the legal
process stopped at Maryland's state line. In commenting on the Supreme
Court appeal, the editors wrote, "It was felt that in so clear a case of guilt
the law ought to be allowed to take its course without obstruction, and that
the technical points to be passed on by the Supreme Court, which might
be tested just as well in any case of less importance, would delay indefinitely
the execution of the sentence or would end, as such delays have often done
before, in a miscarriage of justice."[69] As whites saw it, lynching did not
obstruct the law; appeals through the court system did.

Newspapers across Maryland echoed the *Sun*'s sentiments. "The lynching was the result of an attempt to take Cooper's case on technical grounds
to the Supreme Court of the U.S." The *Frederick Daily News* denounced the
appeal as a way to undermine the law in order to set Cooper free while the
Hagerstown Daily News argued that Cooper's attorneys hoped to "evade
the punishment deserved." The *Rising Sun Journal* in Cecil condemned the
efforts of African Americans to see the case to the Supreme Court. "This
kind of trifling with justice outraged the people," the paper editorialized,
"who cut short the business by hanging the darkey."[70]

It is telling that the mob did not wait for the Supreme Court to hear
the case or issue a verdict. If the ringleaders had been truly worried about
Gray having to testify in a retrial, they could have taken action after the
court rendered its decision. The court would not have compelled Gray to
testify until after they scheduled Cooper's retrial. Instead, the lynchers
mobilized as soon as rumors surfaced that African Americans had cleared
the financial hurdle and the Supreme Court challenge appeared inevitable.

Taken together, the lynching and the subsequent coverage of the crime
rewrote Cooper's plight in important ways. In these accounts, the mob and
the press portrayed African Americans as criminally obstructing justice. The
lynchers became the protectors of law and order as well as righteous aveng-
ers. The praise that newspapers heaped on the mob demonstrated unified
and unquestioned support of white supremacy. Editors also drove home
their contention that Maryland's system of justice was equitable and fair.
In fact, the *Sun* falsely opined, despite evidence to the contrary, that Cooper's jury was "uninfluenced by any such excitement as might have warped

the judgment of a jury of the vicinage."[71] The state press further minimized African Americans' claims that Maryland's judicial system violated the Fourteenth Amendment by repeatedly maintaining that the appeal rested on a technicality. Cooper's lynching served as a stark reminder that in matters of race, white Marylanders were united and above the law.

For African Americans, Cooper's lynching cut deep. Black Marylanders witnessed yet another case of vigilante murder and were robbed of the chance to challenge the prejudicial apparatus that foreclosed the possibility of a fair trial. Black Marylanders expressed many levels of frustration. In most cases, they did not challenge Cooper's guilt, although there is reason to suspect that he did not commit rape. Most likely, this was a strategy born out of self-preservation. In the 1880s African Americans invited bodily harm and even death when challenging the validity of rape accusations. Still, in at least one instance African Americans publically cast doubt on Cooper's guilt. Shortly after Cooper's lynching, fifty African Americans gathered at Bethel AME Church in Hagerstown. The attendees printed resolutions including one that condemned the lynchings of a "great number of colored men accused as criminals who have been lawlessly slain in this State within the past few years." Although they did not explicitly name Cooper in this resolution, the meeting was held as a result of his lynching, and the group did not separate him from the category of "accused."[72]

In other cases, African Americans reacted by offering wide-ranging critiques of race relations and Maryland's criminal justice system. Rev. P. G. Walker, of the Metropolitan Colored Methodist Episcopal Church, rhetorically asked, "What occasion is there for such things in a country of law like this?" He answered his own question by highlighting one of the great hypocrisies at the center of the affair. "Men who want the protection of the law," Walker observed, "should let the law take its due course." Rev. Robert Steele, of Baltimore's Centennial Church, captured the many levels of frustration that African Americans felt in the wake of Cooper's lynching. "Some colored brutes commit such outrages against the virtue of white females," Steele observed, "just as white men did the same years ago in the South upon the chastity of colored women. The difference is that the whites will not tolerate such outrages and take the law in their own hand, while colored men were and are powerless to even expect a fair verdict against the ravishers of their women." Steele concluded by noting, "I have no regret to express at the death of the unfortunate Cooper other than that the law should have been permitted to take its course." One Baltimore County man, who asked the *Sun* not to print his name, also criticized the lynch mob for not allowing the justice system to run its course. His statement subtly acknowledged that he recognized the mob's intent in disrupting Cooper's appeal. He first explained to the reporter that any jury—white or black— would have found Cooper guilty. The man then remarked that if they lynched him "because they knew he had not had the trial the law entitled him to, then it was a greater crime to hang him under such circumstances."[73]

As the unnamed man's statement indicated, black Baltimoreans understood the mob's intended message. They refused, however, to be cowed by racial violence and intimidation. The independent judiciary movement, the *Sue* trial, and Charles S. Wilson's suit demonstrated that the judicial system offered some promise. In all three cases, but especially Wilson's victory, activists scored important successes. African Americans would now be able to hire attorneys committed to providing strong representation and invested in furthering racial equality.

Black Baltimoreans' use of test case challenges revived a strategy that an earlier generation employed to expand their freedoms after the Civil War. Just as African Americans in the 1860s and 1870s challenged transportation segregation and race-based exclusions, activists in the 1880s continued those struggles. In some cases, such as the fight against Maryland's prohibition of black attorneys, they opened new fronts. While activists built on this tradition of activism, they also pushed the strategy in new directions. In the 1860s and 1870s, black Baltimoreans did not often coordinate their strategies; Harvey Johnson and his associates did. Activists methodically planned and executed test cases designed to make Baltimore and Maryland live up to the promises of the Fourteenth Amendment. They first tested their strategy's feasibility with the *Steamer Sue* case. When they met with some success, they next pushed open the city's bar to black attorneys. The two victories changed the trajectory of civil rights in Baltimore and Maryland. As fellow activist William M. Alexander noted, "Process in the courts of law, rather than political agitation" would be the way forward for activists.[74]

As 1885 came to a close, Baltimore's black radicals intended to capitalize on the momentum they had built. Thus far Johnson and his allies helped remake Baltimore's Supreme Bench; his parishioners put their bodies on the line to challenge discrimination and had donated money to fund further legal challenges. At the end of 1885, Johnson set into motion the next step in his plan: to establish the city's first civil rights organization, which would begin the next chapter in the struggle for racial equality.

CHAPTER 3

The Mutual United Brotherhood of Liberty
and New Directions in Black Activism

On 2 June 1885, Rev. Harvey Johnson called five of his fellow clergymen and close confidants—Ananias Brown, William M. Alexander, Patrick Henry Alexander (P. H. A.) Braxton, John Calvin Allen, and W. Charles Lawson—to his Baltimore home. During the previous year, Johnson had orchestrated challenges to public transportation segregation and Maryland's prohibition on black attorneys. Now he hoped to accelerate the fight for racial equality by forming Baltimore's first civil rights organization, the Mutual United Brotherhood of Liberty. As William Alexander, Johnson's friend and protégé, remembered, "The favorable termination of these important cases prompted and hastened the organization of the Brotherhood of Liberty as the most effective medium through which the laws in Maryland and other States repugnant to the interests of the colored people could be most speedily expunged." In the coming years, the group fundamentally altered the fight for racial equality in Baltimore and helped shape the civil rights movement in the United States.[1]

The organization of the Brotherhood of Liberty was a pivotal moment in the history of the black freedom struggle. Active between 1885 and 1891, the Brotherhood was not only Baltimore's first civil rights organization but also one of the first in the nation. During its brief history, the group undertook three key efforts in the late 1880s and early 1890s: the fight to amend Maryland's Bastardy Act, the movement to end inequalities in public education, and the defense of black laborers virtually enslaved on Navassa Island in the Caribbean. In each of these endeavors, the Brotherhood eschewed partisan politics in favor of protests and lawsuits. Black Baltimoreans had conducted court challenges and protests before; however, these initiatives were largely uncoordinated. The Brotherhood built on these earlier efforts but also brought a new level of sophistication and organization to Baltimore's black freedom struggle. Although the Brotherhood possessed a cohort of all male leaders, as was typical for the period, women served as active supporters and participants in Baltimore's black freedom struggle. By organizing test cases and community-based protests, the group built a more inclusive, community-based movement to fight racial inequality.

The Brotherhood's founding came as civil rights activists across the nation debated the direction of the fight for equality. During the early 1880s, journalists, including Ida B. Wells, T. Thomas Fortune, John Mitchell, Jr., and others, used their newspapers to challenge the advent of Jim Crow. In New York, Fortune began promoting the idea of a permanent, nonpartisan civil rights organization in 1884. Although it would take years for Fortune to realize his plan, the Brotherhood quickly incorporated many of his ideas and tested their feasibility in Maryland. The group organized independently, demanded the fulfillment of the Constitution's promises of racial equality, and aggressively challenged discrimination. The leaders of the Brotherhood, like other civil rights activists of the era, saw in the Constitution, particularly the Thirteenth, Fourteenth, and Fifteenth Amendments, a viable path toward ending legalized inequality.[2] Their vision for racial equality, their strategies, and uncompromising demand for civil rights, more so than any group, set the foundation for later national groups such as the Afro-American League and the Niagara Movement.[3]

By the 1880s, Baltimore's black community had taken important steps in developing a nonpartisan reform agenda that paved the way for the formation of the Brotherhood of Liberty. The newly emergent black press was an integral element in spurring this independent political action. African Americans in Baltimore already had access to out-of-state black newspapers, including the *People's Advocate* (Washington, DC) and T. Thomas Fortune's *New York Globe*. Fortune in particular used his paper to rally African Americans around race rather than party, to spark debate, and to issue calls for a national civil rights organization. Baltimoreans not only read these papers but contributed to them as well. Throughout the decade, both newspapers published regular columns written by black Baltimoreans who reported on social events, gatherings, and political protests.[4]

Black Baltimoreans soon founded their own newspapers. Most of these publications only survived for a few years, leading many black Baltimoreans to joke that the city was a "grave-yard for colored newspapers."[5] Neverthe-less, the establishment of an independent press was an important step in organizing black Baltimoreans. In January 1882 the *Baltimore Beacon* became the first black newspaper to appear in the city in more than fifteen years. The next year, political activist and union organizer Isaac Myers pub-lished the *Colored Citizen*. Under Myers's watch, the paper was, according to the *New York Globe*, "intensely Republican in politics." That same year, activist Joseph E. Briscoe started a four-page weekly newspaper, the *Vindi-cator*. Briscoe promised the paper would be nonpartisan. He focused on issues of education and the fight against the state's remaining black laws. An advertisement for the paper in *Rowell's American Newspaper Directory* revealed Briscoe's editorial stance: "*The Vindicator* is devoted to the vin-dication of right and to opposition to wrong."[6] Even though the papers represented different points of view, they collectively created a sense of community and developed a political voice in a rapidly growing city. They provided African Americans a public forum in which to debate, discuss, and critique events in their city free from white editors' control.

Baltimore's growing black Baptist movement further laid the founda-tion for new directions in the struggle for racial equality. It is difficult to overstate the importance of the black church to social activism in the late nineteenth century. The black Baptist church in particular had long been a font of political protests. Throughout the nation, they provided communi-ties safe spaces to articulate their opposition to racism and Jim Crow. The Baptist church also espoused a political and social agenda that emphasized self-help, independence, and resistance. In Baltimore, a few of the city's Baptist churches were rooted in the antebellum era, but many others were founded during the Reconstruction era. In the years after Emancipation, many of them, both established and new, welcomed new ministers. These ministers not only attracted larger congregations but would also lead the fight for racial equality in the coming decades.[7]

In 1872 John Calvin (J. C.) Allen became the pastor of the First Colored Baptist Church. Allen, a recent graduate of Ohio's Iberia College, assumed control of a church with a deep history but small congregation. Moses C. Clayton, a former slave from Richmond, founded the church in 1836 follow-ing an invitation from a white missionary named William Crane. Clayton led the church and early community education efforts during the antebellum era. When Allen arrived in Baltimore, the church stood at a crossroads. One report described First Baptist as "the first in age, but others had outstripped it, and it stood, somewhat in debt, not knowing, but hoping for a future." In a little more than ten years, Allen revitalized the congregation. He grew the membership to 371 and helped raise funds for a new building.[8]

Shortly after Allen's arrival, Rev. Ananias Brown moved to Baltimore from Newport, Rhode Island, to become the minister of a small congregation at Leadenhall Street Baptist Church in South Baltimore. A Richmond native and graduate of Wayland Seminary, Brown inherited a congregation that counted only 147 members in 1875. The white-led Maryland Baptist Union Association built the church in 1870 when they helped parishioners from Providence Baptist Church purchase a lot and construct a new building. When Brown arrived, he grew the membership at a more rapid pace. By 1885 the congregation, now known as Leadenhall Street Baptist, counted six hundred members.[9]

During the 1870s and early 1880s, Harvey Johnson's Union Baptist became the city's most important and influential church. In addition to being the largest African American church in Baltimore, it became the epicenter for a proliferation of new black Baptist churches across the city and state in the 1870s and 1880s. In total, at least fourteen churches and eleven ministers traced their roots to Union Baptist and Johnson's mentorship. The earliest mission to branch off Union Baptist Church was Macedonia. In 1875 Rev. W. Charles Lawson and Leander Jones began to hold small meetings in a horse stable. Within a few years, the growing congregation moved to a new building, where it continued to grow throughout the 1870s and 1880s.[10]

In early February 1878, twelve members of Union Baptist Church formed Calvary Baptist Church. After the arrival of their new pastor, P. H. A. Braxton, in 1879, the church's membership thrived. When Braxton moved to Baltimore from Virginia, Calvary Baptist only had ten members. As was true at Macedonia, Calvary Baptist lacked a home and met in various locations in the city's northwest, including a carpenter shop. Within two years, Braxton began collecting funds to build a proper church while increasing the membership to 125. By 1890, he preached to 550 attendees in a building that one observer proclaimed was the "finest church building used by the colored people of Baltimore."[11]

In 1888 another of Johnson's protégés, Garnett R. Waller, formed Trinity Baptist Church. Like Brown, Johnson, and Braxton, Waller originally hailed from Virginia before moving to Baltimore. Waller became a member of Johnson's Union Baptist Church before he left the city to earn a degree at Pennsylvania's Lincoln University. After finishing his studies at Lincoln, he attended Newton Seminary in Massachusetts before returning to Baltimore. In the early 1900s Waller would become one of the first members of the Niagara Movement and play an instrumental role in opening the Baltimore branch of the NAACP.[12]

Johnson's most important ally, William Moncure Alexander, helped organize Sharon Baptist Church. Alexander met Johnson as a young man in the 1870s. Inspired by Johnson's example, Alexander enrolled at Wayland Seminary before returning to Baltimore in 1882 to take the reins of Sharon Baptist. The congregation's growth mirrored that of the city's other Baptist churches. Sharon Baptist grew out of a Sunday school that originally held services in a vacant lot. When Alexander arrived, the nine-member congregation worshipped in a building that the city's largest black newspaper, the *Afro-American Ledger,* described as "not altogether suitable." Under Alexander's watch, the growing congregation bought a white Baptist church in Northwest Baltimore. Like Johnson, Alexander quickly established himself as a community leader and activist. A 1915 *Afro-American Ledger* article remarked, "As a community worker Dr. Alexander stands in the forefront, there being no racial movement in Maryland within the past three decades with which he has not been identified."[13]

Together, the city's black press and Baptist churches proved to be vital parts of Baltimore's black freedom struggle. The newspapers provided valuable space for activists to reach a wider audience and organize the community. The churches also united black Baltimoreans across the city. First Baptist Church served African Americans living east of the city's downtown. African Americans living in the southern section of the city attended Leadenhall. Union Baptist Church, and the congregations that sprang from it, served citizens living north and west of the city's downtown. Together, the newspapers and churches augmented the political space offered through the black-owned, black-operated Douglass Institute by serving as forums where African Americans discussed, debated, and broadcast ideas. Union Baptist Church hosted temperance meetings, political gatherings, and celebrations to honor legal triumphs. In the 1890s Sharon Baptist Church began to publish the *Afro-American* newspaper, which became one of the nation's leading black papers. Calvary Baptist Church hosted political rallies and meetings to support public education, while women met there to plan mission work. At the churches, ministers also encouraged congregants to become activists and support movements for civil rights. For example, in

Figure 5. Sharon Baptist Church's Rev. William Moncure Alexander, an associate of Rev. Harvey Johnson. He was an activist and education reformer. (Photograph date unknown.) Courtesy of Philip J. Merrill Nanny Jack & Co. Archives.

the *Steamer Sue* case and the protests surrounding Howard Cooper's lynching, Johnson's congregation played key roles as plaintiffs, activists, and fund-raisers.[14]

When Johnson created the Brotherhood of Liberty in 1885, he drew on the church for financial support, to form the organization's leadership, and to provide organizing space. The group, in turn, relied on their faith to guide their principles. "It is a Scriptural truth that God has made of one blood all nations of men," the Brotherhood proclaimed in their Constitution, "to dwell on all the face of the earth." They combined this religious grounding with a faith in the nation's founding documents. "It is equally true, according to the Declaration of American Independence, that all men are endowed by their Creator with certain inalienable rights," they continued, "and that among these are life, liberty, and the pursuit of happiness." Johnson and his cohorts formed the Brotherhood to "use all legal means within our power to procure and maintain our rights as citizens."[15]

The Mutual United Brotherhood of Liberty was determined to follow a legal strategy to challenge racial inequalities and began searching for a legal team. Their search led them to the nation's capital. In June, Everett J. Waring was preparing to graduate from Howard Law School in Washington, DC. Waring possessed the training and background that the Brotherhood desired. He had grown up in Springfield, Ohio, where he succeeded his father as the principal of the city's "colored high school." Waring also edited a local paper, the *Sunday Capital*, before founding the *Afro-American* newspaper in his hometown. The latter paper, according to the *Baltimore Sun*, was instrumental in fomenting an "important revolt of colored people against the republican party." Johnson convinced Waring to move to Baltimore to become the first African American admitted to the city's bar. A few months later, Joseph S. Davis joined Waring. A Virginia native, Davis had graduated from the Hampton Institute in the late 1870s. After a stint as a teacher in his hometown, Davis moved to Washington, DC, to work for the General Land Office and enroll at Howard University. Davis combined his legal training with a firm commitment to civil rights. "Many a brave soldier gave his life for universal liberty," Davis once proclaimed, "and we will be derelict of duty if we fail to labor unitedly in carrying out the principles of justice and liberty for which so many noble lives have been sacrificed."[16]

With their legal team set, the Brotherhood targeted Maryland's Bastardy Act. During the 1860s, reformers successfully fought to overturn some of the state's most discriminatory "Black Laws," including the apprenticeship law (which allowed former slave owners to enslave black children after Emancipation) and a statute that prohibited African Americans from testifying against whites. Maryland's discriminatory Bastardy Act survived this initial onslaught. The law, as it was originally conceived in 1781, allowed women to compel their child's father to provide financial support in cases of abandonment. It originally applied to all women. Then, in 1785, lawmakers narrowed its provisions to free women, regardless of race. In 1860 legislators made the act racially exclusive when they inserted the word "white."[17]

In early 1886 a black Baltimorean named Lucinda Moxley sought the Brotherhood's assistance in prosecuting her child's father, James Smith, under the provisions of the Bastardy Act. From the outset, Waring made it clear that he intended to use Moxley's plight to challenge the law as a violation of both the Fourteenth Amendment and the Civil Rights Act of 1866. The *Baltimore Sun* reported that he was "supported in his efforts by a number of citizens, white and colored, who think that the bastardy law, which discriminates against colored women, is a barbarism, and ought to be done away with." The assistant state's attorney, Edgar H. Gans, supported the effort. It is possible that Smith willingly participated as well. Smith employed Edwin R. Davis, an attorney who previously had tried to change the law in Maryland's House of Delegates. Davis entered a demurrer on Smith's behalf, which claimed that Moxley had no legal ground to file the suit since the law did not apply to black women. By entering a demurrer, which the lower court accepted, Davis opened the door to a hearing before the city's Supreme Bench to determine the Bastardy Act's constitutionality. When Waring presented arguments, he became the first African American to appear before Baltimore's Supreme Bench.[18]

In covering the case, the *Baltimore Sun* predicted that the Supreme Bench would make "the law of general application to white and colored." Yet the Bastardy Act proved a difficult law to challenge. The legislation technically protected the state from having to pay child support by leveling a fine on the father. Therefore, in the eyes of the law, this financial restitution was not a benefit to the mother or child but a way to safeguard the state's economic resources. The law's mechanics further complicated the matter. It required that authorities arrest the woman in question for having a child out of wedlock. Once detained, she could then identify the father to avoid prosecution. In reality, women were rarely, if ever, held. Instead, the state used this threat as leverage to compel the mother to identify her child's father.[19]

Despite the *Sun*'s initial optimism, the Supreme Bench upheld the lower court's decision. The justices ruled that the Bastardy Act did not violate the Fourteenth Amendment since it did not protect an individual. The decision surprised the *Sun*, which saw parallels between it and the court's decision to end the prohibition on black attorneys a year earlier. The justices, however, thought otherwise. The *Sun* reported that, in opening up the bar to African Americans, "the object was to confer a benefit," while the effort to amend the Bastardy Act only "sought to impose a penalty on the colored man."[20] The verdict tightly adhered to the law's language. If the court excised the word "white," the law could penalize African Americans, subjecting both men and women to arrest and fines. Yet the verdict left unspoken the protections that the Bastardy Act extended to whites and the ways in which changing it would benefit African American women. Whether the state chose to acknowledge it or not, the law extended economic and social protections to white women. It provided any white woman with some degree of financial security since she could compel the father of her child to pay support. If the state removed the word "white," they would provide that same economic security to black women.

By failing to overturn the law, the Supreme Bench made important statements on race, gender, and the law. The justices let stand a law that elevated the status of white women. The legislation, in turn, stigmatized black women by insinuating that they were not worthy of the same protections. Waring pressed this argument before the Supreme Bench. The "Bill of Rights guarantees colored women the common law," Waring maintained. "They are on the same footing with white women at common law. Why not under statute?"[21] The Bastardy Law also shielded white men. By excluding black women, the state protected white men from legal proceedings stemming from interracial sex and from having to financially support the children they fathered. In the end, the Supreme Bench was loath to place black women and white women on the same legal plane and expose white men to potential court proceedings.

The justices may have also calculated their decision to send a message to activists. After African Americans notched two victories in the *Sue* case and the fight to overturn Maryland's prohibition on black attorneys, it is possible that the justices wanted to discourage more legal challenges to discrimination. This could explain Judge Edward Duffy's sudden change of heart just a few months later in a case involving a white couple. In August 1886 Sarah E. Clinton charged Thomas B. Driscoll with being the father of her child. In December Driscoll's attorney demurred, arguing that the Bastardy Act was unconstitutional. Duffy upheld the demur on the grounds that the law violated the Fourteenth Amendment's guarantee of equal protection. Duffy explained, "The Bastardy Law denied to a white woman equal protection to a colored woman in this respect, that it made a white woman who had an illegitimate child liable to arrest and prosecution when no such proceedings were provided against a colored woman." He also pointed out, "It denied the colored woman the right to have the father of her illegitimate child compelled by process of law, to support the child, a right accorded by law to the white woman, and was therefore in that respect also unconstitutional."[22] It is unclear why, exactly, Judge Duffy changed his mind. Duffy sat on Baltimore's Supreme Bench and ruled against Moxley. It is entirely possible that Duffy waited to issue this verdict in a case that involved a white couple to avoid or prevent a wider civil rights challenge. Unlike the Brotherhood, Clinton and Driscoll were far less likely to pursue the challenge to the Supreme Court, which would have exposed the state's laws to outside review.

Shortly after Judge Duffy's ruling, two other justices were split over the law's constitutionality in *State v. David H. Neikirk* in Washington County.[23] In an effort to settle the matter, the Maryland Court of Appeals heard a case involving another white couple, Pius L. Plunkard and Annie M. Hamilton. In *Plunkard v. State*, the court ruled in a five-to-one decision that the Bastardy Act did not violate the Fourteenth Amendment. The justices relied on the law's technical details in rendering their verdict. "The procreation of illegitimate children cannot be said to be a privilege or immunity of citizens of the United States," the justices maintained, "nor does the statute give any privilege or confer any benefit upon the mothers of such children." Even though a white mother received a financial benefit under the law, the justices argued that it was not because she was "the mother of the child, but because the child is maintained by her." This decision was not without controversy. The lone dissenting justice, Frederick Stone, retorted, "If the fourteenth amendment to the constitution of the United States means anything it means that there shall not be in any State one law applying to the white race and another and different one applying to the black."[24] It was a strong public rebuke of the Bastardy Act, as well as the court's strict interpretation of the law's language.

Following *Plunkard v. State*, African Americans across the state pressured the legislature to amend the law. In Frederick County, seventy-six black residents signed a petition while 242 others did the same in Allegany County. Nevertheless, the legislature rejected two bills to amend the Bastardy Act in the spring of 1888. At this point, black Marylanders began efforts to mount an appeal before the Supreme Court. An African American newspaper in Baltimore undertook a fund-raising drive to pay the seventy-five dollars needed to file an appeal. The grassroots effort raised sixty of the needed seventy-five dollars, mainly through one-dollar donations, attesting to the black community's widespread opposition to the law. The Brotherhood of Liberty also issued a call for subscriptions to pay for the legal challenge.[25]

Sources are not entirely clear, but at least one group of African American women, possibly two, pitched in as well. Women called an indignation meeting at Baltimore's Samaritan Temple, where they formed an auxiliary to the Brotherhood to raise funds for the legal challenge. The group had roots in another activist organization that had been formed in 1885 to promote black women's occupational opportunities, known as the Women's Protective Association. Another report claimed that a group of more than two hundred women affiliated with the African Methodist Episcopal Church also undertook a fund-raising drive. It is possible that this organization came to be known as the Women's Protective Association, or it could have been a separate organization altogether; the surviving evidence is scant and unclear. At any rate, it is evident that women both supported and participated in the effort.[26]

Faced with mounting public pressure and a possible date before the Supreme Court, the state's stubborn resolve finally disintegrated. In May 1888 attorney John Prentiss Poe was in the midst of codifying Maryland's laws when he "omitted the word white in the Bastardy act and . . . the Legislature had adopted his digest."[27] Poe never explained his reasoning, but his action was not in keeping with his politics. He was a Democrat and a segregationist who in later years would author legislation to disfranchise black voters. As dean of Maryland's law school, he also oversaw the expulsion of black students in 1891. Poe's timing, however, was not coincidental. Faced with the prospects of the case landing before the Supreme Court, Poe removed the word "white" from the code and ended the controversy before activists could press the issue before the federal courts.[28]

The Brotherhood's fight against the Bastardy Act left important legacies. It was the first test of the group's legal strategy, and they prevailed. Not only did the Brotherhood help defeat the law, but they also mobilized African

Americans throughout the state. The fact that the effort attracted women was especially significant. After the fight ended, Alexander credited women's activism "as one of the influences which helped to correct the obnoxious 'Bastardy Act.'" The Brotherhood hoped to build on this foundation and continue to draw on the activist network that they had created. Their next target was a decades-long struggle for Baltimore's black community that sat at the intersection of race, gender, and labor: inequalities in public education.

Throughout the 1860s and 1870s, black Baltimoreans fought long, frustrating battles with the city and state governments over the issue of educational equality. They had made little in the way of progress. Since 1868, black Baltimoreans had been sending their children to public schools that had been neglected and inadequately funded for nearly two decades. By 1885, the school board reported that black schools could accommodate fewer than six thousand students; Baltimore's population of black school-aged children was approximately fourteen thousand. The next year, the *New York Freeman* observed, "The building in which the colored High, Grammar and No. 1 Primary schools meet is in a miserable location" where some students had to "walk at least three miles a day to attend." The black-owned *Cleveland Gazette* added, "The schools for colored youth are in a deplorable condition. The lower grades are illy governed by worse white teachers, and the institutions intended for high and grammar schools are not worth the name, and the buildings are the poorest and most miserable." The Brotherhood's Joseph S. Davis termed the situation in Baltimore an "educational crisis."[29]

African Americans augmented the city's meager public education system with a network of private schools. Since the antebellum era, African Americans maintained private schools in a variety of spaces throughout the city.[30] Henrietta Hucless, Ida Johnson Rollins, William M. Alexander, and his wife Mary Ellen operated a school housed in the Patterson Avenue Church (soon to be renamed Sharon Baptist) that alleviated overcrowding in the rapidly growing black enclaves of Northwest Baltimore. It was a remarkable achievement in self-sufficiency and racial uplift. In two years of existence, 350 students, who supported the endeavor by paying ten cents per week, passed through its halls.[31] Nor was the Patterson Avenue Church School alone. The private schools in existence included those run by Adele Jackson, another administered by a "Miss Mahalla," one conducted in the

Douglass Institute, and another that operated in one of the city's alleys. African Americans also conducted night schools at the Biblical Centenary Institute and another at a church. By 1887, Davis claimed that more than five hundred black children attended private schools in Baltimore.[32]

Funding and poor facilities were only two of the problems afflicting black public education. When the city assumed control of African American schools in 1868, they refused to hire black educators, a policy that survived into the 1880s. Since Emancipation, African American activists had recognized the centrality of labor to civil rights and fought to expand job opportunities. Baltimore's activists attempted to organize unions, built a cooperative shipyard to ease unemployment, and attacked the legal system for prohibiting black attorneys. All of these efforts broadened the job prospects of black men. Reforming education had the potential to similarly expand the employment opportunities for black women. The city was home to a "Colored Normal School"—established during the Reconstruction era—which trained African American educators. Throughout the 1880s, African American women overwhelmingly made up the graduation lists. Baltimore's prohibition on black teachers forced graduates of the Normal School to leave the city for the surrounding counties to find employment in public schools.[33]

From its founding, the Brotherhood targeted education reform as one of its highest priorities. At its inaugural meeting it organized an education committee to lead its efforts. The committee appeared before the city council on numerous occasions to demand new schools and jobs for qualified black teachers. In February 1886 delegations pressed their demands at city hall and before the city council. Mayor Hodges and the city council responded favorably to the delegations. In April 1886 the council passed an ordinance to build a new high school and two primary schools. The initial favorable response, however, soon evaporated. The next year, Mayor Hodges vetoed the legislation, offering to fund the high school but not the two primary schools.[34]

Unsatisfied with the mayor's watered-down proposal, African Americans expanded their fight. In February the *Star*, a black newspaper edited by the Brotherhood's lawyer, E. J. Waring, championed the issue. Waring, according to the *New York Freeman*, "called upon the mechanics, professional men, business men, laborers, women, children, in fact every one, to join the army and storm the fortress that denied us [equal employment and opportunities in the schools]." At a meeting in Calvary Baptist

Church, Rev. T. R. Wilkins urged black Baltimoreans to take direct action. "If we do not get better schools we ought to send our children to the white schools as they did in Kentucky," Wilkins advised. "And when they are refused admittance we should appeal to the law and have the question settled."[35]

The Brotherhood's education committee helped found the Maryland Educational Union (MEU) to chart this more militant path forward. The group elected Braxton to lead the fight. Braxton used his opening remarks to connect children's education to the "highest rights" of being American citizens. He promised that the MEU would "continue to labor and wait until our right is recognized and enjoyed." Following the meeting, the group collected reports from city wards and recommended that citizens form "auxiliary unions" to assist in the effort.[36]

In early May 1887, the MEU issued a blistering report that castigated the mayor and city council "who have turned a deaf ear" to the "appeals of the colored citizens to better the educational facilities of their children in this city." They also rebuked the city council, which on the previous night "refused to pass the ordinance appointing colored teachers in the colored schools." The MEU called on "the citizens in every locality to protest against such disregard of our rights." In addition, they threatened that these protests would continue until the city reversed its prohibition on hiring black teachers. These were not idle threats. At the end of May, the organization attracted nine hundred people to one of its meetings held at Braxton's Calvary Baptist Church.[37]

During the summer of 1887, activists' and educators' frustrations with the city government continued to boil over. In July the Colored Teachers' Association of Maryland forcefully rebutted the council's refusal to pass an ordinance that would have authorized the hiring of African American teachers. Formed in 1886, the statewide organization pressured the state to improve black education. At their second annual gathering in 1887, the association did not mince words when they announced that they "deplore and condemn the action of the City Council," after the council failed to authorize the hiring of black teachers. They further termed this discrimination a "disgrace" to the city. In a move that signaled their determination to keep pressuring the city, the group changed its name to the Maryland State Progressive Teachers' Association. Many members felt that the word "colored" was "inconsistent in view of the concurrent effort to have the word 'white' stricken out of the State laws."[38]

After spending the spring and early part of the summer conducting protest meetings, gathering information, and fund-raising, as well as organizing local unions and female auxiliaries, the MEU sprang into action.[39] At a 19 July meeting, a teacher at the Normal School, Mary Saunders, addressed the audience and, through the medium of the *Baltimore Sun*, the city at large. Saunders railed against the inequality in public education. "The colored teachers of this city and State feel keenly the unjust treatment they have and are receiving at the hands of the school commissioners of Baltimore city. We are discriminated against," Saunders protested, "not on the ground of incompetency, but because of the color of our skin." Saunders was not the only one running out of patience. Braxton announced that he had consulted attorneys who assured him that if the MEU wanted to pursue legal action, they would meet with success. "I have always been of the opinion," he announced, "that we will not get what we want until we take this matter into the courts." Braxton then offered fifty dollars as an initial contribution to fund the legal effort. Braxton's resolution was "unanimously adopted," but the MEU apparently never followed through. The Brotherhood of Liberty, who had previously threatened a lawsuit, continued to pressure the city council's educational committee to appropriate funds for a school in Northwest Baltimore.[40]

Throughout the remainder of 1887, the city government refused to budge. Then, early the next year, external political events gave activists the leverage they needed to nudge Baltimore's recalcitrant government. The city hoped to annex some of the outlying suburbs in Baltimore County (known collectively as "the Belt") into Baltimore proper. The idea was controversial and city officials scrambled to secure every vote possible. For African American voters in the Belt, one of the issues in the proposed annexation was the fate of black public schoolteachers employed in the suburbs. If the city incorporated these schools, African American teachers would lose their jobs. Black voters in the Belt threatened to vote against annexation.[41] The city council finally relented. They voted to allocate $25,000 to purchase a lot and fund the building of a new school for African Americans. They also agreed to hire only black teachers to staff the new school, but they stipulated that the schools remain segregated. Finally, in May 1888, Baltimore's new mayor, Ferdinand Latrobe, signed the ordinance that, at least for African Americans, made sweeping changes in the city's education system. Not only did African American teachers win the right to teach in the city; they were also promised the same pay as their white counterparts.[42] After twenty years of fighting, black Baltimoreans had finally won some meaningful education reforms.

In the span of two years, activists pressured the city to open its public schools to African American educators and improve the available facilities. In a practical sense, these triumphs alone made an enormous difference. When the 1888 school year began, Roberta Sheridan became Baltimore's first African American public schoolteacher. Then, on 10 October 1888, the new black high school formally opened, though only after white residents made a last-ditch appeal to block its construction. The school proved to be an immediate success. Within three days of opening it was already over-crowded.[43]

Across the city, African American educational opportunities improved as a result of the pressure exerted by the Brotherhood of Liberty, the Colored Teachers' Association, and the Maryland Educational Union. The city increased its funding from $75,834.21 in 1886 to $111,890.42 in 1888. Their expenditures dropped the next two years but did not plummet to the paltry sums allocated in the early 1880s. Despite these victories, the state of black education in the city continued to pale in comparison to white education. As a result of increasing segregation in the 1890s, African Americans would eventually fight to compel the city to improve its educational facilities and employ more black teachers. Despite these problems, the disparities between white and black education in Baltimore were not as drastic as they were prior to the 1880s.[44]

In the early 1890s the battle over public education temporarily cooled down after the city began hiring African American teachers. The timing was fortuitous. Within a year, events on Navassa Island commanded the attention of Baltimore's black community. Since 1854, the Baltimore- and New York–based Navassa Phosphate Company claimed the island, exploiting both the land and its black employees. Located near Haiti, Navassa was, in the words of the *New York Times*, "a barren island, of no value except for its phosphates."[45] In order to extract the island's supply of guano, agents for the Navassa Phosphate Company recruited men in urban areas—particularly Baltimore—with the promise of a well-paying job on a Caribbean paradise. Once on the island, workers encountered starkly different circumstances from those recruiters had described.[46]

In 1889 eleven white officers ensured that conditions for their 137 black laborers matched the island's harsh landscape. Workers toiled on the island for tours that lasted at least fifteen months at a time. Stooped over, the hot Caribbean sun unrelentingly bearing down on their backs, they wielded picks and shovels to separate the valuable bird dung from limestone. After completing the collection process, the barefoot men loaded their harvest onto a cart that they pushed across the island to the harbor. Laborers' grievances extended beyond working conditions. The men subsisted on a gallon of water per day, which one investigator described as "brackish, not fit to drink." The workers complained of food that was "insufficient in quantity and consisted mainly of herring, hard tack, and 'salt horse.'" Edward Smith, an employee on the island, stated that he survived on a diet of "corned beef, hard tack, and boot-leg coffee." For dinner the men ate "spoiled fish pickled beef and beans." The *New York Times* found that the poor diet led to an outbreak of scurvy and reported that there "was no evidence that anything was done to alleviate their sufferings."[47]

Employees of the Navassa Phosphate Company also struggled to collect money for their labors. The company contracted workers for wages that equaled eight dollars per month but found numerous ways to cheat employees out of their earnings. With no other commercial outlets, laborers shopped at a company store that charged exorbitant prices for all basic supplies. If a worker required medical treatment, they paid fifty cents for each day in Navassa's hospital and forfeited a day's wages. The expenses quickly added up. In his investigation of the company store, Rev. John H. Collett, of Baltimore's Ebenezer AME Church, concluded, "This is worse than slavery—it is oppression and robbery." To further exacerbate an already dreadful situation, the company's contract stipulated that they would settle their accounts with workers only after returning to Baltimore. However, if the workers "should fail to obey the orders and instructions of said Navassa Phosphate Company, or its agents, or refuse at any time to labor, they shall forfeit all claim for wages and compensation which may be due them." This was a loophole that the company exploited with regularity.[48]

Tensions between employees and management on Navassa came to a head on 14 September 1889. That morning, the managers had been particularly abusive. One worker, Charles H. Davenport, reported that some of their bosses had been drinking that morning. When one of the employees (sources disagree whether it was Edmund Francis or James Phillips) arrived late from a stint in the hospital, supervisor Charles Roby reportedly pointed a gun at him and threatened that "the next grave I measure out will be yours." The workers responded with violence, wounding their supervisor. After the initial tensions abated, another officer, Samuel Marsh, advised the men to take their grievances to the superintendent. The superintendent met the workers' entreaties with more threats. The laborers left the meeting and initiated an impromptu strike, refusing to return to work until they received better treatment. During the confrontation that followed, one of the officers shot Phillips in the face, after Phillips allegedly refused to resume working and turn over Roby's firearm.[49]

Following Phillips's shooting, the situation on Navassa deteriorated further. Armed with stones and a few firearms, the laborers chased their supervisors into a nearby house. According to the workers, the supervisors continued to fire at them. The workers made two demands: cease firing and hand over James Mahon. The latter demand was particularly important. Mahon, "the mining and car boss," had repeatedly abused his workers. According to them, Mahon made them push cars full of guano across the island in bare feet, forcing them to choose whether to walk along the blistering hot rails or the island's jagged rocks. In another incident, Mahon had tortured one of the employees, C. H. Smallwood, who refused to work on account of illness. Workers wanted a measure of revenge for the violence that Mahon had committed against them. Holed up in the house, the supervisors refused to give in to either demand. The workers responded by planting dynamite in an attempt to flush them out. As some of the officers fled, workers killed three of them. Others surrendered. Finally, the violence subsided. The only one missing was Mahon, who had fled in fear of his life. An hour after the uprising ended, an employee named George S. Key found Mahon hiding underneath his bed. Key shot the supervisor twice, killing him in a final act of revenge.[50]

In late October and early November, the laborers arrived in Baltimore ahead of their trial. The men's appearance as they marched through the city streets made an unforgettable impression on black Baltimoreans. One report noted, "Eye witnesses said that they had never beheld men in such a degraded condition before." Many of the prisoners did not have winter clothing or shoes. In an image that harked back to Baltimore's slaveholding past, the alleged ringleaders, dressed only in rags, were bound in chains. Over the course of five indictments, the government indicted eighteen men for the murders. They charged seven of them—George S. Key, Henry Jones, Caesar Fisher, Edward Smith, Stephen Peters, Charles H. Smith, and Chas. H. Davis—with murder. They charged the remaining eleven with aiding and abetting. A number of others would face lesser charges. When the defense challenged the legality of trying all of the defendants together, the judges decided to hold five separate trials that they later consolidated to three.[51]

Under the best circumstances the defendants faced long odds. Their trial was in a state and city with a long history of racial prejudice in the courts of law. Moreover, the men already stood convicted in the court of public opinion. From the outset, newspapers across the nation sided with the company's officers who had tormented their workers. A *New York Times* headline screamed, "Hunted Down by Negroes," while the *Washington Post* published a salacious account of the events under the headline "A Horrible Butchery." The *Post* based its reporting on the uncorroborated account of one of the white superintendents who spun a tale of unrestrained violence and black laborers "uttering fiendish yells that a Comanche Indian would have envied." A number of other newspapers provided their own lurid, racialized coverage. The *New Orleans Daily Picayune* described the workers as "a murderous gang of mutineers," the *Galveston Daily News* termed them "Black Butchers," and the *Milwaukee Daily Journal* called them a "Mob Without Mercy." The *Sun* initially showed restraint, but it proved short-lived as it sought to match its counterparts. The paper soon reported on the "butchered" men and published a "special report" that described the laborers as a "fine a collection of scoundrels as could be gathered together in any jail in the country."[52]

The African American press had a different understanding of the events on Navassa. The black press presented a range of reactions and interpretations. Some of the papers found ways to qualify the descriptor "rioters." For instance, the (Detroit) *Plaindealer* termed the laborers "the so-called Navassa rioters." In its coverage, the *Cleveland Gazette* frequently printed the word "rioters" in quotation marks. The *Plaindealer* also found ways to contextualize the events, which white newspapers often failed to do. In one editorial, the paper contended that the laborers in Navassa had "very successfully imitated white brutality in the recent troubles on the island of Navassa." In another case, they reprinted an op-ed from the white *Pittsburgh Dispatch*, which presented a more nuanced account of the violence. "Two stories of the Navassa riots have been told," the editorial read, "and so far as the public can judge that of the workmen sounds altogether the most probable."[53]

For the Brotherhood, the Navassa case encapsulated all that they and other activists had been fighting against since the Civil War ended. The case concerned unrestrained racial violence. The Navassa Phosphate Company's exploitation and inhumane treatment of its African American laborers bred the violence that swept over the island that hot September day. The case involved labor rights: the workers on the island possessed no power to dictate the terms of their employment or earn a decent wage. The case also concerned issues of law and order. Although US maritime law technically governed the island, the practical reality was that the Navassa Phosphate Company wholly controlled affairs at the work site. The company's labor contract stipulated that they created the laws and instilled discipline "for the better protection of life and property." This meant, among other things, that the company acted as a private police force with the power to imprison its employees in a jail that one reporter found to be "so stifling as to cause me to cut my investigations short." The upcoming trials afforded the Brotherhood a chance to illustrate to the nation the brutality of racial discrimination.[54]

After the men arrived back in Baltimore, A. J. Reed, the Brotherhood of Liberty's president, quickly dispatched Waring to represent the prisoners. By the time the case went to trial, white attorneys Archibald J. Stirling, his son J. Edward Stirling, Robert B. Graham, James D. Cotter, and the Brotherhood's other attorney, Joseph S. Davis, rounded out the defense team. On 3 November Waring entered a writ of habeas corpus on behalf of Henry Jones, who had been identified as one of the leading conspirators. Waring hoped to convince the court that the United States did not have jurisdiction over Navassa. Since the late 1850s, both the United States and Haiti laid claim to the island. Viewed in the short term, the strategy was a long shot. Officials from the Department of Justice had already considered this possibility and dismissed its validity. Waring's move, however, was more than just a legal haymaker: the defense hoped to establish a foundation for an appeal before the Supreme Court, which had yet to rule on jurisdiction over the island. As expected, the US District Court turned down Waring's petition and the preliminary stages of the trial proceeded as planned.[55]

Outside of the courts, African Americans rallied public support for the accused. Rev. W. A. Credit, who worked as an agent for the Brotherhood, delivered a speech and solicited donations in support of the laborers at the Fifth Baptist Church in Washington, DC. At Baltimore's Leadenhall Baptist Church, the Brotherhood held a mass rally. The *Indianapolis Freeman* reported that "a very large crowd" heard numerous speeches about conditions on the island as well as descriptions of the Brotherhood's activism.

Throughout the course of the trial, black beneficial groups such as the Order of Galilean Fishermen in Baltimore and the Central Relief Bureau in Washington raised money for and/or awareness about the case. Their efforts were needed: the *Washington Bee* estimated the costs of the initial trials would total $1,350.[56]

Between November 1889 and March 1890, Baltimore hosted three trials to determine the fate of the Navassa laborers. The defense did not deny that their clients participated in the uprising, but they argued that it was not the result of a conspiracy. The defense maintained that the company's supervisors instigated the violence by mistreating workers. According to the laborers, tensions began to mount approximately a week and a half before the uprising when the previous superintendent, George W. Tipton, died and Charles D. Smith replaced him. One of the workers, James Johnson, remembered that before Smith became superintendent, "there was no such thing as calling men black ———— ———— dogging them around and putting them in jail."[57] Even the prosecution's carefully constructed portrait of conditions on Navassa crumbled during the defense's cross-examination of the state's key witnesses. When the prosecution secured the cooperation of seven laborers, they hoped that their testimony would bolster their case, which in large measure it did. As the prosecution intended, the men detailed a conspiracy that went back days, perhaps even weeks. Nevertheless, the men also testified to the horrible conditions on Navassa and spoke openly about them with the press. In the end, the prosecution's own eyewitness undermined their contention that conditions on the island were not as bad as workers described. For instance, when Waring cross-examined William James, one of the state's witnesses, James readily detailed the rotten food, overwork, and exploitative prices in the company store.[58]

On 2 December the all-white jury announced their verdict in the first trial. They found Key guilty of murder, acquitted Moses Williams, and deadlocked on the remaining sixteen men. The defense considered the outcome a partial victory since they were able to convince jurors that the violence was not the result of a conspiracy. The next two trials, however, produced diminishing returns. In the second trial, the jury found nine of the defendants guilty and two not guilty, and they deadlocked on the remaining seven. Of the nine guilty, the jury convicted Henry Jones of murder and eight others of manslaughter.[59] The third and final trial resulted in the biggest disappointment for the defense. The jury found three men—Key, Smith, and Jones—guilty of murder and others of crimes ranging from manslaughter to participating in a riot. The judge condemned the men convicted of murder. He sentenced the eight convicted of manslaughter to ten-year sentences, gave four men five-year terms, and sent two others away for two years of hard labor. The court sentenced twenty-three others convicted of participating in the uprising to terms of six months in the House of Correction.[60] All told, the verdicts were bittersweet. The fact that a court convicted African American men, regardless of circumstance, for murdering white men was not surprising. The cards were decidedly stacked against the defendants. Yet the Brotherhood, along with other activists in Baltimore and Washington, DC, rallied to save "fifteen of the doomed men from the gallows." In an era plagued by racially motivated legal and extralegal violence, this was no small feat.[61]

Following the trials in Baltimore, the defense appealed their clients' murder convictions. On 29 October 1890 the US Supreme Court heard the case of Key, Jones, and Smith. Both Davis and Waring, the Brotherhood of Liberty's lawyers, traveled to Washington on behalf of their clients. Technically, the defense did not contest the verdicts but rather the constitutionality of US jurisdiction over the island. Nevertheless, they continued to press their case against the company that had enslaved its workers. Waring pointedly remarked, "It is very strange that although the Government of the United States has claimed jurisdiction over Navassa for thirty-three years, although there are from 150 to 200 men at the island, all the time, the United States has never yet placed a government official on the island. . . . It seems strange that so many men should be left to the mercy of an arbitrary and tyrannical owner or corporation."[62]

After nearly six years of struggle, the Brotherhood finally saw a case to the Supreme Court. The *New York Age* proudly pointed out the historic import of the day. When Waring presented his argument, he became the first black attorney to argue before the Supreme Court. "On Wednesday of last week one of the most impressive and significant events in the jurisprudential history of the Republic transpired at Washington," the paper remarked, "and none the less so because the leading papers of the country allowed the event to pass without emphasizing it in any manner." The paper refused to let the event pass without comment. The *Age* put the hearing in perspective by noting that the Supreme Court, just thirty-four years earlier, rendered the Dred Scott decision. "Mark the change. Thirty-four years after the rendering of this monstrous decision," the editors wrote, "three 'Negroes' appear before the same Court, full-fledged attorneys and counselors at law, residents of the erstwhile slave State of Maryland, and argue a question of Federal jurisdiction."[63]

Despite the historic nature of the hearing, the Supreme Court ruled against the defense. The only remaining avenue for redress was a presidential pardon. Although in a legal sense the Brotherhood of Liberty's strategy failed, they made considerable inroads in swaying public opinion. This made it easier for them to gather signatures in support of clemency. During the trials, the defense convincingly painted a picture of deprivation and brutality among laborers on the island. This loomed large in the coming years. The organization noted after the first trial, "The general verdict of the public, so far as could be obtained, at the conclusion of this trial, was that the riot was the result of the cruel treatment which the men received, and not, a malicious conspiracy."[64]

The defense's arguments convinced at least one newspaper to change its position. The *Washington Post*, which initially publicized the case in lurid detail and couched its condemnations of the uprising in racialized terms in 1889, spoke in favor of clemency in an 1891 editorial. The *Post*'s editors argued, "The men employed by the Navassa Phosphate Company were subjected to brutal and inhuman treatment of 'bosses' worse than the worst of the proverbial overseers of old slave times, and that there was great provocation for the outbreak and mutiny which culminated in the murder of five of the white men who had themselves precipitated the riot." The editorial revealed important shifts. This time the paper placed the blame squarely on the shoulders of the officers. They also trumpeted the defense's claims that Navassa approximated slavery. In 1889 the editorialists could have chosen any number of strikes and labor uprisings as their point of reference. Instead, they found slavery to be the most apt metaphor, but they used it to illustrate that conditions on Navassa were even more dire.[65]

The defense also persuaded others to support clemency, including some of the jurors in Smith's original trial. The jurors felt compelled by law to convict Smith of murder but later signed their names to the Brotherhood's petition "on account of tyrannical and brutal treatment, bad food, long hours of hard and severe labor" that, in their opinion, led to the rebellion. The Baltimore Federation of Labor held a protest meeting in support of the laborers. Others, including "leading citizens of Baltimore, officers of the Y.M.C.A., State Temperance Alliance, Prison Reform Association, S.S. Union, eminent lawyers, leading ministers of different denominations, physicians, merchants, &c." signed the petition. J. T. Ensor, the US attorney for the district of Maryland, spoke out in favor of commuting the condemned men's sentences. In early 1891 Ensor penned a letter on the men's behalf to President Harrison. Ensor's message noted that the testimony in the cases was contradictory and singled out Charles D. Smith and Mahon's callous treatment of their workers. "Expediency and justice," Ensor concluded, "justify the exercise of executive clemency in these cases."[66]

On 1 April 1891 a committee that included the Brotherhood's William M. Alexander personally delivered the petition to President Harrison. The men brought with them an appeal authored by the defense team and another written by Maryland congressman Isidor Rayner. A month later, Harrison announced his decision. "The conditions surrounding the prisoners and their fellows were of a most peculiar character," Harrison explained. "They were American citizens under contracts to perform labor upon specified terms within American territory removed from any opportunity to appeal to any court or public officer for redress of any injury or the enforcement of any civil right. Their employers were," the president maintained, "in fact, their masters." Harrison sharply criticized the Navassa Phosphate Company's practice of torture and imprisonment, contending that this "state of things generally . . . might make men reckless and desperate." Harrison refused to pardon the laborers, but he commuted the sentences of the three condemned men to life in prison.[67]

In the ensuing years, labor problems continued to plague the island. But the work of the Brotherhood changed the national public conversation about the Navassa Phosphate Company's treatment of its workers. When laborers went on strike in 1891, the *New York Times* covered the dispute under the headline "Slaves Under Our Flag." The report further explained, "It is into the methods of the Navassa Phosphate Company itself that inspection is needed. With its operations in a country which is practically foreign, and with little or no communication with the outside world," the story continued, "with no responsibility to any law and no supervision or knowledge of its methods, it has for years been run with a brutal selfishness that would be amazing were it not the well-known tendency of all corporations whose operations are screened from the public eye." The *New York Times* further criticized the company's labor practices in subsequent articles. Other major papers, including the *Chicago Daily Tribune* and the *Washington Post*, continued to cover events on the island after the uprising. Rather than denouncing laborers using racialized language as they had done in 1889, the papers condemned the company's actions and publicized laborers' own accounts of the mistreatment they endured on the island.[68]

As politicians, citizens, and the courts slowly rolled back the modest gains made during Reconstruction, the Brotherhood of Liberty challenged the dictates of the emerging Jim Crow era. Their strategies galvanized the wider community and incorporated women as supporters and activists. In 1891 the organization listed among its "Life Members" four women. It remains possible that other women belonged as well, but their use of initials makes it impossible to determine their precise identities. In addition to the Life Members, the Brotherhood listed six other women as contributors. Included in this group were Martha E. Stewart and Mary M. Johnson, two of the four litigants in the *Steamer Sue* case.[69]

By the early 1890s the high-profile battles waged by the Brotherhood of Liberty had a noticeable effect on Baltimore's racial climate. When P. B. S. Pinchback, the former Reconstruction-era African American governor of Louisiana, traveled through the city in 1891, he remarked that he was "at last in a free country."[70] Looking back over the previous five years, Waring agreed. He remarked, "The 'Brotherhood of Liberty' has accomplished more good in Maryland than any other secular organization ever established in the State. Its efforts to open the bar of the State to colored men, to change the Bastardy law, to protect colored women, to secure additional school facilities were highly successful." Waring observed that the organization had "assisted largely in liberalizing the sentiments and opinions of the white people of the State toward the colored people."[71]

Although efforts to overturn black codes, reform education, and defend the Navassa workers ostensibly had little in common, activists realized that they had much to say about perceptions of race in the United States. In taking up these challenges, they authored a counternarrative to a racial discourse that increasingly marginalized African Americans and formed the foundation for Jim Crow segregation. The work of the Brotherhood reenergized Baltimore's activist community and blazed a path for further political advancement. On the heels of the Brotherhood's legal victories, black Baltimoreans helped elect Harry S. Cummings to the Baltimore city council. He was the first African American to hold elected office in Maryland. Cummings, who worked as an attorney, directly benefited from Johnson's successful fight to open the bar to black lawyers. While it is unclear if

Cummings became a member of the Brotherhood, he did make financial contributions to the organization.[72]

Even as the organization faded in the early 1890s, it left behind other important legacies. Johnson and Alexander continued to lead a variety of movements for racial justice in the city. Johnson would become one of the earliest members of the Niagara Movement, the forerunner to the NAACP, while Alexander organized efforts in the early 1900s to stop Jim Crow disfranchisement. On 13 August 1892 Alexander published the first issue of the *Afro-American* from Sharon Baptist. In the years to follow, the *Afro-American* became a potent counterweight to the often-prejudicial coverage in the city's white papers, including the *Sun*. At the same time, it became a platform for black businesses, churches, and individuals to reach a wider audience throughout the city and the United States. But, perhaps most importantly, it served to highlight nationwide and local racial injustices, as well as the efforts of activists to fight them.[73]

For many black Baltimoreans, the modest steps toward equality in the Reconstruction era did not occur between 1865 and 1877. Instead, they began when Harvey Johnson spearheaded judicial challenges to inequality and organized the United Brotherhood of Liberty. The Brotherhood's use of test case litigation would reverberate throughout the nation. In 1887 T. Thomas Fortune contemplated similar strategies for his Afro-American League, the first nationwide civil rights organization. The Brotherhood's attorney, Joseph S. Davis, wrote to Fortune's *New York Freeman* to offer his support and weigh in on the deliberations. "The time has come when we have got to fight our greatest battles," Davis declared, "and win our greatest victories in the courts and at the bar of public opinion." Davis proposed pursuing test cases to achieve civil rights to "try the strength of our great Constitution." "To accomplish this result we must follow such cases as are suitable from the station house to the Supreme Court. We must employ the best legal talent attainable," Davis argued, "and we must pay these men and pay them well. Here the League can make itself heard, felt and respected."[74] This was a vision that the Brotherhood of Liberty had already put into practice in Maryland. Now it would serve as the blueprint for the work of other national civil rights groups through much of the twentieth century.

The activist foundation of newspapers, churches, and organizations painstakingly built by Baltimore's African American activists in the 1880s would become even more important in the decades to follow. Beginning in the mid-1890s, white politicians and citizens across the South renewed efforts at blunting black political power and instituting Jim Crow. Baltimore followed these national trends. Segregationists responded to the gains made by the city's black community by hastening the advent of the Jim Crow era. But the city's black population would have a firm foundation on which to fight these efforts.

CHAPTER 4

The Creation of Baltimore's Racialized
Criminal Justice System

On the evening of 31 October 1903, Maryland's senator Arthur Pue Gorman climbed onto the stage of Baltimore's Lyric Theatre. It was the last night before the statewide election, which Gorman and his Democratic Party viewed as crucial to their political fortunes. As they had done for the previous five years, the party exploited supposed connections between politics, race, and criminality. Gorman maintained that when Republicans controlled Baltimore and Maryland during the mid-1890s, African Americans felt that they had "license to commit crime." He further alleged that "while the negroes comprise only one-fifth of the population of Baltimore, more than one-half of the crimes were committed by them during these four years."[1] Gorman was not the only one to make these unsubstantiated claims during the 1890s, but as a senator with presidential aspirations, his views were broadcast far and wide.

In the 1890s Baltimoreans linked race with crime to systemically arrest and incarcerate African Americans as well as change city governance, politics, and the criminal justice system. The creation of the carceral state needs to be understood as a reaction to the gains that African Americans had made toward equality in the previous decades. Historians have widely recognized that the struggle for civil rights born in the Reconstruction era remained unfinished by the time the federal government abandoned African Americans in 1877. They have less frequently explored how segregationists' efforts to secure white supremacy similarly remained incomplete and were in a constant state of flux in reaction to African American activism.[2] Unlike the better-known Jim Crow legislation initiatives that segregationists passed to curtail black rights, disproportionately targeting African Americans for arrest did not require legislative approval. Nor did it run the risk of being overturned in a court of law. The outcome, however, was often the same: African Americans were socially marginalized, spatially restricted, and increasingly incarcerated.

For black Baltimoreans, the advent of the carceral state proved just as damaging as Jim Crow legislation, if not more so.[3] Although the trope of the "black criminal" had long been a staple of white supremacist thought, these ideas took on an aura of scientific certainty during the Progressive Era, replacing older markers of supposed African American inferiority.[4] In Baltimore the racialization of crime functioned as efficient shorthand to encapsulate a variety of fears. Segregationists linked alleged instances of black crime with concerns over the safety of white women, growing African American political power, and public behavior. By deploying racialized notions of crime and criminality, segregationists curtailed African Americans' civil rights. They used ideas of black criminality to limit freedom of speech, the right to peaceably assemble, and the ability to move unfettered throughout the city they called home. Segregationists also used fears of black criminality to undermine African Americans' right to a fair trial and burdened them with unduly harsh punishments. The story of Baltimore demonstrates that from its inception, the building of the carceral state and the institution of Jim Crow jointly attacked democracy.

The public rhetoric connecting race, crime, and politics first intensified in the city's police courts and was subsequently amplified by Baltimore's newspapers. Prior to 1898, the phrases "negro rowdyism" and "negro disorder" rarely—if ever—appeared in the Baltimore Sun. This changed in March after the police arrested William Brown for "obstructing the free passage of persons along the public highway." According to the Baltimore Sun, Brown (and an unnamed accomplice who eluded apprehension) approached two women, Miss Ray Hess and Miss Barbara Hammel. Brown "grabbed Miss Hess and made an insulting proposition." The women fled, but Brown caught up with Hess while Hammel summoned a nearby patrolman who promptly arrested Brown.[5]

Although statistics are fragmentary for the period, extant sources indicate that Baltimore's crime rate was on par with, if not slightly lower than, that of other cities. In 1893 the Department of Labor commissioned a report on the "slums" of Baltimore, Chicago, New York, and Philadelphia. The report found that Baltimore's police made one arrest for every fourteen people. In comparison, police in Chicago made one arrest for every eleven citizens, while in Philadelphia and New York the rate was one to every eighteen residents.[6] Still, Baltimore's Western, Northwestern, and Central Police Districts developed reputations as high crime areas by the turn of the twentieth century. As a rookie reporter for the *Baltimore Morning Herald*, the famed newspaperman H. L. Mencken recalled covering "Afra-American [*sic*] razor parties in the Northwestern." He described the Western District as containing "the largest and busiest of Baltimore's five Tenderloins" and the Central as having "the busiest of the police courts." A *Baltimore Sun* report depicted the Western District as a lawless zone within the city. "A group of low caste white men, maintained in ease by its outcasts, constituted its senate," the report read. "They held the balance of power politically and the police were their slaves." The paper depicted the Central District in similar terms.[7]

Police apprehended Brown in the Western District. Following his arrest, his next stop was the Western District Police Court. Baltimore's police courts, located in each district's station house, were the first stop for all arrested for criminal offenses punishable by fines of less than a hundred dollars.[8] The "old fashioned brick building" that housed the Western sat on Pine Street; when it closed in 1951, the *Baltimore Sun* marked its passing by deeming it a "red brick monstrosity, built between Lexington and Saratoga streets when Baltimore architecture was at its lowest point. The old place is a municipal eyesore." Inside this "municipal eyesore," the police court was a hive of activity. "Here, if you are at all interested in the study of your fellow-man," the *Baltimore Sun* reported, "you should some day make your way [to the Western District Police Station], for here can be felt the pulse of Baltimore's Tenderloin."[9]

Brown, who proclaimed his innocence, realized he was in trouble. He told one of the arresting officers that he had heard that the Western Police District magistrate, Eugene E. Grannan, had a reputation for harshly punishing "such offenses." He had good reason to fear the judge. Grannan began his career as a reporter in Cumberland, Maryland, before the Baltimore and Ohio Railroad hired him in 1875 as a private detective. For the next twenty-one years Grannan worked for the company, eventually ascending to head of detectives. In 1896 the state's Republican governor, Lloyd Lowndes, made Grannan, a Democrat, the police magistrate of the Western with a mandate to clean up the district. Grannan intended to see this directive through.[10]

Brown appeared before Grannan to answer for "Disturbance of the Public Peace," an expansive charge that included obstructing a sidewalk. Brown now had a choice to make: he could stand trial in the police court where Grannan alone would decide his fate or take his chances with a jury. City law mandated that magistrates inform defendants of their right to a jury trial, an option that Brown exercised.[11] Although Grannan would not hear the case, he was not yet finished with Brown. He informed the *Baltimore Sun* that Brown's arrest was a prime example of the recent increase in black criminals in sections of the city. Grannan told the *Sun* that "it is not safe for a woman to walk alone in the western district after nightfall. I would not let my wife enter the district after dark unless she had an escort." He continued, "and I should advise all of my friends to be equally as careful."[12] Grannan's unsubstantiated statements concerning a suspect who had yet to stand trial made news in most of the city's papers.

In the days that followed, two fellow police magistrates bolstered Grannan's contentions. Magistrate Henry Krug, Jr., who had spent two days temporarily presiding over the city's Central District Police Court, detailed to the *Sun* a "daily increase in cases in which the tough coon figures." Krug further opined that the "good citizens among the colored population . . . are very much in the minority." The city's justice-at-large, W. B. Schoen, also noted the supposed increase in lawlessness among African Americans, explaining that it was no longer safe for white or black females to roam the city streets.[13]

The magistrates' comments ignited a firestorm. Throughout April, the *Baltimore World* printed lurid tales of black criminality, reporting in breathless fashion that "orgies were being held and the [Central District] was being converted into bedlam."[14] While less melodramatic, the *Baltimore News* published stories of "negro disorder."[15] With stunning rapidity, "negro rowdyism," "negro disorder," and "negro toughs" became watchwords used by the press, magistrates, and citizens to connect a wide array of unrelated misdemeanors, including nonviolent offenses such as swearing in public or disturbing the peace as well as assaults. To what extent this attention factored into Brown's case is impossible to know with any degree of certainty. It should be noted, however, that Judge John J. Dobler sentenced Brown to sixty days in the House of Correction. A conviction for Brown's offense normally carried "a fine of not less than one dollar" and required the defendant to pay the costs of prosecution.[16]

The extant evidence indicates that this conflation of race and crime was more rhetorical than real. White Baltimoreans and the press relied almost solely on observation and anecdotal evidence to document the alleged growth of black crime. For example, Nicholas Burkart, the reverend of the German Lutheran Church, claimed that he noticed an increase in crime among black Baltimoreans. The *Baltimore News* published uncorroborated accounts from citizens who documented the "outrageous disorder" caused by African Americans. The *Baltimore Sun* added that there appeared to be a "growth of an insolent spirit of disorder and aggression" on the part of African Americans. The paper further proclaimed that African Americans "appear to seek crime deliberately" while noticing that they had become more "unruly" in recent years. Although the *Sun* claimed that statistics on race and crime did not exist, they still leveled serious charges by estimating crime rates and then relaying them as fact. "It is a noticeable fact that a majority of the murders and homicides in Maryland are committed by the negro population," the *Sun* proclaimed in one story, but "only about one-fifth of the people of the State belong to that race. And yet, while we have no statistics at hand," the paper continued, "it is safe to say that fully one-half of the work of the criminal courts of the State comes from disorders among the colored population."[17]

For their part, the city's police board of commissioners maintained that the charges of increased black crime were exaggerated. Shortly after the *Baltimore Sun* published Grannan's charges, the board convened hearings in front of a packed house at police headquarters. During the proceedings a number of policemen testified that they had actually encountered fewer problems than in years past. Captains Lewis W. Cadwallader (Western), Thomas Barranger (Central), and John Baker (Northwestern) all testified that conditions in their respective districts had improved in recent years. Residents and business owners mostly corroborated these accounts. Jordan Stabler, who worked at a grocery, claimed that he did not witness any increase in black criminality. Two other residents, Dr. Duncan McCalman and Henry Rosenthal, agreed with Stabler. A third witness, Henry Thomas, asserted that conditions in the neighborhood were better than they had been in the last twenty years. Numerous other observers presented similar testimony. Of all the witnesses, only one affirmed that conditions had recently deteriorated.[18]

By the end of the hearing, the president of the police board of commissioners, Daniel C. Heddinger, had concluded that the whole affair was "much ado about nothing." The surviving evidence supports Heddinger's conclusion. Although the *Sun* claimed that crime statistics were not available, some data did exist. In his study *Some Notes on Negro Crime, Especially in Georgia*, W. E. B. DuBois concluded that the number of African Americans sent to jail in Baltimore, while higher than the rates found in Charleston or Saint Louis, had remained relatively stable throughout the 1890s. In addition, the arrest rate of African Americans in Baltimore slightly decreased after 1896 and remained steady between 1897 and 1899.[19]

Baltimoreans also had crime rate statistics. At the police board hearings, Captain Cadwallader furnished data on arrests for "disorderly conduct" going back to 1894 in the Western, Central, and Northwestern Districts. Although the numbers fluctuated year to year, the arrest rates in each case were lower in 1898 than they were in 1897.[20] The *Baltimore American* provided statistics for the three-day period from 12 to 14 April 1898, the days that Justice Krug claimed to have witnessed an increase in black-perpetrated crime. The paper tallied the arrests at the Central Police District and found that the police arrested white offenders in greater numbers on two of the three days. On the third day, the police apprehended an equal number of black and white offenders. The editors further demonstrated that arrests in the city had dropped on a year-to-year basis beginning in 1894.[21] The *Baltimore World* painted a similar picture of crime rates in Baltimore. The daily compared 1895 (the last year of Democratic governance) and 1898. Although African Americans had a higher arrest rate than whites in 1898—not surprising given the police's increased surveillance of black Baltimoreans—the crime rate among whites was actually growing at a faster rate.[22]

Rather than reflecting growing black crime rates, these accounts reveal white Baltimoreans' anxieties concerning what they perceived as African Americans' growing political power. These fears increased racial tensions on the streets. White fears of black political power have historically fueled street confrontations, which served as the settings for proxy battles over racial equality. In times of political tumult, these clashes assumed greater importance and had more deadly consequences. In 1879, for instance, a coalition of black and white voters in Virginia propelled the upstart Readjusters into state office. African Americans made modest political and social gains under Readjuster rule. As they did so, whites became more sensitive to what they considered rude or untoward behavior on the part of African Americans, which they interpreted as a reflection of growing black political strength. During the 1883 election season, tensions in Danville, Virginia, ran high. Days before ballots were cast, a white pedestrian sparked a race riot over a perceived violation of street etiquette. During the subsequent violence, white rioters killed seven African Americans. In the aftermath, Democrats defeated the Readjusters and ushered in the Jim Crow era in Virginia.[23]

In many respects, the atmosphere in late nineteenth-century Baltimore bore a striking resemblance to Readjuster-era Virginia. In the decades after the Civil War, activists in Maryland (especially Baltimore) challenged segregation on public transportation and expanded public education. They contested laws that banned intermarriage, defended black laborers who rebelled on Navassa Island, and opened up the courtrooms to black witnesses and attorneys. In the political realm, Harry S. Cummings became the first African American to serve on the city council when he was elected in 1890. Then, in the 1895 election, black voters helped Republicans defeat Maryland's Democratic Party, which had dominated the city and state since the Civil War. For the first time in Baltimore's history, African American votes proved decisive in an election.

In this context, white Baltimoreans almost certainly invested political meanings in African Americans' public behavior. In many reports of "negro disorder," it is difficult to find evidence of any criminal wrongdoing. Instead, witnesses focused on the ways that African Americans comported themselves in public. Throughout early 1898, papers often described African Americans refusing to cede a walkway or swearing in public. It remains a strong possibility that African Americans who cursed at whites, refused to cede sidewalks, and/or asserted their dignity in the city's public spaces were engaged in acts of everyday resistance. Unfortunately, the papers rarely investigated these interactions, opting instead to simply report them as instances of "negro disorder."[24] Other Baltimoreans commented on the interracial mingling they witnessed. In his testimony before the police board, Justice Grannan blamed two black nightclubs for fostering disorder. He also conjured fears of miscegenation—or possibly the "black male rapist"—by claiming that "a white girl was taken from one of [the clubs] recently." Arrest reports paint similar pictures. African Americans were arrested for "cursing" at whites, causing disturbances, or "jostling" white customers in stores.[25]

In other cases, white Baltimoreans overtly articulated their fears of black political power. For example, Justice Grannan relayed the story of an African American who, on being incarcerated, threatened to use his "pull at the city hall" to have the arresting officer fired. The *Baltimore Sun* claimed that African Americans "have been emboldened by the knowledge that their political friends are in power." In another report, the paper blamed "bad and partisan administration" for creating the conditions that allowed black criminals to thrive. The *Baltimore News* declared that a "dangerous element of Republican negro politicians has sprung up of late" with more "pull" than African Americans had had in the past. These charges became so commonplace that police board president Heddinger felt the need to directly address them. "I think politics is in this charge," he explained, "and behind it is an effort to play upon factional differences."[26]

By late 1898, events in Wilmington, North Carolina, bolstered white Baltimoreans' fears of growing black political power. Throughout November, the Baltimore press covered white supremacists' coup d'état that ousted Wilmington's biracial government and led to the deaths of fourteen African Americans. In addition to its regular coverage, the *Baltimore Sun* shared various firsthand accounts of events in Wilmington. The *Sun* interviewed Baltimore businessman and former city councilman Richard J. Biggs, who had just returned from North Carolina. Biggs wrote that black voters in the state represented a "serious menace to law and order and threaten[ed] the safety of the homes of white people in a most alarming way." He then drew explicit comparison to Baltimore, claiming to have witnessed multiple cases of "negro ruffianism" in the forty-eight hours since returning. He warned readers that unless the authorities took action, the events of Wilmington might repeat themselves in Baltimore.[27]

Other "experts" on race relations shaped public opinion by weighing in on Wilmington. Johns Hopkins University's Guy Carleton Lee published a series of articles in the *Baltimore Sun* that used the racial violence in Wilmington to more widely examine the fate of African Americans following emancipation. Steeped in the language of turn-of-the-century racist thought, Lee contended that African Americans had "degenerated" and that the Republican Party permitted a rise in black crime. Notably, Lee focused on African Americans' public behavior. "The race seemed intoxicated with newly given power," Lee argued of Wilmington's black population, "and manifested elation by increasing insolence to the whites." Lee contended that black criminals increased "over 85 per cent" and, in a charge that echoed Grannan's claims, made the streets unsafe for white women "after nightfall."[28] Lee's articles painted Wilmington as a postslavery dystopia where African Americans, emboldened by Republican electoral success, ran roughshod over an entire city. For white Baltimoreans concerned with crime and black political power, it must have been difficult to read Lee's articles as anything but a cautionary tale.

Unlike Virginians and North Carolinians, white Baltimoreans did not respond with wholesale violence. Instead, they marshaled the power of the police and magistrates. African Americans immediately recognized the political motives and dangers that this strategy posed to the gains they had made in the previous decades. In April 1898 the editors of the *Afro-American Ledger* contended that "whether it be detected under the form of Klu-Kluxism, mid-night marauders, ballot-box stuffing, or political disfranchisement, or in many other forms that have been employed from time to time, to the same end, the once fixed purpose of Negro humiliation can be most plainly discerned."[29] In a letter to the *Baltimore News*, a local resident, John E. Board, disputed claims of black criminality. Board claimed that these accusations were exaggerated and a "political trick." He chalked up the charges to the fear that African Americans were gaining political ground. He concluded that the "police justices of the Western district have greatly exaggerated the condition of affairs."[30] As many black Baltimoreans predicted, Democrats recognized that the issue of black crime resonated with many white Baltimoreans, and they intended to use it for political gain.

For Maryland's Democrats, the public concern over black crime arrived at a particularly opportune moment. In 1895 Maryland Republicans ousted the Democratic machine that had controlled the city and state for a quarter of a century by running on a plank that promised to bring back "good government" by restoring order, ending political corruption, and tackling the ills of urbanization. Democrats were desperate to regain power after losing again in 1897. The party co-opted the Republicans' "good government" message but added an explicitly racial component by interjecting concerns over "negro domination." In the late 1890s the phrase "negro domination" had a precise meaning and represented an important shift in the rhetoric of white supremacy. In the first decades following Reconstruction, white supremacists used the phrase "negro rule" as shorthand to demonize black politicians who gained office throughout the South. By the 1890s, however, this charge held little resonance because whites had largely forced African Americans out of government positions. Instead, segregationists replaced the phrase "negro rule" with "negro domination." The latter phrase located the supposed threat that African Americans posed not in the few government positions they held but rather in the black vote that could influence politicians.[31]

The Democratic Party made race a central plank in their campaign by connecting "negro domination" with Progressive concerns over "good government." For Democrats, the two issues were inseparable. "There is another aspect of the question of good government that is too serious and too palpable to be obscured," Democratic Party operative Isaac Lobe Straus contended at one rally. "I refer to the danger of negro domination." Later in the speech Straus was even more direct: "The pull they [African Americans] have with republican politicians makes them defiantly indifferent to the law." Democrats promised to end "negro domination" and restore order to the streets by arresting and incarcerating African Americans.[32] At the first Democratic rally of the season, the assembled audience burst into the "wildest enthusiasm" when a group paraded through the hall displaying a banner that read "This Is a White Man's City." Maryland's former governor, Frank Brown, told the Democratic faithful, "I believe that the white men, both democrats and republicans, realize that a crisis is on, and that the future of the city is at stake." Stereotypical images of black criminals, "tough looking" African Americans in the words of Democratic supporters, illustrated rally signs that read "No Coons for Me." At another meeting in the city's Fourteenth Ward, the home of Hiram Watty, an African American candidate for city council, a Democratic speaker contended that Baltimore "cannot be a white man's city until negro rowdyism and lawlessness is suppressed."[33]

Democrats racialized crime throughout the campaign. At a rally in April, Alonzo L. Miles, a former Dorchester County representative, condemned African Americans and the Republican Party for outbreaks of black crime. Other speakers contended that African Americans were antithetical to good government. Strauss argued that African Americans were "disturbing the peace and order of the city with a riotous indifference to the laws." James R. Wheeler, the president of the Commonwealth Bank, proclaimed that the previous two years of "negro rowdyism . . . have been enough for everybody." At another rally, Martin Lehmeyer blamed both Republicans and African Americans, contending that politicians encouraged blacks to flout the law and disrespect "our women." Another Democratic official, William B. Rayner, called on voters to end black crime and guard the city's women by electing Democrats who would harshly punish "negro ruffians."[34]

Politicians were not alone in connecting race with crime to advance their political agenda. At least one rival paper claimed that the *Baltimore Sun* manufactured stories for partisan reasons. With the election season in full swing, the *Sun* published the tale of Lucy Price's confrontation with a "colored thief." According to the paper, Price found herself face-to-face with a man who was in the midst of robbing her house. She screamed, attracting a crowd and compelling the would-be robber to flee. The *Baltimore World* challenged the *Sun*'s coverage. The *World* contended that the robber was not a man but rather a "little colored boy" who occasionally ran errands for the Price family. The alleged crime involved the youngster attempting to steal two "pewter spoons." The *World* chided its rival for its intentional exaggeration, in this and other cases, in an effort to "keep up the race prejudice."[35]

African Americans continually contested depictions of black criminality in the press. As Election Day approached, a group of black ministers wrote to the *Baltimore Sun* to protest the way the paper connected race and crime for "political reasons." They criticized the *Sun* for its penchant to devote "columns of its valuable space to the criminal escapades of a few irresponsible rowdies [while finding] little or no space to make honorable mention of the deserving ones among that same race."[36] The ministers understood that unlike the city's white population, one alleged black criminal's actions stood as an indictment against the entire community.

In the end, the election of 1899 proved the power inherent in the coupling of race, crime, and political corruption. In early May the Democratic mayoral candidate, Thomas Gordon Hayes, defeated William Malster. The Democrats had won not only the mayoralty but also majorities in the first branch of the city council, capturing eighteen of a possible twenty-four seats, and sweeping the second branch of the city council. The editors of the *Afro-American Ledger* were troubled by the results. While hoping that the mayor-elect would treat them with respect, they also noted he had no reason to do so since African Americans voted against him "with practical unanimity."[37]

In the aftermath of the municipal race, city officials, the press, and the police sustained their campaign against alleged black criminals to tilt the fall's statewide races in their favor. Shortly before Election Day, Democrats ran a two-column ad in the *Baltimore Sun* attacking Republicans for, in their view, allowing the level of black crime to reach alarming proportions. "Negro rowdyism, disorder and law breaking has reached such a pitch in

Baltimore as to cause general alarm," the ad read, "and it has been asserted in the newspapers that there are parts of the city where it is unsafe for a white woman to venture unprotected on the streets."[38]

At rallies across the state, Democrats linked Republicans with alleged black criminals. Herman Stump, a former congressman, recalled Democratic rule as a time when African Americans were happy and black crime did not exist. The Democrats' gubernatorial nominee, Col. John Walter Smith, citing newspaper coverage, claimed, "It is a well-known fact that violations by [African Americans] have been more frequent during the last four years in this State than ever before in its history."[39] Isidor Rayner, another former congressman, further drove the point home by painting a picture of Baltimore and Maryland at the mercy of black criminals and rapists. Addressing an audience at a rally in October 1899, he remarked that the Republican administration gave "rise to a succession of crimes that almost daily send a thrill of horror to every fireside and home in the State. There are highways in this city," he continued, "infested by these creatures, upon which we ought to plant a sign board of danger, so that unprotected women could avoid them." Looking back at the election, Arthur Pue Gorman noted that these appeals secured the election for Democrats.[40]

By the turn of the twentieth century, segregationists had firmly established the trope of the black criminal, which had a number of repercussions for African Americans. For years, black Baltimoreans lodged numerous complaints alleging police harassment. In 1895 Harvey Johnson claimed that police departments across the country engaged in "lawlessness, bloodshed and riot everywhere with no power anywhere to check it."[41] The *Afro-American Ledger* argued that the police enforced laws disproportionately against black Baltimoreans: "Whenever a new law is passed or some incident happens whereby some person must be made an example of, it always happens that it is a poor Negro that is the first to get into the toils."[42] The paper contended that persecution became so widespread that "no decent, self-respecting colored man or woman is safe, on street or cars."[43] In 1906 J. H. N. Waring, the principal of Baltimore's Colored High School, argued that the police overzealously arrested young African Americans for minor offenses when they could have issued warnings. Because of these widespread problems, the *Afro-American Ledger* remarked that it "is not at all strange that ignorant and vicious Negroes should view the police force as already prejudiced, in advance, against them."[44]

It is also clear that black Baltimoreans faced an overtly biased judiciary after the police arrested them. There are a number of problems with quantitatively determining if police magistrates systematically punished black Baltimoreans more severely than their white counterparts. The justices possessed a wide degree of latitude when sentencing defendants and did not need to publicly justify their decisions. That fact, coupled with incomplete and unreliable record keeping, makes it impossible to render a comprehensive statistical portrait of racially biased sentencing.

Nevertheless, a host of qualitative evidence points to the fact that justices consistently leveled tougher penalties on the African Americans that stood before them in court. Justices such as Grannan often punished African Americans with severe fines. For example, Grannan fined two African American men, Thomas Lewis and Thomas Mason, for using profanity in public, a charge that fell under the umbrella of "Disturbance of the Public Peace." Although the conviction carried a fine of "not less than one dollar," Grannan fined Lewis twenty-five dollars and Mason fifty, plus the costs of their prosecution. In another case, Justice Loden fined Joseph Purcell twenty-five dollars for the same charge after three white women claimed that he followed them down the street and touched one of them on the arm.[45] Even more telling is that the public record is replete with examples of Baltimore's police magistrates boasting of ways that they disproportionately punished African American defendants. Justice W. B. Schoen proclaimed that if "any [African Americans] are brought before me they will get the fullest penalty that I am permitted under the law to impose." Police magistrate George T. Leech remarked that he planned "to do everything in my power to break up negro rowdyism in this section of the city." Justice Loden also promised longer prison terms and steeper fines for African American offenders.[46]

Newspapers frequently commented on the severe punishments doled out to black defendants. The *Afro-American Ledger* reported that many African Americans opted to stand trial in criminal courts because "as a rule, the magistrates sitting at the several police stations take a special delight in giving the most severe sentences to Negro criminals who are unfortunate enough to be brought before them."[47] The *Afro-American Ledger*'s editors further alleged that magistrates subjected black Baltimoreans to heavier fines and longer terms of incarceration. "Colored women are arrested and locked up in station houses and in many instances refuse[d] bail for the most frivolous cases," the paper contended. "The heaviest fines are imposed for the most trivial violations of the law." White papers also noted the justices' propensity to more severely punish African Americans. On numerous occasions, the *Baltimore Sun* reported that magistrates (particularly Loden and Grannan) handed out "heavy" sentences to black defendants. The *Baltimore News* accused Justice Llewellyn of exacting more severe fines on black defendants, saddling him with the nickname of "$25 Llewellyn" for his penchant to fine black defendants in that amount.[48]

Justice Thomas Ireland Elliott, of the city's Supreme Bench, also noticed this trend. In 1909 two African American men, Peter Tenant and Henry Daniels, appealed their sentences before the Supreme Bench. Justice Loden had previously sentenced the men to long jail terms in separate unrelated cases in his efforts to thwart "negro rowdyism." Tenant was charged with attempting to rob a tobacconist. His would-be accomplices allegedly informed the police of his plans after "hearing Tenant's proposition to way-lay" his intended victim. In what the *Baltimore Sun* termed "one of the longest sentences ever given by a police magistrate of this city," Loden sentenced Tenant to ten years in jail.[49] It is unclear what Daniels did to receive his five-year sentence from Loden. Attorney Thomas J. Mason submitted writs of habeas corpus on behalf of the two men, contending that the length of the prison terms constituted "cruel and unusual punishment." Judge Elliott agreed, releasing the men and admonishing the police magistrates who "either from mistaken zeal or ignorance . . . sometimes impose sentences which would not be imposed by courts in the cases of people who are not able to defend themselves properly."[50]

Conditions in Baltimore were indicative of wider trends in the United States. According to the *Afro-American Ledger*, blacks across the South encountered a criminal justice system where, "for the slightest infraction of the law, no mercy is shown, but off to the chain gang or the stockade, or workhouse they are sent for not less than thirty days while white men and boys are given a chance to recover themselves, if possible and are let out on a very light fine or possibly a reprimand." The *Afro-American Ledger* concluded that the South's criminal justice system engaged in the "wholesale manufacturing of Negro criminals." In this, the paper was partially correct. As W. E. B. DuBois demonstrated in his landmark study *The Philadelphia Negro*, African Americans in the North were also subjected to disproportionate arrests and longer terms of incarceration.[51]

Not only were the police increasingly scrutinizing and arresting black Baltimoreans; officers were also complicit in allowing crime to occur in

African American neighborhoods. In some cases they ignored the complaints of black residents. In the early 1900s black residents in the Lower Druid Hill neighborhood of Northwest Baltimore claimed that white-owned saloons enjoyed police protection. Booker T. Washington speculated that "it was, perhaps, true also that in Baltimore, as in some other cities, saloons and dens of vice which were not allowed to exist in other parts of the city were permitted to take refuge in the districts where the masses of the colored people lived." Washington wrote that the police and the liquor boards ignored the complaints of black residents due to the "general feeling that colored people were either themselves so criminal, or so disposed to shield and protect criminals of their own race, that their protests against lawlessness and lawbreaking were not to be taken seriously."[52]

In response, black reformers formed the Colored Law and Order League to document the saloons and "disorderly houses" that proliferated under the nose of the police. When the city's liquor board held hearings to discuss the league's findings, more than a dozen officers provided false testimony to protect the saloons. Because of the conflicting testimony offered by the police and reformers, members of the liquor board traveled to Druid Hill and witnessed the conditions in the neighborhood firsthand. It was only after being confronted with these surroundings that the liquor board denied the renewal applications for eleven saloons. In the wake of the hearings, the *Baltimore News* sharply criticized the more than a dozen police officers that they claimed "whitewashed [the saloons] completely and comprehensively" in their testimony.[53]

African Americans also faced recriminations when they alleged police misconduct and/or corruption during the city's turn-of-the-century campaign against cocaine. Beginning in 1903, sporadic stories appeared in the *Baltimore Sun* documenting the alarming rise of cocaine abuse. At the time, the city did not criminalize the sale of cocaine or other narcotics; consumers could purchase them in drugstores. In 1904 the city slightly modified its laws, limiting the amount of cocaine that could be sold, before entirely prohibiting the trade two years later. The effort to eliminate the burgeoning cocaine industry hit full stride near the end of 1906. Just as he did in 1898, Justice Grannan once again publicly connected African Americans to this newly created category of crime. Grannan contended that the drug's abuse was confined "almost exclusively" to African Americans and "degraded white women." According to his own estimates, which he offered without corroborating evidence, "90 per cent" of the black offenders who entered his courtroom were addicted to the drug. Grannan was not alone in his conviction. Justice Loden estimated that 70 percent of the African Americans appearing before him were addicts. He further asserted that cocaine was responsible for "half of the assaults of these beasts upon white women."[54]

In 1908 a letter from an African American inmate named James Wesley sparked a police backlash against Baltimore's black community. Wesley, together with four other inmates, contended that four officers either allowed the cocaine trade to flourish or received protection money. The police board initially suspended the policemen before holding hearings. Within days, another patrolman was suspended facing similar accusations. Eventually, two more witnesses—Abe Hill and Henry Hamilton—lodged similar charges.[55] The case was complicated. By their own admission, the witnesses were involved in the cocaine trade; many of them were also serving jail sentences after being arrested by the officers they accused of misconduct.[56] But it still came as a surprise to the local press when the police board abruptly exonerated the suspended officers halfway through the scheduled hearings. The *Baltimore World* noted that at the very least, the sudden end to the trial gave rise to questions about whether the police engaged in a cover-up. The *Baltimore Sun* pointed out that the widespread existence of the cocaine trade gave some credibility to the witnesses.[57]

In the aftermath of the acquittal, Baltimore's police department exacted a measure of revenge on the city's black community. The reinstated officers were not transferred to another beat. Instead, they were ordered to their old posts with a mandate to clean up the neighborhood in thirty days' time. Now with an ax to grind, reputations to rehabilitate, and orders to demonstrate results, the cops hit the streets. The results were not surprising. The next day police moved in on the city's Central District, arresting Louisa Brown and Rosa White, both African American, for "acting in a disorderly manner on the street." Justice Grannan leveled a fine of a hundred dollars on each of the women and committed them to the jail when they could not afford to pay. The next evening, police arrested more black men and women. Among the arrestees was Abe Hill, one of the witnesses who had detailed police corruption during the abbreviated hearings. Other African Americans were arrested on a variety of charges ranging from vagrancy, "creating a disturbance," and disorderly conduct.[58] From the extant evidence, only one of the arrestees was suspected of using cocaine. The police did not detain anyone for possessing or selling cocaine. Rather, they used the opportunity to arrest African Americans for a variety of unrelated charges.

The fact that the conflation of race and crime had repercussions for the wider black community was not coincidental but by design. The press, magistrates, and citizenry applied the trope of the "negro rowdy" to all African Americans, not just those who ran afoul of the law. The *Afro-American Ledger* recognized that "every crime committed by a member of the Negro race, is by concurrent action, upon the part of the white press, so pictured and paraded, as to make the whole race partakers of the short-comings of one member of the race."[59] The rhetoric of black criminality also made all African Americans accessories to crime. In at least four instances, the *Afro-American Ledger* pointedly criticized white Baltimoreans' penchant for claiming that the black community harbored criminals. Although white society barred African Americans from serving on the police force, it expected them to become amateur detectives or else be branded as criminals themselves for allegedly sheltering fugitives.[60]

Stories of black crime effectively dehumanized all African Americans. The *Baltimore Sun* used supposed outbreaks of disorder to categorize African Americans as "barbarians" and "warring savages" while likening their presence to a "black plague."[61] They also referred to black Baltimoreans as "roughs" and "rowdies" while police magistrates spoke openly of the "coons" that stood before them in the city's courts. In one case, Justice Grannan contended that "disorderly" African Americans were the "scum of the city." These stories provided narrative examples that complemented social scientists' concurrent efforts to use statistics to link race and crime in northern urban cities.[62] It is not surprising in this context that African Americans faced instances of police violence. By 1904, the *Afro-American Ledger* complained that "men are shot down in their tracks by zealous policemen, for supposed infraction of the law."[63]

For black Baltimoreans, simply being in public could lead to police harassment. In one example, the Baltimore Police Department arrested a number of African Americans during Fourth of July celebrations for igniting fireworks but ignored white revelers engaged in the same activity. In another instance, the *Afro-American Ledger* reported that a policeman in the city's northwest harassed African Americans—including two mothers holding their infants—while sitting on steps. Then, in 1909, the Baltimore Police Department hauled in more than one hundred men because of alleged "disorderly" behavior. As the *Afro-American Ledger* pointed out, many of the arrests were unwarranted, and the presiding magistrate immediately released twenty-five of those detained.[64]

The racial prejudice that African Americans encountered in their dealings with the police and judges continued after sentencing. Black teenagers confronted the prospect of being sentenced to the Colored Reformatory at Cheltenham if they were not remanded to the city jail or House of Correction. For years, African Americans condemned the reformatory. In 1901 the *Afro-American Ledger* railed against "brutal" reformatory agents after a young child was found handcuffed with a ball and chain attached to his legs. The paper remarked that the institution was "doing the young Negroes of this State more harm, if such a thing is possible, than the Baltimore City Jail." Less than a year later, the paper alleged that employees neglected sick children and claimed that the white teachers' racial prejudice made them "unfit" for the job of rehabilitation.[65]

Many adults convicted of minor offenses, such as William Brown, were sent to the Maryland House of Correction in rural Jessup. Nicknamed "The Cut" for its proximity to a Baltimore and Ohio rail line that ran (or cut) through the wooded area, the institution faced numerous allegations related to substandard facilities and its brutal treatment of inmates. In 1897 the *Baltimore Sun* reported severe overcrowding at the facility: the institution housed 489 inmates even though its capacity was only 300. To compensate, prison officials forced two prisoners into cells big enough for one mattress. These crowded conditions and the lack of employment opportunities led to tensions that frequently resulted in fights between inmates and attacks on guards. In 1900 Dr. C. P. Carrico, the institution's newly appointed physician, reported an outbreak of scurvy resulting from what prisoners described as food that contained little to no vegetables.[66]

The city and the *Baltimore Sun* boasted of a number of improvements made to the Cut after its expansion in 1906. Yet troubling reports continued to emerge about its sanitary conditions and treatment of prisoners. When Dr. E. Stagg Whitin, the secretary of the National Commission on Prison Labor, visited in 1911, he found a number of problems including substandard food, poor sanitation, and physical abuse. Notably, Dr. Whitin also contended that many inmates should not have been committed to the prison. "It seems an admitted fact," Whitin's report read, "that habeas corpus proceedings would release a large number [of inmates]."[67]

African Americans sent to the Maryland Penitentiary might have suffered an even worse fate. Convicts entered an institution that became infamous by the early 1910s for its horrid treatment of inmates and wretched living conditions. The aging penitentiary, which occupied six and a half acres of land, was opened in 1811 on the eastern bank of Jones Falls in Baltimore. In 1899 a new wing was added to the original structure to increase its size to 1,350 cells. In 1912 Governor Phillips Lee Goldsborough sent the Maryland Penitentiary Penal Commission to investigate the prison facilities, its staff, and its warden, John F. Weyler. The three-member panel issued a scathing report. Investigators found cells in "filthy condition" and a bedbug infestation throughout the entire complex, including the hospital. In one of the wings, "we found men there confined in darkness without beds or mattresses, with nothing but a board slightly elevated from the brick floor, the underside of the board covered with cobwebs and every crack lined with a white row of bed-bug eggs, and infested with live bedbugs, the men complaining of sleepless nights due to the prevalence of vermin and the presence of rats." Inmates described the food as "rancid and nauseating," as well as frequently infested with cockroaches.[68]

For black Baltimoreans, the criminal corrections system offered little chance for rehabilitation. When Marylanders began agitating for a state reformatory at the turn of the twentieth century, Weyler opposed it. He contended that only a fraction of the inmates sent to the penitentiary would be eligible for a stint at a reformatory. Of those qualified, in his eyes, none were black. Weyler contended that African Americans, "on account of their low order of mentality, their almost utter lack of moral sense, are not nearly so susceptible to the influences tending toward their reformation as are many of the whites."[69]

In lieu of rehabilitation, Weyler's penitentiary doled out severe physical punishment. Until the early 1900s, the institution whipped prisoners with a cat-o'-nine-tails before Weyler discontinued its use over sanitary concerns. Nevertheless, guards still "cuffed-up" prisoners, a painful form of torture that involved hoisting an inmate by their wrists until their feet no longer touched the ground. Investigators determined that guards frequently used this punishment on inmates "for their first infraction upon the rules, and that some of these punishments were inflicted within a week after the man's admission to the Institution." In addition, guards locked prisoners in solitary confinement without adhering to "proper safeguards and regulations." Other states had already abolished similar forms of punishment. The penal commission pointed out that "corporal punishment occupies no part of the disciplinary system of a modern Penitentiary." They also remarked, "In no penal institution that we visited did we find the dark cells used."[70]

The move by politicians, the press, and city officials to criminalize African Americans redefined politics and the workings of the criminal justice system by the 1900s. The story of Walter White illustrates many of the problems African Americans faced as a result of segregationists' persistent linkage of race, crime, and politics. White supported his three children and wife by working as a dump picker. The job was difficult. Each morning he set off at 5:00 A.M. to arrive at the dump by 5:30. There he worked until "well after the sun has set."[71]

In the predawn hours of 15 October 1909, White crossed paths with Officer Adam Klingenburg, who arrested him. Klingenburg suspected that White had stolen a "coil of new rubber hose" but could not provide evidence to support his suspicion. It is likely that White found the hose at the dump. A few days following his arrest, a resident named John Smeltzing stepped forward to claim the hose. If it were indeed his, Smeltzing's claim would have demonstrated that White had stolen it. However, when the police presented him with the hose, he did not recognize it. "Well—er, it's red all right, and it looks like my hose," Smeltzing uttered, "but I believe my hose was a little redder than that." The officer, in an effort to lead his witness, retorted that "this hose would be redder if you wet it." This response, according to the Baltimore News, prompted a bystander to quip that it "would be redder than that if you painted it." The paper reported that a number of witnesses, contrary to Klingenburg's contention, also claimed that the hose was not new but was in poor shape. The hose "bore every appearance of having been thrown away and lain discarded for some time," the News sarcastically noted, "just such a piece of hose as might been found on a dump."[72]

The circumstances surrounding White's arrest point to the probability that he was arrested because he was black. Officials provided various reasons for apprehending White. Justice Llewellyn claimed that the police had received reports of "petty thefts" in the area committed by a person matching White's description. The judge only made this claim on one occasion, and no one else involved with the case repeated it. Klingenburg, for his part, provided two reasons. He claimed that an unnamed source or sources reported White had been spotted in the neighborhood throughout the week carrying "a sack full of things." Klingenburg also asserted that "he looked like a suspicious character and as he was carrying a bag I thought he might be up to mischief." The *Baltimore News* remained dubious of these explanations. The paper asked the patrolman if White had been "making any loud noises or disturbing the peace of the neighborhood." "No," Klingenburg responded, "he was not making any fuss but he acted suspiciously." Even though the officer could not find evidence that the hose White had on him was stolen, he arrested him anyway.[73]

Race continued to influence White's treatment during his trial. When White tried to explain himself before Justice Llewellyn, the magistrate abruptly interrupted and admonished him to "Hurry up, now. We haven't got time to fool with you." In two minutes, Llewellyn rendered his guilty verdict for a crime, disorderly conduct, which White did not commit. The magistrate left little doubt of what he thought of White. "I can't understand why so much fuss should be kicked up over a man," Llewellyn told the *Baltimore News*, "who is nothing more than a negro bum." Despite the lack of evidence, Justice Llewellyn arbitrarily charged White with "disorderly conduct" and fined him twenty-five dollars and the costs of prosecution. When White could not afford to pay the penalty, the magistrate committed him to jail for twenty-seven days.[74]

White's saga substantiated African Americans' numerous allegations of official malfeasance and racism in Baltimore's criminal justice system. The police arrested White for a minor offense with no evidence. Once in court, White faced a hostile justice uninterested in hearing his defense; the justice, it would seem, was already convinced of his guilt. Like many other poor black defendants, White was unable to pay the excessive twenty-five-dollar fine and was instead remitted to jail. In the end, White was fortunate. Following his initial trial, George Drenford, an attorney and Catholic priest, volunteered his services and worked arduously to secure White's freedom. Most African Americans were not as lucky and instead were remanded to one of the state's correctional institutions.[75]

Segregationists' persistent racialization of crime demonstrated the resiliency and flexibility of white supremacy. White Baltimoreans—from politicians, the press, and magistrates to everyday citizens—affixed in the public's mind a connection between crime and African Americans. The Democratic Party recognized the power inherent in these ideas and used the trope of the black criminal to regain control of Baltimore and Maryland. Once in power, Democrats trumpeted these concerns to suppress the black vote and erode democracy. Once again, the story of Walter White is instructive. Justice Llewellyn sentenced White to twenty-seven days in jail. This sentence, as some observers noticed, was just long enough to keep him from voting in the upcoming election. This was not an isolated incident. Weeks prior to the election, the *Afro-American Ledger* warned black Baltimoreans to stay away from police stations or risk being sentenced to "30 and 60 days in jail," which would be enough time to keep them from missing Election Day. White's arrest and sentence did not surprise the *Ledger*'s editors. "We know the tricks of the enemy so well, that some time ago we called attention to the importance of our people keeping their distance from the police courts. Some of our pastors have," the paper continued, "in their pulpits, called attention to the same thing, for from now on, these Democratic justices will use almost any pretext to put the offending Negro in jail to a period past the day of election."[76] The city's strategic use of arrest and incarceration to suppress the black vote augured a wider assault on democracy that would occupy activists for the next decade.

The creation of the racialized carceral state raises important questions concerning notions of Progressive Era racial progress. Although white Baltimoreans had long exploited fears of black criminality, these ideas found new life in the Progressive Era. The ostensibly race-neutral language of Progressive Era concerns with "good government" provided segregationists with the framework to halt the steps that African Americans had made toward equality since the Reconstruction era. In the coming years, segregationists continued to rhetorically link race and crime to justify constitutional disfranchisement and legalized residential segregation. Instead of continuing their efforts to tackle inequalities through the courts or protests, African Americans would instead spend the first two decades of the twentieth century defending gains that they had already secured in previous decades, as we shall see in the next two chapters.

CHAPTER 5

"The Wave of Disfranchising Deviltry Has Gone to Its Utmost Northern Limits"

On 23 January 1904 the *Afro-American Ledger* published an urgent editorial. "On next Tuesday morning at 12 o'clock, in old Bethel church," the paper announced, "a grand mass meeting of extra-ordinary and far-reaching importance will be held." The editorial combined themes of religious duty, civil rights activism, and American history in its call to action. The *Afro-American Ledger* implored black Baltimoreans to fight Maryland's recently proposed disfranchisement initiative, known as the Poe Amendment, by "[consecrating] ourselves anew to the service of God and the Brotherhood of all mankind." They invoked the memories of Benjamin Banneker, Frederick Douglass, and abolitionist Henry Highland Garnet and reminded readers of the "great cost whereby human freedom was obtained for us." Three veteran activists, Sharon Baptist's Rev. William M. Alexander, civil rights attorney W. Ashbie Hawkins, and Trinity Baptist's Rev. G. R. Waller, organized the meeting at Bethel where they formed the Suffrage League to fight the initiative.[1]

At Bethel Church, black Baltimoreans created a statewide movement that would consume activists' energy for the better part of the next decade. Between 1904 and 1911, Maryland segregationists attempted to pass three separate disfranchisement amendments: the Poe Amendment in 1904–1905, the Straus Amendment in 1908–1909, and the Digges Amendment in 1910–1911. In each case, black Baltimoreans organized grassroots movements to help defeat the amendments. Their efforts not only stopped the spread of Jim Crow disfranchisement but also preserved democracy in the face of segregationists' attempts to make Maryland a one-party state. In fighting Jim Crow, activists used their struggle for racial equality to counter segregationists' efforts to cast disfranchisement as a progressive reform and articulated their own vision of a just society that positioned African American voters as a safeguard against political corruption, oppression, and disorder.[2]

Black Marylanders' fight against disfranchisement was more than just a local struggle. African Americans in Maryland confronted the prospect of disfranchisement in the midst of important national developments in the black freedom struggle. As Jim Crow spread across the South at the dawn of the twentieth century, African American activists across the nation stood at a crossroads. The Afro-American Council (AAC) had led the resistance to Jim Crow as the only national black civil rights organization. However, the group's lack of tangible successes, along with the widening rift between the conservative Booker T. Washington and more radical activists such as William M. Trotter and W. E. B. DuBois, led many African Americans to rethink their strategies. DuBois and Trotter split from the AAC and in the summer of 1905 formed the Niagara Movement. The new organization promised to meet racial injustice with uncompromising protest and targeted preserving the right to vote as one of their highest priorities. In their Declaration of Principles, the group proclaimed, "We believe that [African Americans] should protest emphatically and continually against the curtailment of political rights." Black Marylanders stood ready to answer the call.[3]

Black Baltimoreans' campaign against the Poe Amendment became the first test of the Niagara Movement's more forthright style of resistance. Black Baltimoreans, many of whom participated in the Niagara Movement, led the effort to fight disfranchisement. They drew inspiration from the new organization, but also from the activist traditions and networks they had created during the previous decades. They also expanded their protests. Black men and women organized new civil rights groups, led consumer boycotts and impromptu strikes, held protest meetings, mobilized voters, and conducted voting schools across the state. Their activism demonstrated to the country that an uncompromising stance, coupled with mass protest, could be an effective means of fighting Jim Crow. Following their victory in 1905, black Marylanders confirmed that their success was not a fluke when they helped defeat two additional attempts to institutionalize Jim Crow voting restrictions by following the same strategies. These latter victories came as activists, including DuBois, began organizing the National Association for the Advancement of

Colored People (NAACP), an organization that many Baltimoreans supported from the outset.[4]

In some respects, Maryland's journey to constitutional disfranchisement followed familiar southern patterns. In the two decades following the Civil War, Marylanders, like their southern counterparts, relied on violence, fraud, and intimidation to suppress the African American vote. In the 1890s, however, the state's path diverged from that of their southern neighbors in key respects. Unlike many southern states, Maryland did not pass legislation—for example, a poll tax or literacy test—to explicitly undermine the black vote during the nineteenth century.[5]

By southern standards, Maryland's voting laws remained largely fair and nonpartisan into the late 1890s. Maryland Democrats, however, changed that after they suffered a series of electoral defeats between 1895 and 1897. During the 1899 election season, the party sought to reverse their losses by making the fear of "negro domination" a central component of their campaign at the city and state levels. In rally after rally, Democrats argued that African Americans felt emboldened to commit crime so long as Republicans held office. As Baltimore's spring municipal elections came to a conclusion, Democrats had so effectively stigmatized African Americans as inherently criminal that they no longer felt the need to explicitly draw these connections. At one campaign rally, Democrat Hugo Steiner told his German American audience, "This matter of negro domination has received a great deal of attention in the campaign, but I will not insult your intelligence by discussing it further tonight. You all know how to vote," he continued, "to get rid of this lawless element."[6] In the end, Democratic charges of "black lawlessness" proved doubly effective, propelling Democrats back into office across the state in 1899 and marginalizing African Americans.

The Democrats' pledge to end "negro domination" served as the opening salvo in their fight to scale back democracy. In fact, it became Democrats' first tool to disfranchise black voters. During the late nineteenth century, states across the South used arrests and criminal convictions, often for petty crimes, to disfranchise African Americans prior to using more familiar legislative means.[7] At the turn of the twentieth century, Baltimoreans followed a similar strategy. In 1901 the *Afro-American Ledger* alleged that the Baltimore police apprehended blacks close to Election Day to keep them from voting. "The unfortunate soul, that happens to be black, will have to be a little careful of himself," the paper quipped, "or he will find himself rounded up and sent to moralize at Hotel Doyle [the city jail] until after [the] election." Democrats continued to use the criminal justice system to limit the black vote throughout the decade. In 1909 the *Afro-American Ledger* warned its readers to keep their distance from police stations or risk being sentenced to jail until after the voting concluded. Two weeks later, the editor's fears proved to be founded. The *Baltimore News* alleged that police magistrate William J. Llewellyn leveled steep penalties on four African Americans to keep them from voting. Llewellyn knew that the city would incarcerate the men until after Election Day in the likely event that they could not afford to pay the excessive fines.[8] Even without criminal convictions or legislation, Democrats' fight against "negro domination" chipped away at African Americans' right to vote.

Democrats soon complemented their ad hoc policy of disfranchisement through arrest with legislation. During the 1901 election, Arthur Pue Gorman's senatorial seat hung in the balance. In an effort to ensure victory, Democrats passed the Wilson Law prohibiting the printing of party symbols (which made it easier for illiterate or semiliterate men to vote) on ballots in Republican strongholds throughout Maryland. They also reorganized the ballot alphabetically (instead of by party affiliation) and set strict rules that enabled them to disallow returns marked incorrectly. According to the Reform League, a nonpartisan organization composed of elite white reformers, the bill was an invitation to outright fraud that sought to disfranchise illiterate voters, of which a disproportionate number were black. Ultimately, the Wilson Law, like disfranchisement through arrest, was a half measure that proved only partially effective: Democrats triumphed on the strength of the rural vote but lost ground in Baltimore where the legislation did not apply.[9]

The Democratic Party intended the next election in 1903 to serve as a public referendum on race and the franchise. The party's gubernatorial nominee, Edwin Warfield, launched his campaign with an open appeal to white supremacy. "The great and pressing problem of the day, not only in Maryland, but in every section of our common country—North as well as South, East as well as West—is the 'negro question.'" Warfield deployed the trope of the black criminal to punctuate his message. "We have experienced in this State in recent years the effects of Republican supremacy on the emotional and excitable negro mind," Warfield remarked. "It brought [an] increase of lawlessness among the colored population of our chief city," he continued, "and multiplied crime throughout the State." Warfield, to "great applause," implored "all citizens, irrespective of party, who love and honor the State, to lend their earnest and active support in this contest for the supremacy of the white race, for the cause of civilization and good government." Warfield's remarks presaged a virulently racist campaign that carried Democrats to the governor's mansion and earned them a two-thirds majority in the General Assembly.[10]

As Maryland Democrats launched their campaign against democracy, African Americans were losing their right to vote in most of the South. By the turn of the twentieth century, many southern states moved from voter suppression to using constitutional means to fully eliminate the black vote. Their timing was not coincidental but rather intensified after the federal government weakened laws designed to ensure universal male suffrage following the Civil War. In 1890, Maryland's Arthur Pue Gorman orchestrated a Democratic filibuster to defeat the Lodge Bill, which would have made it far easier for citizens to request federal supervision of elections. The Democratic defeat of the Lodge Bill marked the last time the Republican Party attempted to strengthen the Reconstruction measures it passed to ensure African Americans' right to vote. Then, in 1893 and 1894, Democrats (now holding a majority in Congress) repealed the Reconstruction-era federal laws that enforced the Fifteenth Amendment. With that, the federal government abandoned efforts to ensure fair voting in the South. For Maryland's Democrats, national developments, together with their electoral gains in the state, left them well positioned to launch an effort to formally disfranchise African Americans.[11]

Maryland Democrats hoped to follow in their southern neighbors' footsteps by reestablishing the antebellum status quo. The newly elected speaker of the Maryland House of Delegates, George Y. Everhart, reminded his colleagues in 1904, "The majority of you were elected upon a platform which committed you to preserve in every conservative and constitutional way, the political ascendancy of the white race in Maryland."[12] Gorman had already set the wheels in motion. Maryland's senior senator asked his friend and dean of the Maryland law school John Prentiss Poe to craft the state's disfranchisement legislation. The plan (which came to be known as the Poe Amendment) hinged on two mandatory "saving clauses." The first was a temporary grandfather clause (which would expire in 1906) that required all voters to prove that they had a male descendant eligible to vote in 1869. The second was a permanent "understanding clause" that mandated that registrants read and give a "reasonable" explanation of the Maryland state constitution or interpret a selection read to them by an examiner. Even by early twentieth-century standards the legislation was severe. Its requirement that all voters, not just African Americans, satisfy its provisions and its use of a permanent "understanding clause" invested an inordinate amount of power in registrars to determine a voter's eligibility. Nevertheless, with a two-thirds majority in the state legislature and a Democrat in the governor's mansion, the proposed amendment seemed destined to pass.[13]

Maryland's disfranchisement movement placed black Marylanders in a precarious position. Democrats successfully ran on an openly racist platform. At the same time, African Americans could not rely on the state's Republicans. The party largely ignored the concerns of their black constituents, paying lip service to equality only when courting African American votes. As early as 1899, the editors of the *Afro-American Ledger* lamented, "It is the Negro's vote and that alone in which [Republicans] are greatly interested; not the Negro, but his vote." The *Baltimore Sunday Herald* declared that opponents of the Poe Amendment viewed black voters as an "undesirable ally."[14]

Lacking reliable white political allies, African Americans took the lead in the effort to defeat the Poe Amendment. On 23 January 1904 an estimated four hundred black Baltimoreans braved poor weather conditions to organize the Suffrage League at Bethel Church. Attendees selected a cross section of Baltimore's most venerated activists to fill out the organization's ranks. They elected one of the titans of the city's civil rights movement, Rev. Dr. Harvey Johnson, to lead the new organization. In addition, they selected other movement veterans, including William M. Alexander, W. Ashbie Hawkins, George F. Bragg, Jr. (pastor at the Protestant Episcopal Church), Harry S. Cummings (a lawyer and politician), and Hiram Watty (a city councilman) to serve on the advisory board. Johnson, citing poor health, declined to serve as president and left the organization in the hands of his protégé, Reverend Alexander.[15]

Under Alexander's stewardship, the Suffrage League capitalized on the infrastructure that activists had built in the 1880s and 1890s. The nascent organization leaned heavily on Baltimore's churches for logistical support. Although African Americans lived throughout Baltimore following the Civil War, by the early twentieth century they increasingly resided in Baltimore's northwest.[16] The black churches that followed the city's internal migration, including Union Baptist, Sharon Baptist, and Sharp Street Memorial United

Methodist Church, became the heart of the resistance effort. Churches and ministers throughout the city also played key roles. First Baptist, Bethel AME, and Waters AME on the city's east side, the south side's Leadenhall Street Baptist Church and Ebenezer AME, and the west side's Allen AME and Perkins Square Baptist Church hosted either Suffrage League meetings or indignation meetings, or their ministers spoke out against the Poe Amendment.[17]

Baltimore's network of churches provided the Suffrage League with coverage that spanned the entire city. On 28 February 1904 thirteen African American preachers—all members of the Suffrage League—launched a coordinated assault on Jim Crow in their Sunday sermons. At Sharon Baptist Church, Alexander told his congregation that the law branded African Americans as an "inferior element of society." Rev. Reuben H. Armstrong proclaimed that Jim Crow laws "disrupt democracy" and labeled them "absurd, foolish, cowardly; they are marks of littleness." Rev. J. T. Jenifer combined religion and American ideals by labeling the Poe Amendment as "unchristian" and "opposed to every tradition and principle for which the American Republic stands." Others mixed condemnation with a call to action. Trinity Baptist Church's G. R. Waller exclaimed that African Americans "must contend for full recognition of all the rights incident to manhood and American citizenship."[18]

The *Afro-American Ledger* helped further spread the organization's message.[19] The paper became black Marylanders' most important source for information on the league's meetings and upcoming events. It also helped define the stakes of the fight for the black community. The *Afro-American Ledger*'s editors labeled the Poe Amendment as an act of "political lynching" and a piece of "un-American legislation." They also pushed black men to register to vote. Alexander used the paper to disseminate the Suffrage League's message. He regularly wrote letters to the *Afro-American Ledger* that explained the group's objectives and rallied community support.[20]

African Americans across the state also formed chapters of the Suffrage League. A week after the league's founding, a black resident of Frostburg wrote the *Afro-American Ledger* to report that Allegany County, in the state's western panhandle, had organized a chapter. The letter writer proclaimed, "We do not intend to sit down and whine and bemoan our fate, but we intend to fight; fight hard and continue to fight until we win or go down in defeat." In Easton, on Maryland's Eastern Shore, black residents organized a chapter of the Suffrage League in January 1904. Although the fight against disfranchisement originated in Baltimore, it quickly became a

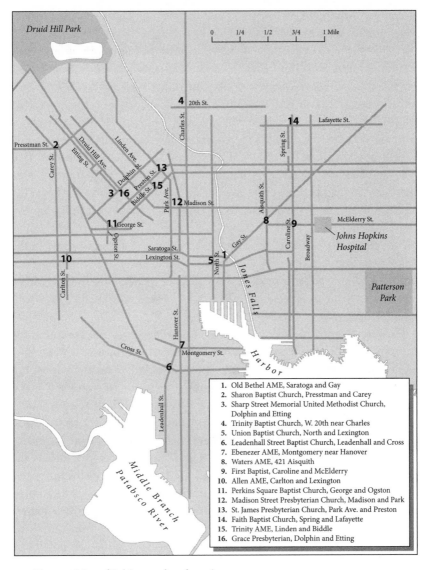

Figure 6. Map of Baltimore churches, circa 1905.

Map labels:

Druid Hill Park

0 1/4 1/2 3/4 1 Mile

4 | 20th St.

14 | Lafayette St.

Presstman St. 2

Druid Hill Ave.

Linden Ave.

Etting St.

Carey St.

Charles St.

Spring St.

Dolphin St.

13

Preston St.

3 16

15

Biddle St.

Park Ave.

12 | Madison St.

Aisquith St.

McElderry St.

11 | George St.

Ogston St.

8

Caroline St.

9

Broadway

Johns Hopkins Hospital

Saratoga St.

Lexington St.

Gay St.

10

Carlton St.

5 | 1

North St.

Patterson Park

Jones Falls

Hanover St.

Cross St.

7 | Montgomery St.

6

Harbor

Leadenhall St.

Middle Branch Patabsco River

1. Old Bethel AME, Saratoga and Gay
2. Sharon Baptist Church, Presstman and Carey
3. Sharp Street Memorial United Methodist Church, Dolphin and Etting
4. Trinity Baptist Church, W. 20th near Charles
5. Union Baptist Church, North and Lexington
6. Leadenhall Street Baptist Church, Leadenhall and Cross
7. Ebenezer AME, Montgomery near Hanover
8. Waters AME, 421 Aisquith
9. First Baptist, Caroline and McElderry
10. Allen AME, Carlton and Lexington
11. Perkins Square Baptist Church, George and Ogston
12. Madison Street Presbyterian Church, Madison and Park
13. St. James Presbyterian Church, Park Ave. and Preston
14. Faith Baptist Church, Spring and Lafayette
15. Trinity AME, Linden and Biddle
16. Grace Presbyterian, Dolphin and Etting

statewide movement. Eventually, the league had auxiliaries or members in ten counties throughout the state.[21]

The Suffrage League immediately leveraged the black community's economic clout to resist Jim Crow. In addition to passing the Poe Amendment in 1904, Maryland's General Assembly instituted a segregation law on railroads and steamships. At the Suffrage League's initial meetings, speakers urged black Baltimoreans to boycott excursion lines, while the *Afro-American Ledger* encouraged its readers to boycott public transportation. These boycotts lasted throughout the summer. Alexander explained that "since [black customers] paid the corporations $200,000 a summer, if we keep our money in our pockets as an expression of our protest against the Jim Crow law, the corporations for self interest will use their influence and money to elect men to the next legislature who will repeal Jim Crow laws." Throughout the summer, the league placed various advertisements in the *Afro-American Ledger* urging African Americans to forgo excursions. They also asked the paper's readers to report any unequal conditions they encountered on public transit and further requested that ministers help spread the word.[22]

Although it is impossible to gauge how widespread the boycotts were in 1904, anecdotal evidence indicates that they were successful. The *Afro-American Ledger*'s Frostburg correspondent reported, "We do not intend to run any excursions this year, and the Afro-Americans who attempt such a thing should be driven into obscurity and be compelled to remain there." The paper reported that several groups had cancelled their planned trips. Perhaps most telling were Annapolis and Baltimore Short Line Railroad's advertisements in the *Afro-American Ledger*. Signed by S. B. Hughes, the black minister of Baltimore's Saint Paul Methodist Episcopal Church and an agent for the rail line, the advert sought to assure black Baltimoreans that the company's employees were only directing passengers to an alternate entrance because of nearby fire damage, not because of Jim Crow. The *Afro-American Ledger*'s editors did not buy this explanation and noted that Hughes's own congregation refused to go on their excursion that year on account of Jim Crow. The paper further reported that business remained "dull" in July on account of the boycotts.[23]

As African Americans registered their opposition to Jim Crow, legislators encountered problems of their own making. Within a matter of weeks both Governor Warfield and the state's attorney general, William S. Bryan, Jr., announced their opposition. The two men, while segregationists, objected to the power that the law invested in registrars. Their opposition notwithstanding, the legislature voted to pass the bill by a two-thirds majority vote. Yet when Governor Warfield refused to sign the amendment, Democrats temporarily pocketed the legislation. For the next year, the amendment languished in a state of limbo. In late November, Murray Vandiver, the chairman of the Democratic State Central Committee, pushed Governor Warfield to publicly state if he would ever sign the amendment. After Warfield declined, Vandiver carried the case to Maryland's Court of Appeals. Since the General Assembly passed the amendment with a veto-proof majority, Vandiver maintained that the amendment did not require the governor's signature to stand for public ratification. In March 1905 the court sided with Vandiver and the amendment's supporters.[24] The state's voters would now decide the fate of the amendment in the upcoming fall election.

Black Marylanders faced the possibility of disfranchisement as a number of important changes occurred in the national struggle for racial equality. In 1905 DuBois and Trotter finalized their plans for the Niagara Movement. The organization championed a more proactive style of activism that appealed to many Baltimoreans. In addition, the group identified preserving the franchise as one of its top goals.[25] Trinity Baptist's G. R. Waller, one of the early organizers of Maryland's Suffrage League, served as Maryland's representative and attended the Niagara Movement's first meeting in Buffalo, New York, in the summer of 1905. The next year, the Niagara Movement counted a number of Baltimoreans among its ranks, including Waller, Hawkins, and Harvey Johnson. It also gained the support of the *Afro-American Ledger*, which announced that it stood with the organization "heart and soul."[26]

It is too simplistic to say that the Niagara Movement changed the course of black activism in Baltimore. Rather, the organization's founding validated ideals and strategies that had guided black Baltimoreans since the mid-1880s when Harvey Johnson established the Mutual United Brotherhood of Liberty. In fact, Baltimoreans' early participation in the Niagara Movement may have shaped the organization's initial ideals. In its Declaration of Principles, the Niagara Movement declared, "We refuse to allow the impression to remain that the Negro-American assents to inferiority, is submissive under oppression and apologetic before insults." The Niagara Movement called on men and women to rally against racial injustice, urged the black clergy to take leadership positions in the struggle, and called for

vigorous and uncompromising protest against oppression. Black Baltimoreans had already professed these ideals and had been practicing these strategies for decades.[27] Yet the founding of the Niagara Movement came at the
perfect moment for black Marylanders. Their struggle against the Poe
Amendment became the first local test for the more forthright style of activism advocated by the Niagara Movement. Black Marylanders knew from
past experience that this style of activism could work. Now they would
demonstrate for the country the promise and effectiveness of the Niagara
Movement's strategy.

As the 1905 election approached, the *Afro-American Ledger*'s editors
hoped to build on the successes of the transportation boycotts they helped
foment during the previous year. This time, rather than just transportation
companies, they targeted amendment supporters. Black Marylanders' use
of boycotts and financial pressure made the resistance movement a community affair. In August the paper urged its readership to "carry your politics into your business" by not giving money to someone who would "then
immediately politically lynch them." The *Afro-American Ledger*'s editors
especially urged women to find out how the white men with whom they
did business intended to vote. "If they say they are going to vote for it," the
paper counseled, "give them to understand, that they are both ungrateful
for the patronage received from Negroes, and secret enemies to the very
people whose hard earning[s] are keeping afloat their respective business
enterprise."[28]

Women built on the consumer boycott efforts by leveraging their labor.
Black domestic workers organized an impromptu strike that targeted families where "any member is in favor" of the Poe Amendment. The *Baltimore
Sunday Herald* reported that when African American women negotiated
their employment with white families, they first asked if "there anybody in
this house who favors that amendment that the democrats want to pass to
keep colored people from voting?" If the prospective employer answered
yes, the women refused to work or demanded higher wages. As one
unnamed African American woman explained, "We propose to show the
white people that we can take a part in this business as well as they, and we
mean to do it."[29] These domestic battles matched the racial and political
tensions in the city. Amendment supporters had justified disfranchisement
as a way to undermine growing black political power. Although the setting
was the home and not the political arena, black women's protests prompted
similar complaints. The *Evening Herald* sarcastically dubbed one striking

domestic a "queen of the kitchen." White housekeepers accused strikers of being "brutally arrogant" and possessing a "dictatorial attitude." The domestic workers' strike also drove a political wedge between husbands and wives. As one white housekeeper complained, "The whole thing is a carefully concocted plan to force voters, through the persecution of their wives, daughters, or mothers, into casting their votes against the proposed amendment." Another white housekeeper confessed that she had gone "weeks" without help. By the eve of the election, the *Baltimore Sunday Herald* estimated that "nearly 40 per cent of the homes in some sections are without domestic help." The *Afro-American Ledger* reported that white Baltimoreans were having a difficult time finding domestic help because of the "abuse that has been heaped upon the heads of the colored people for the past three or four months in the newspapers."[30]

Black women's contributions to the fight against disfranchisement were not limited to boycotts and strikes. On at least one occasion, women organized a public protest against the Poe Amendment. On 23 October 1905 "100 or more" African American women held an indignation meeting at the Perkins Square Baptist Church. The women implored the men in the audience to work to defeat the legislation. The church's minister, Frank R. Williams, encouraged the women to continue their work. "I should like to suggest that you devote special attention to the young gentlemen," Reverend Williams remarked, "and that you visit them and sit and talk with them about the great issue involved. The liberties of our people are at stake." Alexander attended the rally and asked the women to get their husbands out to the polls to vote against the legislation.[31]

By actively recruiting women, Baltimore's activists broke with their Niagara Movement peers. In its early days, the Niagara Movement repeatedly termed civil rights activism as a "manly duty"—a term that Baltimoreans used as well—and initially barred women from membership. In Baltimore, however, Alexander made numerous overtures to black women to play active roles. Alexander asked women involved in "benevolent and secret society work" to use their statewide contacts to rouse men into action. He called on women to help open "places of instruction in every town and precinct throughout the State." Alexander also stressed the potential of day-to-day interactions. "You can help us by speaking one to another," Alexander wrote in a letter published in the *Afro-American*, "and by urging the men to see that their liberty, civil and political, and the general welfare of their wives and children, are largely dependent upon the result of the next election."[32] Although their efforts are impossible to document, women probably rallied support to defeat the Poe Amendment in the privacy of their homes or in quick conversations with friends, neighbors, coworkers, or family members as well.

As Election Day approached, the Suffrage League focused on registering voters. The group called on "the pulpit, the press, and every other educating agency" to urge voters to exercise their franchise.[33] The voter registration drive paid dividends. Democrats in Baltimore openly worried at the sight of so many African Americans registering to vote. Alexander wrote that "I think it is safe to say that we have more colored men on the registration books in Baltimore city and throughout the State who can vote at the coming election than have been at any time in the past."[34] Alexander's initial optimism soon faded in the face of Democratic chicanery. On the day after the registration period ended, the *Baltimore Sun* confidently crowed that the number of voters would "be reduced." In the end, officials removed 5,500 voters from the lists. These decisions fell heavily on the city's black population. White voters saw an increase of 611 over the previous year, while African Americans lost 194 votes despite their intense voter registration drive. Still, the number of African Americans who attempted to register indicated the community's commitment to fighting the Poe Amendment.[35]

Although Democrats successfully barred some black voters, they continued to face strong headwinds from various quarters. In addition to the state's black population, foreign-born voters registered strong opposition, fearing that registrars could arbitrarily disfranchise them. Most ominously for amendment supporters, many Democrats who opposed the state's Gorman-Raisin political machine denounced the initiative as corrupt.[36] With the amendment already on life support, Maryland's junior senator, Isidor Rayner, delivered a crushing blow. In the late nineteenth and early twentieth centuries, Rayner engaged in the same racial politics as his fellow Maryland Democrats. But Rayner, the son of a Bavarian immigrant, opposed the Gorman machine and the threat that the amendment potentially posed to immigrants. Less than three weeks before the election, Rayner announced his opposition via an open letter published in the *Baltimore Sun*.[37]

Despite the Poe Amendment's dim prospects, African Americans were not going to leave their voting future to chance. The *Afro-American Ledger* published weekly editorials and short articles up to Election Day highlighting the importance of defeating the measure. "Not only our suffrage but our very liberties are at stake," the paper reminded readers in one editorial. The paper also pushed voters to turn out for the election. "The way to vote early and often is first to vote yourself and then see to it that your neighbor votes." The *Afro-American Ledger*'s most poignant pleas contextualized the fight against conditions in the South. One editorial proclaimed, "To be without our franchise is to be next door to slavery in its vilest form." In another, the *Afro-American Ledger* framed the vote as a way to avoid the "peonage system" found in Georgia or the fate of Mississippians and Louisianans who were "deprived of educational facilities."[38]

On 7 November Marylanders voted on the Poe Amendment. It must have been a nerve-racking night for the men and women who worked tirelessly against disfranchisement. The state's electorate ultimately rejected the legislation by a margin of 33,946 votes.[39] The newspapers did not print a racial breakdown of the vote. African Americans, however, made their voices heard. The *Philadelphia Inquirer* reported that "the colored vote in all precincts was exceptionally heavy." The city's largest concentration of African Americans resided in the northwest's Seventeenth Ward, where black voters provided the amendment its largest margin of defeat, rejecting it by 2,400 votes.[40] Harry S. Cummings highlighted the role that black voters played. "Of one feature of the result am I especially proud," he told the *Baltimore American*, "and that is the commendable way in which the colored voter of the city and state did his duty to himself and the community." The *Afro-American Ledger* proudly proclaimed, "Maryland was the first Southern state to give the 'Jim Crow' law a black eye."[41]

Activists scored a remarkable victory in defeating the Poe Amendment. As the *Afro-American Ledger* pointed out, "Negro domination; Negro criminality, and all other phases of the Negro bugaboo had been exploited for months after months, and the daily papers teemed with article after article why the Negro should be deprived of the right to vote." The *Voice of the Negro*, the monthly journal of the Niagara Movement, remarked that the legislation's defeat "means first that the wave of disfranchising deviltry has gone to its utmost Northern limits." In another editorial, the journal noted, "It is a significant fact that Maryland is the first Southern state to turn down the Negro disfranchisement amendment when passed by a legislature and submitted to the people."[42]

Despite black Marylanders' victory, the issue of disfranchisement was not dead. Many white voters still supported Jim Crow disfranchisement in principle and voted against the Poe Amendment only because they feared the initiative's particular mechanics. This set the stage for segregationists who would launch a second attempt at disfranchisement in a matter of a few short years.

Maryland's Democrats regrouped amid a great deal of change following the defeat of the Poe Amendment. Six months after Marylanders rejected the amendment, Arthur Pue Gorman, the man that the *Voice of the Negro* dubbed as "one of the high priests of Negro-haters," died. Isaac Freeman Raisin, his machine counterpart in Baltimore, passed away shortly thereafter.[43] Despite their deaths, Democratic politicians continued to eye black disfranchisement. In 1908 Maryland's attorney general, Isaac Lobe Straus, appointed a subcommittee of nine Democrats and independents to craft a new amendment. Straus chose men who supported the Poe Amendment and others who opposed it, hoping that their combined efforts would avoid previous mistakes.[44]

In January 1908, the group authored the Straus Amendment. The initiative contained a standard grandfather clause dated back to 1869. The amendment, however, allowed immigrants and their male descendants to vote if they were naturalized between 1869 and 1908. In effect, the two provisions, according to the *Baltimore Sun,* placed "the naturalized citizen . . . upon an absolute equality with the native-born American and under these two alternatives . . . all white citizens of Maryland will come in." By doing so, the law placated Poe Amendment critics. It was designed to appease those who felt that amendment too vague or that it invested too much power in registrars, as well as immigrants who feared that they could not satisfy the grandfather clause. For African Americans, who could not meet the requirements of these two provisions, the Straus Amendment contained an arbitrary education requirement that tested an applicant's ability to name the president, a Supreme Court justice, the state's governor, and a judge sitting on the Maryland Court of Appeals. If the applicant was a Baltimorean, it further specified that the person identify the city's mayor. The bill's final provision stipulated that males who owned property worth at least five hundred dollars for two years could exercise the franchise. The Straus Amendment passed through the General Assembly with a three-fifths Democratic majority, and Governor Crothers promptly signed it. Once more, the state's voters would have the final say as to whether black men would retain their right to vote.[45]

Black Marylanders also regrouped against the backdrop of some significant national changes in civil rights activism. The years between 1906 and 1908 were particularly important in the black freedom struggle. Two events in 1906 galvanized activists: the 1906 Brownsville shooting affray and the Atlanta race riot. In late 1906 the US military blamed black soldiers in the Twentieth Infantry for a shooting spree in Brownsville, Texas. Without conclusive evidence, President Theodore Roosevelt discharged the accused without honor. Roosevelt's actions, coupled with Booker T. Washington's conciliatory response, angered activists across the country. A few weeks later, whites in Atlanta killed ten African Americans and injured sixty more over the course of a multiday race riot.[46]

Events in Brownsville and Atlanta brought together activists and incited more forthright activism around the country. In Baltimore, African Americans deepened their support in the fight for civil rights in the aftermath of these two events. Black Baltimoreans participated in the Constitution League, a biracial civil rights organization. Waller served as one of the organization's officers; he also served along with Hurst, Hawkins, and Johnson on the executive committee. A host of other Baltimoreans participated in the organization as well.[47] Many black Baltimoreans also joined the Niagara Movement. Activists George F. Bragg, W. Ashbie Hawkins, Mason Hawkins, H. T. Pratt, John Hurst, and G. R. Waller traveled from Baltimore to Harpers Ferry, West Virginia, to represent Maryland at the organization's second meeting in 1906. Although Harvey Johnson did not attend, he continued to support and participate in the organization. By 1908 the Maryland chapter of the Niagara Movement listed twenty-two members.[48]

Black women lent their support to the Niagara Movement as well. Twenty-four women—including Minnie L. Gaines (wife of activist and pastor Rev. A. L. Gaines), W. Ada Hawkins (the mother of Harry S. Cummings), Amelia Johnson (wife of Harvey Johnson), and Lelia G. Waller (wife of G. R. Waller)—formed an auxiliary to the Niagara Movement in early 1907 that they named the DuBois Circle. The women formed the social group to "take up literary work as the special feature of the circle." Yet the organization engaged in activism both publicly and behind the scenes. The women investigated school conditions, published their results in the *Chronicle* (the newspaper they founded), and resolved to undertake a campaign to address these concerns. They worked as ushers for the 1907 Constitution League meeting in Baltimore. They also wrote a letter of appreciation to

Ohio senator Joseph B. Foraker for his statements in support of the black soldiers in Brownsville and donated funds to the Niagara Movement. In addition, they contributed money to help fund a lawsuit against the Pullman Company for discriminating against black passengers.[49] As they had throughout the 1880s and 1890s, Baltimorean women continued to play vital roles in the city's black freedom struggle.

The changing tenor of the national civil rights movement permeated Baltimore as well. Activists targeted not only Democrats but also Republicans. In part, these criticisms stemmed from the previous fight against the Poe Amendment. Maryland's Republicans made no secret of their animosity toward the black voters they relied on to stay in office. During the 1905 Republican state convention, the *Chicago Daily Tribune* reported that the party "took great pains to keep the negro in the background." In their platform, they declared that "the Republican party of the state of Maryland favors no social equality among the races." Even as they fought against the amendment, the party nearly adopted a plank that would have barred African Americans from holding office. As the *Washington Post* explained, "The Republicans are no more enamored of negro suffrage than the Democrats." These events left a sour taste in the mouths of many activists. Shortly after the General Assembly passed the Straus Amendment, Alexander called a meeting to reorganize the Suffrage League. At the gathering, the *Afro-American Ledger* reported that a number of elected officers "brought forth spirited speeches, in which a number of those present avowed their hostility to the Republican machine in this state."[50]

Black Baltimoreans did not limit their criticisms to the state Republican Party. When Baltimoreans hosted a mass rally sponsored by the Constitution League in 1908, a few weeks after the Suffrage League meeting, a number of attendees harshly criticized William H. Taft and Theodore Roosevelt for their stance on racial equality. W. Ashbie Hawkins delivered a particularly scathing denunciation of Taft and his role in allowing disfranchisement to spread throughout the South. "In striking the names of Negroes from the poll books and closing the election booths to them," Hawkins remarked, "Republican government in the South has been wiped out. This is what Maryland wants and this is what Hon. William H. Taft has endorsed as a 'turn for the better.'"[51]

The *Afro-American Ledger* also ramped up their attacks, specifically targeting Jim Crow. The paper's most pointed critique linked the Straus Amendment with physical violence. In one editorial cartoon, sarcastically

Figure 7. "Uplifting the Afro-American." Editorial cartoon published in the 2 October 1909 issue of the *Afro-American Ledger*. The illustration connected physical violence to the Straus Amendment and its supporters. Courtesy of the *Afro-American*.

titled "Uplifting the Afro-American," prominent supporters of the Straus Amendment—Straus, Governor Austin Crothers, Warfield, and Rayner—are pictured pummeling an African American man with clubs labeled "disfranchisement." Lurking in the background, an angry, club-wielding mob labeled "Democratic Politicians" waits to take their shots. The satirical caption connected the image to politicians' cynical contention that the amendment would benefit African Americans. "The Amendment will have a tendency to make the Negro a better citizen," the caption read. "It will stimulate the Negro to thrift and education and create a better feeling between the races." The illustrator credited the quotation to "Warfield, Rayner, Straus, and Granny Sunpaper [the *Baltimore Sun*]."[52] Far from uplift, this narrative marked the Straus Amendment as oppressive and the legislative equivalent of racial violence.

A host of other groups joined the *Afro-American Ledger* and the Suffrage League in protesting the Straus Amendment. At the Maryland Co-Operative Baptist State Convention in June, the group (which included Waller and Johnson among its ranks) pledged "to do all in our power to defeat at the polls the recent amendment passed by the Legislature." When they met the next year, they printed another resolution condemning the amendment.[53] Black churches across Baltimore organized against the amendment as well. Bethel AME Church advertised a "special discourse on the Straus Amendment" to be delivered by its pastor, Rev. D. G. Hill. Waters AME Church hosted a sermon that promised to show how the disfranchisement amendment was "analogous to the treacherous plot of Ahab against Naboth." A group composed of "Young Men" also lent their support. They formed the Young Men's Anti-Amendment League and held rallies throughout October at Sharp Street Memorial and Asbury ME church.[54]

Black women also continued to fight against disfranchisement. Women, according to Alexander, were "in the hottest of the fight" against the Straus Amendment. Eliza J. Cummings, Minnie Gaines, Sarah B. Holmes, Mary F. Handy, Florence K. Owens, Martha E. Murphy, Emma J. Truxon, and Charlotte Davage organized the Women of Baltimore Against the Disfranchisement Amendment. Many of the women had familial ties to male activists but also participated in various racial uplift programs. Among their many other affiliations, Cummings worked on behalf of the Women's Christian Temperance Union and the Metropolitan Church. Murphy (the wife of the *Afro-American Ledger*'s John H. Murphy) served as the head of the (Colored) YWCA and contributed to the Fresh Air Society as well as the Empty Stocking Circle. Truxon was the first to graduate from the State Normal School before teaching in schools across the state. She was also active in teachers' associations. The women's work put them in frequent contact with black Baltimoreans and positioned them to follow the *Afro*'s advice to keep "a copy of the amendment in your pocket and read and explain it to our people, on the street cars, street corners, barber shops or anywhere else you happen to find men who are not alive to the situation." This strategy expanded a practice common throughout the city. Black Baltimoreans often read the *Afro-American Ledger* aloud to illiterate African Americans.[55]

In late September the Women of Baltimore against the Disfranchisement Amendment organized a meeting at Grace Presbyterian Church for the "purpose of arousing their husbands and sons in the coming election." The organizers encouraged the attendees to ensure that the men registered to vote so they could "stand up and be counted on the day of election." Women also raised funds for the Suffrage League so it could continue its fight. In the ensuing months, the group held meetings at various churches throughout the city "to pray, talk and plan against the proposed Disfranchisement Amendment." The women also formed the Woman's Civic League in a further effort to fight disfranchisement efforts. Finally, they made home visits, where they "aroused the men and opened the eyes to danger." There is little doubt that women were instrumental in helping defeat the Straus Amendment, but it remains difficult to obtain a full picture. Immediately after the election, the women of the DuBois Circle sent an article to the Niagara Movement's *Horizon* to document "the work of the women of Md. toward defeating the suffrage amendment." For reasons that remain unclear, the *Horizon* never published it. Nevertheless, from pushing their family members to vote, to holding rallies, to educating voters, black women played numerous roles in preserving African Americans' right to vote in Maryland.[56]

The Suffrage League joined these groups in fighting the Straus Amendment. Beginning in September, the organization conducted a series of gatherings in the city's churches and at the YMCA. They also used the pages of the *Afro-American Ledger* to encourage potential voters to register. In September 1909, for instance, Alexander and William C. McCard placed a notice in the *Afro-American* reminding all black men to register or update their voting information.[57]

The Suffrage League's largest effort centered on coordinating "night schools" to educate voters. The night schools were truly a community effort that required a tremendous financial commitment. The Suffrage League devoted more than half of its budget to their operation. The organization staffed the schools from 6:00 to 10:00 P.M. each day during the final two weeks before the elections. The schools provided both information and instruction so that black voters could understand the ballot and vote against the Straus Amendment. Across the city, Trinity AME Church, Zion Baptist Church, Macedonia Baptist Church, Eastern ME Church, and many others opened their doors to host the schools. Citizens pitched in by operating at least four of the schools out of their homes. George W. Howard and Mary J. Howard opened their house on North Schroeder in West Baltimore; John Ives and Peter Gray hosted a school in their residence on West Preston

Street in the Northwest; Jacob Addison and E. Louis Gray's house on Latrobe Street in North Baltimore served as the setting of another school; and William P. Wilson allowed the league to use his residence on Leadenhall Street in South Baltimore.[58]

On 2 November 1909 Baltimoreans soundly defeated the Straus Amendment by 11,772 votes; statewide, Marylanders rejected it by a total of 16,155 votes. The *Afro-American Ledger* celebrated the defeat of the amendment with the simple words, "'Twas a glorious victory."[59] The victory was remarkable in many respects. Black Marylanders once again defeated the Democratic Party, which was intent on imposing race-based disfranchisement. They had to contend with the *Baltimore Sun*, which strongly supported the amendments and frequently disparaged the state's black population. In the face of these obstacles, African Americans organized, attended rallies, raised money, engaged in boycotts, educated each other, and voted to once again stop the tide of disfranchisement that had swept over the South.

Even though African Americans helped defeat segregationists at the polls on two separate occasions, Democrats did not give up on their dream to disfranchise black voters. In 1910 William J. Frere and Walter M. Digges, Democrats from Charles County, located in the southern tip of the state, coauthored a third disfranchisement initiative that came to be known as the Digges Plan. The complicated provisions of the proposal were astonishing in their unambiguous intention to undermine the US Constitution. After much debate, the General Assembly passed five laws as part of the plan with the first two provisions being the most pertinent. The first provision mandated new voter registration for the 1911 election. Registration would only be open to white applicants who would subsequently vote on the second provision, which authorized the Digges Amendment. The amendment sought to permanently disfranchise all African Americans, except those owning at least five hundred dollars in property.[60]

Unlike other disfranchisement measures passed throughout the South in the late 1890s and early 1900s, the Digges Plan was stunning in its naked ambition and racism. As many contemporary observers recognized, the Digges Plan was a bold attempt to nullify the Fifteenth Amendment by explicitly denying African Americans the right to vote by virtue of their race. Since Maryland did not ratify the Fifteenth Amendment in 1870, Frere and Digges (along with the measure's supporters) argued that its provisions should not apply to the state. Baltimore city solicitor Poe did not even bother to hide the law's intentions to violate African American voting rights, telling the *Baltimore Sun* that "by adopting this plan, the white people of the State alone would pass upon [black voting]. In my judgment, it is impossible to adopt a suffrage amendment as long as 60,000 negroes are allowed to vote solidly against it."[61] Although Governor Crothers supported black disfranchisement, he soon faced widespread pressure, especially from outside the state, to veto the legislation. Because the Digges Amendment was so blatantly unconstitutional, southern segregationists feared its inevitable legal challenges would shine an unwelcome spotlight on their states' more carefully crafted amendments. Alabama congressman Hilary A. Herbert fretted that "some radical measure like the Digges bills" would empower "extremists" in Congress to mount an assault on disfranchisement throughout the South.[62] Crothers chose to split the difference. Rather than sign the bill, he vetoed the law that barred black registration but allowed Marylanders to vote on the amendment. His decision, however, ensured that both black and white Marylanders would have the chance to vote.[63]

Activists wasted little time organizing against the Digges Amendment. Once more, the *Afro-American Ledger* played a crucial role in publicizing the grassroots effort to block the amendment. The paper published numerous articles decrying the Digges Amendment. Its editors pushed male readers to register to vote and included detailed instructions on how to do so. For the third time, Alexander reorganized the Suffrage League. Baltimore's network of black churches also pitched in. At Union Baptist Church, the *Afro-American Ledger* reported that Johnson told his congregation that the "rights of the race were at stake." At Sharp Street Memorial, Rev. W. A. C. Hughes connected the struggle against disfranchisement to the colonists' fight to obtain their freedom. Alexander also used his Sunday sermon at Sharon Baptist to urge his congregation to not only vote against the amendment but also elect "candidates who we believe will put an end to the ballot box frauds."[64]

For the first time, activists also received a hand from the state's Republican Party. Although Republicans had largely ignored African American voters in 1904 and 1909, they changed course in the fight against the Digges Amendment. Initially, Maryland's Republican Party chose a white man, Alfred Schultz, to help organize black voters. The *Afro-American Ledger* immediately protested the decision and called on the party to choose an

African American to lead the effort. "The Republicans have blundered enough in dealing with the race," the paper exclaimed, "and what the race demands is that colored men of probity be placed in charge of the political affairs of the race." For once, Maryland's Republicans heeded black Baltimoreans' demands. The party invited Dr. Ernest Lyon, a minister and former ambassador to Liberia, to head the Auxiliary Republican Committee. The group's executive committee included Alexander, Cummings, and the *Afro-American Ledger*'s John H. Murphy, among other ministers and activists. The Republican Party also formed an "advisory committee of two hundred ministers and laymen, selected from the city and state."[65]

The Auxiliary Republican Committee largely followed the blueprint that the Suffrage League had created during the previous decade. They called on ministers to donate needed contributions, disseminate information, and rally support against the amendment. In addition, the group established night schools to help black voters decipher the ballot and noted that their headquarters would be "opened morning, noon and night for instruction." The Republican Auxiliary Committee also encouraged women to participate in the movement. Along with Lyons, "several hundred" African American women formed the Anti-Digges Amendment League. The women, including E. J. Cummings, canvassed neighborhoods to rally support against the legislation. They also organized meetings in churches throughout Baltimore.[66]

In the final weeks before the election, activists and the *Afro-American Ledger* intensified their efforts. At least eight Baltimore churches—with the help of the Colored Republican Auxiliary—held mass meetings to rally black voters. At a "monster mass meeting" at John Wesley AME Church, an estimated 1,200 citizens attended to hear speakers—both white and black—from throughout the state assail the Digges Amendment. A group of sixty-five women volunteered to help African Americans understand the state's convoluted ballot. The *Afro-American Ledger* contributed by publishing a slew of articles encouraging its readers to vote. On the eve of the election, the paper printed directions on how to vote against the amendment, which appeared not as the Digges Amendment but rather "Chapter 253," including its location on the ballot.[67]

Marylanders soundly rejected the Digges Amendment by more than twenty thousand votes. For the third time in the span of a decade, African Americans helped successfully save their right to vote. "In this battle against the Digges Amendment, the Negroes for the most part bore themselves like men," the *Afro-American* wrote, "and their conduct on election day elicited the highest praise from the party leaders in both city and state." Numerous publications, including the NAACP's *Crisis* and the *Afro-American Ledger*, also credited women with their work fighting the amendment. "The women helped greatly," the *Afro-American* wrote. "It pays to get on the good side of the female contingent. When they take hold something will be done." Not only had African Americans defeated the Digges Amendment, but they also helped elect Phillips Lee Goldsborough, a Republican, as Maryland's next governor. With Goldsborough in office, Democrats were not able to mount another attempt to disfranchise black Marylanders.

During the late nineteenth and early twentieth centuries, white Marylanders, in the name of progressive reform, waged an assault on democracy by using the predominant concerns of the era as a weapon against African Americans. Maryland segregationists exploited anxieties surrounding public order and political corruption to first marginalize African Americans and then frame black disenfranchisement as a needed corrective. When Isaac Lobe Straus stumped for his Democratic Party and the disfranchisement amendment that bore his name, he demonstrated how easily Democrats could make disfranchisement appear as a progressive measure. "There is not a single progressive reform which the Democratic party is not vigorously pressing forward," Straus contended. "There is not a single progressive reform upon which the Republican party has not turned its back. Nominations by direct popular vote, oyster culture, the arresting of bribery at elections," Straus remarked, "and the restriction of illiterate negro votes are illustrations."[68] Although Democrats contended that black disfranchisement was key to restoring order and ending corruption, black Marylanders did not let these claims go uncontested.

In fighting disfranchisement, African Americans reclaimed from segregationists the language of progressivism. The fact that scholars have largely left African American activists out of accounts of the Progressive movement reflects, at least to a certain extent, problems of perception. Segregationists used their considerable resources, including elected office, political campaigns, and the press to position black Marylanders as the targets of progressive reform, not as part of the solution to society's ills.

Histories of the Progressive movement have primarily focused on the expansion of rights and the government's place in society. Progressive reformers expanded the power of the popular vote with the passage of the

Seventeenth (direct election of US senators) and Nineteenth Amendments (women's suffrage). They enlarged the federal government's regulatory roles in the realms of labor, city management, and the economy in countless ways. But for African Americans, the dawning of the Progressive Era meant possible contraction. Black Baltimoreans, like African Americans throughout the South, faced the possibility (and oftentimes the reality) of losing the franchise, a right that they had earned a generation earlier. By forcing African Americans into a fight to retain their rights, rather than expand them, segregationists found a way to slow the pace of the black freedom struggle even as they failed to institute disfranchisement.

Yet if progressives deserve credit for their efforts to make the country more democratic—even if these efforts did not extend to everyone—the work of African Americans needs to be included in this discussion. In the early twentieth century, African American activists not only saved black men's right to vote but also helped preserve democracy in Maryland. Although most whites could not or would not admit it, they benefited from African Americans' steadfast resistance. Maryland's Democratic Party certainly hoped to disfranchise African Americans, but their larger goal was to institute uncontested rule in the state. In particular, the Poe Amendment's reliance on partisan registrars posed a grave threat to Republicans and immigrants who rightfully feared that it could disfranchise them as well. Even when Democrats solely targeted African Americans, as they did in 1909 and 1911, they could have drastically changed Maryland's voting landscape. As the *Afro-American Ledger* pointed out, "If 30,000 or 40,000 Negroes are disfranchised, the whites of the State who sincerely believe in Republican doctrines and the thousands of white Independents who believe in good government without respect to party, will be powerless against the permanently intrenched [*sic*] Democratic machine."[69]

Activists knew that their struggle represented a stand against the spread of an undemocratic and un-American Jim Crow system that had rolled back the progress the country had made following the Civil War. The *Afro-American Ledger* sized up the fight against the Poe Amendment as a moment that would decide "whether we are to continue to breathe the pure air of freedom, as guaranteed to us by the Fourteenth and Fifteenth amendments . . . or whether we shall be stripped of every vestige of that freedom and reduced to the condition of vassals." In another editorial celebrating the defeat of the Digges Amendment, the *Afro-American Ledger* noted that the initiative "would have turned free Maryland into an oligar-chy . . . bringing about a condition which would give one voter in Maryland as much power as six voters in New York and Ohio."[70] In the eyes of black Marylanders, they were not only saving their right to vote but also protect-ing the state and nation from the corrupt nature of the Jim Crow South.

In fighting disfranchisement, African Americans staked a public claim to the central roles they played in addressing many of the most pressing concerns of the age. While segregationists blamed African Americans for urban disorder and the corruption that plagued Maryland's politics, black Baltimoreans answered them by highlighting their sacrifices and contribu-tions to democracy. William M. Alexander reminded the *Sun*'s readers that black voters had been a force of positive reforms in the city. "For the last 20 years the colored voters of Baltimore and the State of Maryland have voted with the reformers," Alexander recalled, "more to secure good gov-ernment than for political advantage to themselves. We helped to break the ring in 1895, and we want to maintain the right to vote, so as to help to save the body politic from ring rule in the future." In repeated instances, black Baltimoreans used the fight against disfranchisement to highlight their patriotism and commitment to democratic principles. Not surpris-ingly, the *Afro-American*'s editors concluded their first call to action by connecting their struggle to the United States' revolutionary past when they quoted Patrick Henry: "Is life so dear, or peace so sweet, as to be purchased at the price of chains and slavery? Forbid it, Almighty God! I know not what course others may take; but as for me, give me liberty or give me death."[71]

African Americans' fight against disfranchisement also had an impact on the many women who played key roles fighting the three amendments. Women's involvement made them important players in one of the domi-nant political battles of the early twentieth century. Although little evidence survives, women's participation prompted some to grapple with their own lack of voting rights. Shortly after they helped defeat the Digges Amend-ment, members of the DuBois Circle agreed that women should also be able to vote. Warner T. McGuinn, an activist and attorney, also announced his support for women's suffrage in the wake of the victory over the Digges Amendment. McGuinn noted that many of the arguments against extend-ing the right to vote to women were the same as the arguments segregation-ists used to justify black disfranchisement.[72]

Black Marylanders' three successful stands against disfranchisement
provided them with a greater national profile. The Niagara Movement's
Voice of the Negro followed the activists' struggle and celebrated their victories. In the 1910s the NAACP's *Crisis* covered black Marylanders' fight
against the Digges Amendment. In organizing, championing, and publicizing black Marylanders' resistance, the once-struggling *Afro-American* established itself as a major voice in the black freedom struggle. During the first
decade of the twentieth century, the paper's circulation expanded more
than 1,000 percent and was sent to locations outside of the state farther
south. Its early support for DuBois and the Niagara Movement, coupled
with its steadfast opposition to disfranchisement, grew its popularity with
activists who favored a more uncompromising stance against racial injustice.[73]

Despite their vital contributions to saving democracy, the battles over
disfranchisement exacted a heavy price on black Marylanders. In most
cases, white opponents of the amendments voted against it to protect their
own interests. African Americans were the only constituency that consistently emphasized the racial animus at the center of the legislation. When
members of Baltimore's Reform League read a report on the Poe Amendment at their 1905 annual meeting, for instance, they hardly mentioned
African Americans. Instead, they repeatedly emphasized the threat that the
initiative posed to white and immigrant voters. The situation in 1909 was
not markedly different. The Reform League urged voters to oppose the
measure because it endangered the white vote and ran counter to the Constitution. On the night before the election of 1911, the Maryland Republican
Party held a rally and segregated African Americans who attended. The
Afro-American Ledger noted, "The Republican Party of this State is clearly
a white man's party, and when once this state is firmly established on the
suffrage question so that our votes will be counted as cast, it will probably
matter little to us which is in power."[74]

White opponents of disfranchisement also rarely challenged the racial
reasoning undergirding the initiatives. As the *Baltimore Sun* pointed out,
"In all the earnest and fervid discussion of the franchise amendment
scarcely a word has been said by its opponents in favor of the negro or his
right to vote."[75] In many cases, the amendment's opponents actually added
to the racial animus. When editorializing against the legislation, the press
often placed African Americans at the bottom of a racial hierarchy. The
Baltimore American, one of the most consistent critics of the amendments,

published an editorial cartoon titled "The Way the Amendment Would 'Work.'" In the drawing, "red tape" straps a white citizen to wooden beams labeled "crooked" and "polls" before a registrar representing "Boss Rule." The citizen meekly complains that he cannot be disfranchised since he is "no black man." The registrar responds by asking, "Is that so? Well, say, you'll look so much like one to me when I get through with you that my conscience won't allow you no vote." The registrar proceeds to paint the man with "amendment black paint" using the brush of "absolute power at polls."[76] For white voters the message was clear: they should oppose the amendment because of the potential danger to their vote. But it also warned white voters that the amendment, if carried, would put them on equal footing with African Americans.

Even as the amendments failed to gain voter approval, the message of black inferiority remained unchallenged except in the pages of the *Afro-American Ledger* and at the meetings of black protesters. In March 1910 William M. Alexander and William C. McCard (an attorney and activist) wrote to Maryland's legislature on behalf of the Suffrage League. "As to the persecuting effect of the Digges Election law will have on the colored people in this State," Alexander and McCard wrote, "it cannot be expressed in words." The men further noted that "during the campaigns when the Poe and Straus amendments were the issues our people, without exception, were defined in print and by campaign orators as a menace to civil society. Even men of the race who by industry and economy had acquired property were stigmatized as dangerous invaders on society."[77] It was a remarkable letter outlining the social and cultural costs of fighting Jim Crow. Even when activists waged a successful battle, they suffered from the rhetoric that justified the measures.

Even in victory, African Americans remained vulnerable to racial oppression. As segregationists watched as their prospects of voting disfranchisement faded, they opened up another front in their effort to marginalize African Americans. This time, they waged a battle along Baltimore's northwest racial frontiers where white residents had been agitating for legalized residential segregation. The two battles shared deep connections. Both the Straus and Digges Amendments relied on a property qualification, a fact that did not go unnoticed by black Baltimoreans. At least one African American bought a home to stave off the possibility of losing his vote.[78]

The reliance on the property qualification was not coincidental. As voters prepared to pass judgment on the Straus Amendment, the *Baltimore*

THE WAY THE AMENDMENT WOULD "WORK"

CITIZEN—You can't prevent me from voting—I'm no black man!
REGISTER—Is that so? Well, say, you'll look so much like one to me when I get through with you that my conscience won't allow you no vote.

Figure 8. "The Way the Amendment Would 'Work.'" Editorial cartoon published in the 20 October 1905 issue of the *Baltimore American*. Although the
paper was a consistent critic of the disfranchisement movement, this image
demonstrated how even white opponents of the Poe Amendment placed African Americans at the bottom of a racial hierarchy.

Sun traveled to the Seventeenth Ward in the city's rapidly changing northwest to interview concerned white residents. "If for no other reason," one
man exclaimed, "the white people of Baltimore should vote for the suffrage
amendment because of serious conditions existing in the Fourth legislative
district, and especially in the Seventeenth ward." Chief among this man's
concern was black political power. "There is now," the man explained,
"absolute negro domination in the Seventeenth ward where there are about
800 more negro than white voters."[79] The *Baltimore Sun* followed this interview with another article published three days later. In this article, a "dis-
gusted property owner" claimed that the original story only scratched the
surface of a deeper problem. The property owner claimed that a "partisan

Republican" was spearheading the movement of black Baltimoreans for political and economic gain. The interviewee claimed that the Republican agent gained politically by ensuring another voter in the ward. He also profited handsomely either through the sale of the house or by using the threat of a potential black neighbor to compel others nearby to sell their homes.[80] Just as issues of race, crime, and politics fueled disfranchisement efforts, they also drove white Baltimoreans' desire to draw racial dividing lines in the city's residential districts.

CHAPTER 6

"The Struggle for Land and Liberty"

On the afternoon of 30 September 1913, George Howe and his family were spending time at their new house on Harford Avenue, a "fashionable street" in North Baltimore. Then the chaos began. The angry shouts of men and the sounds of shattering glass pierced the evening's tranquility. A "large crowd" of white youths playing outside of Howe's door "suggested bombarding his house." Within moments, a crowd of fifty to two hundred men joined the fracas and, according to the *Baltimore Sun*, "in a twinkling the trouble was on." Faced with these daunting odds, Howe, who was black, grabbed a shotgun to defend his family and property. From the second floor, Howe met bricks with bullets, wounding four white youths. Some in the crowd began to shout for his lynching. Finally the police arrived, setting about their work to disarm and arrest Howe. As they did so, the mob turned its attention toward James Nelson, an African American bystander who happened on the scene at precisely the wrong moment. Both Howe and Nelson, whom the crowd severely beat, were lucky to escape with their lives. The only person detained that night was Howe, whom police arrested for "assault with intent to murder, three charges of common assault, and a fifth charge for carrying concealed weapons."[1]

The violence at Howe's residence was a microcosm of the two decades of controversies brewing in Baltimore's residential districts between the late 1890s and 1918 over residential segregation. The attacks demonstrated the precision with which segregationists sought to enforce Baltimore's racial lines. In 1913 Harford Avenue was divided into racially exclusive sides: black residents occupied one side of the street and white residents the other.[2] Howe violated this arrangement when he moved to the all-white side of the block. The major players in this drama also enacted the roles they played in other disturbances throughout this period. Howe—like many African

Americans at the time—sought better housing in Baltimore's northern residential enclaves. White youths and men, frustrated by the city's inability to halt what they termed a "negro invasion," harassed their would-be neighbors. The police served as the final arbiters, in most cases arresting the African American at the center of the controversy.

Historians have analyzed Progressive Era residential segregation from legal, governmental, and reform standpoints but have neglected the vantage point of the street where segregation actually occurred. This street-level history of housing segregation in Baltimore challenges existing Progressive Era historiography in key ways.[3] In addition, it uncovers a deeper story of the fight over residential segregation. The effort to maintain race-exclusive blocks in Baltimore dates to the late 1890s and did not begin, as previous scholars contend, with the legislative controversies of the 1910s. African Americans and white Baltimoreans battled over racial segregation on the streets before the city council and the law intervened. Even after politicians and the justice system became involved, the issue of racial segregation was contested, promulgated, and nourished at the grass roots.[4] A street-level analysis also emphasizes the roles that violence, white supremacy, and black resistance played in Progressive Era segregation efforts. The movement to segregate Baltimore's residential districts was not a sincere but misguided effort by Progressives to forge a safer social order.[5] Instead, segregationists hoped to institutionalize white supremacy, suppress African American political power, and limit black mobility by legally segregating Baltimore's residential districts.

Focusing on events on the streets makes the expansive roles that African Americans played in defeating residential segregation apparent. African Americans made political statements when they purchased real estate in knowing violation of the law. Many, when necessary, defended their property (and that of others) with arms. Black Baltimoreans repeatedly defied the law throughout the 1910s, and their resistance provided the newly organized NAACP with one of its first test cases. By 1918, black Baltimoreans had done more to remake the city's racial geography than the failed segregation ordinances.

Although African Americans repeatedly defied the laws and consistently defeated them in court, Baltimore's attempt to impose legalized housing segregation left behind a poisonous legacy. The legislation fundamentally changed discussions of race, property, and social order in Baltimore and across the nation. The city's residential segregation laws, and similarly minded efforts modeled on them, built on segregationists' linkage of race and crime. The laws legitimized segregationists' conflation of African Americans with community degradation, crime, and plummeting property values. This pernicious association long outlived the ordinances themselves and continued to fuel efforts at restricting African Americans' residential options well into the twentieth century.[6]

The wave of violence that eventually crashed on George Howe's doorstep had been building for years. Prior to Emancipation, Baltimore's free black population outnumbered slaves, a circumstance that shaped the city's residential patterns. The extent to which neighborhoods were integrated was largely due to the presence of live-in servants and domestic workers who resided in the shadows of their employers' homes. Otherwise, blacks and whites lived in separate sections of the city, with African Americans residing primarily in pockets of the southern, central, and eastern portions of Baltimore.[7]

By the 1880s, a number of factors had converged to alter the city's racial geography. With slavery's demise, the city's black population exploded. Between 1860 and 1880, twenty-five thousand black migrants moved to Baltimore. Beginning in the 1880s, civil rights activist and attorney W. Ashbie Hawkins contended that black Baltimoreans sought better housing in the northwestern portion of the city. This movement was accelerated in the 1890s after Sharp Street Memorial United Methodist Church, Union Baptist Church, and the city's black high school relocated to the northwest. Other factors also pushed African Americans into the northwest. The city turned over tracts of land to the Baltimore and Ohio Railroad, displacing black residents, while immigrants crowded African Americans out of sections of East Baltimore. At the same time, wealthier whites increasingly moved to the suburbs, leaving behind desirable housing. By the early years of the twentieth century, half of the city's black population lived in the neighborhood known as Old West Baltimore, which encompassed the section of Druid Hill in the northwest.[8]

Initially, white Baltimoreans tried to maintain the color line by refusing to either live near black neighbors or sell or rent to African American customers. By the beginning of the twentieth century, black Baltimoreans encountered a racially limited housing market. A 1903 article published in the *Nation* contended, "It rarely happens that enough negroes can be found able and willing to buy or rent all the houses of one of these rows. The builder would not dare to sell some of them to or for negroes unless he were sure that he would be able to sell all for the same purpose, because he could escape having the remaining houses left on his hands only by selling them far below the cost of erection."[9] Yet whites failed to maintain a stranglehold on housing. A three-decade-long slump in the housing and rental market dropped prices and compelled some property owners to sell or rent to African Americans. In fact, white property owners found that they could overcharge black Baltimoreans, since "they will frequently pay more than a reliable white tenant will."[10]

The arrival of a black tenant or family prompted at least some whites to quickly sell. The Very Rev. John R. Slattery, of Saint Joseph's Seminary in Baltimore, noted in the *Catholic World* that "whenever a negro moves into a street the whites flutter away." White Baltimoreans' panicked decision to sell further depressed property values and exacerbated racial tensions. "Every white man who moves, and every white man whose property has become less valuable," the *Nation* reported, "ascribes all his inconvenience and all his loss to the negroes, although it often happens that they have been only partly responsible."[11]

In the waning days of the nineteenth century, some white residents decided to fight rather than "flutter away." The first documented incident of violent intimidation over residential space occurred in September 1899, when a fifty-five-year-old black construction worker named John Lang and his family moved into a house on Druid Hill Avenue. When Lang returned from work the next day, he found his family bunkered in the house behind locked doors. Lang's wife reported that a group of boys and young men had broken nearly all of the windows in the rear of the house. The following day an angry crowd smashed more windows. It is not entirely clear what happened to Lang and his family. Lang, however, did remark to the *Baltimore Sun* that he was willing to move if his landlord returned the rent money.[12]

For the next several years, scattered controversies arose when African Americans breached, or attempted to breach, the city's color line. When Union Baptist Church tried to buy a lot in the northwest in 1901 to open a boarding school, residents raised the specter of the "black rapist" in their campaign against the purchase. In 1902 someone shattered windows and smeared tar across the front steps of the house where Fannie Williams lived. When contacted by the *Baltimore Sun*, Williams remarked, "This is not the first time the windows were broken. Once before—about six weeks ago—every pane in the parlor windows and two on the second floor were broken." The next year, an African American congregation tried to purchase Saint Paul's English Lutheran Church on Druid Hill Avenue. After deliberation, the Saint Paul's council refused the offer, publicly burning their mortgage to the applause of a white audience and resolving never to sell property to African Americans. Later that year, residents at Saratoga and Mount Streets protested a proposed black school, fearing that parents of children attending the school would "have a tendency to move into [the] neighborhood."[13]

One of the early turning points in the battle over residential segregation occurred in 1906 after the Colored Independent Methodist Church bought property on North Gilmor Street with the intention of converting it into a "colored orphan society."[14] White residents reacted by forming the Harlem Park Protective Association. Their protests seemingly worked: the sale was annulled and the property put up for auction. Much to segregationists' chagrin, however, Harry S. Cummings, the city's first black councilman, purchased the house in the second auction. Cummings's acquisition rankled the nascent protective association. Its secretary warned that they would "fight anything likely to degrade the neighborhood. It's not only for Gilmor street and the vicinity that we intend standing for, but it's for the whole west end."[15]

The creation of the Harlem Park Protective Association was a watershed moment in the saga of Baltimore's increasingly contested residential color line. Beginning in the 1880s, white Baltimoreans formed numerous neighborhood associations. Initially, these organizations lobbied for structural improvements to their neighborhoods or sought to protect the property value of their enclaves. By the turn of the century, they became accepted cogs in the city's political apparatus, working closely with politicians and City Hall. But up to this moment they had not been involved in segregation efforts. Now residents had a group that not only united them around the issue of segregation but also pointedly took a confrontational stance. The Harlem Park Protective Association spearheaded a successful effort to block the sale of the house to the Colored Independent Methodist Church and then worked assiduously to stop black tenants from occupying the building after Cummings purchased it. For two years the building sat unoccupied before Cummings finally sold it at a loss to a nearby resident.[16]

Although the protective association won the first battle, shoring up the color line proved to be a more difficult feat. Access to good housing remained a pressing issue in the early twentieth century for many African Americans. In 1903 the Baltimore Association for the Improvement of the Condition of the Poor, alongside the Charity Organization Society, began an investigation of local housing conditions. By 1906 the two groups decided to focus on the "more congested and poorer quarters of the city." Hiding behind the veneer of scientific inquiry, their report amounted to a voyeuristic tour of Baltimore's immigrant and black neighborhoods. Janet E. Kemp, an experienced investigator who conducted a similar study in Washington, DC, led readers on an itinerary that included damp and dilapidated houses lacking modern amenities. She documented high rates of tuberculosis that saddled a section of the primarily poor black neighborhood of Lower Druid Hill, located in the city's northwest, with the derisive moniker of "the lung block." In Kemp's estimation, African Americans' "low standards and absence of ideals" were at least partially to blame for the state of the neighborhood.[17] While Kemp's racial biases skewed her findings, her report demonstrated through photographs and descriptions the overcrowded and substandard housing that many African Americans occupied in the city.

Black Baltimoreans voiced their own concerns about the state of Lower Druid Hill. In 1905 *Charities* published an article written by J. H. N. Waring, a physician and the principal of Baltimore's Colored High and Training School. Waring's investigation, like Kemp's, explored some of Baltimore's black communities. Unlike Kemp, however, Waring shifted blame away from residents by chastising the owners of alley homes and the American people who allowed these conditions to exist in the first place. In 1909 Booker T. Washington wrote that conditions in Lower Druid Hill were primarily the result of the white-owned saloons in the neighborhood and the police protection they received. Washington based his reporting on the ongoing investigation of Baltimore's Colored Law and Order League, a reform organization founded to tackle crime in Druid Hill. Washington argued that the city allowed "saloons and dens of vice which were not allowed to exist in other parts of the city . . . to take refuge in the districts where the masses of the colored people lived." These charges gained wider publicity in Baltimore when the Colored Law and Order League, also headed by Waring, published its findings. The report focused on the deleterious effects that poor living conditions had on children and women. It was the only report of its kind to identify root causes of the problems plaguing the neighborhood, offer a solution, and place housing into the wider realm of racial inequality.[18]

Black civic leaders found themselves in a difficult position when dealing with the housing crisis. Segregationists often equated substandard housing with personal failings and then used this association to contend that African Americans lowered property values. These contentions had particular resonance for Baltimoreans. In the previous decade, segregationists steadfastly connected race and crime. This was a key justification for segregation, and it made it difficult for African Americans to publicly broach the issue without running the risk of confirming segregationists' specious coupling of race and crime. In other cases, this linkage made it difficult for African Americans to improve Lower Druid Hill. After the liquor board and police board ignored black churches' complaints about conditions in Lower Druid Hill, Booker T. Washington explained, "There seems to have been a general feeling that colored people were either themselves so criminal, or so disposed to shield and protect criminals of their own race, that their protests against lawlessness and lawbreaking were not to be taken seriously."[19]

The exposés of Lower Druid Hill and the failures to exact reform surely compelled many African Americans to move to Upper Druid Hill and the environs just beyond. This desire to secure better housing was, in many cases, facilitated by Hugh M. Burkett, an African American real estate agent. Burkett arrived in Baltimore in 1899 and opened a real estate business, the Exchange Building and Loan Association. For the next two decades, Burkett was the only African American real estate agent in the city. Burkett found immediate success. By 1914, Burkett reportedly did $50,000 a year in business. One story in 1916 estimated that he helped more than five hundred black families secure housing. In fact, the *Crisis* proclaimed that Burkett was "one of the prime causes of the Negro segregation agitation in [Baltimore.]" More important for black Baltimoreans, Burkett did not engage in the exploitative business practices of many white agents. He was an associate of Hawkins and Harvey Johnson, became an early member of the NAACP, and was active in movements (particularly surrounding education) to improve the lives of African Americans. On his death, the *Afro-American Ledger* eulogized him as "diligent and honorable in his business, and used his fine talents for the betterment of his people."[20]

Burkett's assistance undoubtedly eased the financial and social burdens accompanying the movement of African Americans into Upper Druid Hill. Yet black Baltimoreans continued to encounter resistance from white residents. On the evening of 27 September 1907, nearly a hundred white residents of Northwest Baltimore gathered into Whatcoat Methodist Episcopal

Church. It would be the most militant and belligerent meeting yet to take place over the issue of residential segregation in the city. At the gathering, Frederick C. Weber, a local businessman and civic leader, spoke to the audience about the challenges they faced. "Within the last few years," Weber remarked, "an undesirable element has come into the neighborhood, and as a result our property is being woefully depreciated. It seems to me that the resident of Northwest Baltimore is blessed," Weber sarcastically quipped, "with a superabundance of negroes."[21]

Staring at the prospect of a "negro invasion," residents formed the Neighborhood Improvement Association. In the coming months Weber, along with representatives of similar neighborhood associations, ratcheted up their opposition to integration. At a meeting before the Harlem Improvement Association—which had its roots in the Harlem Park Protective Association—Weber hit on common racialized fears when he asked, "Shall we allow our toddling tots to associate with negro children? Shall we let them suffer the contamination that ensues?" Then, in a letter published in the *Baltimore Sun* less than a week later, he invoked the trope of the black male rapist. "The hundreds of assaults upon weak and defenseless womanhood in recent years from Texas to Maryland by the negroes," he remarked, "should cause any man to hesitate from coddling or truckling to these outcasts."[22]

Weber's remarks were just the tip of the rhetorical iceberg. Various popular and social scientific discourses converged in 1907 as white homeowners in Northwest Baltimore attempted to thwart the African American "invasion." An ideal of the home and its centrality to white male political, cultural, and social identity lay at the heart of these discussions. Advocates of segregation envisioned white space as pure and respectable, while seeing black space (and by inference African Americans themselves) as dangerous and uncouth. Several segregationists also tapped into discourses of civilization to portray African Americans as unworthy of the refinement offered by homes in some of the city's residential districts. At one of the Harlem Improvement Association meetings, J. J. McNamara protested, "Negroes are but 400 years from savagery" compared to the four thousand years accumulated by the "Aryan race."[23]

Local political events further exacerbated racial tensions in Baltimore. In the early 1900s, segregationists failed to disfranchise African Americans, and black political power was clearly a concern. Before the meeting of the Neighborhood Improvement Association, Col. Winfield Peters—a locally

celebrated Confederate veteran—railed against the city government's pref-
erence to "give the negro power over the white man." Weber felt that a
"negro-ridden" Baltimore spelled doom to city and state politics as blacks,
buoyed by their success in securing the best housing in the city, and reinforced by southern migrants, would drown out the voices of the white
taxpayer. Another member of the organization, W. J. Bracken, chastised
lawmakers who could have thwarted black mobility but instead "rested
supinely in their easy chairs." The words of Peters, Bracken, and Weber
illuminated the perceived threats posed by black mobility. The three men
felt that African Americans were slowly wresting control of politics from
white males. With African Americans primarily clustered into the city's
Seventeenth Ward (in Northwest Baltimore), black political power
remained limited. If black Baltimoreans dispersed throughout the city,
these men surmised, their political power could not be so easily contained.[24]

The perceived threats to white political hegemony, coupled with the
specter of a "negro invasion" of white residential spaces, fueled racial antipathy in Baltimore. Segregationists began to openly speak of the duty that
white property owners had to stand firm against the "negro invasion." But
by 1910 it was apparent that segregationists had failed to disfranchise African Americans and halt black mobility. Despite calls on the part of protective associations to codify racial segregation, their protestations had not
resulted in any remedial legislation.[25] Baltimore's northwest was now a
powder keg waiting for a spark.

In 1910 the racial tensions caused by black mobility, poor housing, and
white political frustration came to a head. In May, W. Ashbie Hawkins
purchased a home in an all-white block on McCulloh Street in Northwest
Baltimore. Hawkins, for reasons that remain unclear, never occupied the
house. Instead, he leased it to his business partner, an African American
lawyer named George W. McMechen, who moved in that June. In short
order, three more black families joined McMechen in integrating the neighborhood. Measured by distance, the move by the four black families was
not significant. McCulloh Street was just a block east of, and ran parallel
to, the primarily black Druid Hill Avenue. Whites, however, envisioned
Druid Hill Avenue as a boundary that separated the races, and the neighborhood that encompassed McCulloh Street was considered prestigious.
Locally known as the "favored fan," the area had lost some of its exclusivity
in the early twentieth century as wealthy whites pushed the boundaries of

the city. Nevertheless, it was home to prominent white Baltimoreans, including attorney William L. Marbury, city councilman Samuel L. West, and city solicitor Edgar Allan Poe (grandnephew of the famous author).[26]

In the coming months white residents in and around McCulloh Street welcomed their new neighbors with verbal and physical confrontations. On his first night in his new home, McMechen reported that someone broke "the front windows and flung a brick through my skylight." Shortly thereafter, M. J. Hammen, the president of a white neighborhood protective organization, happened on William B. Hamer, who was black, busily moving furniture into his new home on McCulloh Street. Approaching the man, Hammen asked his new neighbor why he did not buy a house on "Druid Hill avenue or in some other negro district." "I thought he was foolin' at first," Hamer told one reporter, "but when I saw he was in earnest I sent him on his way." Actually, after arguing with Hammen for a few moments, Hamer lost his patience and warned Hammen that he either move on or risk being "brain[ed]" by a nearby chair. After this incident, the *New York Times* reported that there "ensued more or less lawlessness on the part of small boys and hoodlums in the neighborhood." These "small boys and hoodlums" vandalized the homes of their new neighbors by pelting them with bricks and assorted projectiles. McMechen, Hamer, and Hamer's brother-in-law (who had also recently moved to McCulloh Street) all had their windows broken. Hamer complained that between his house and his brother-in-law's, only three windows remained intact.[27]

Although intimidation worked in the past, the events on McCulloh Street in 1910 played out quite differently. W. Ashbie Hawkins was not just any buyer. Hawkins was well known by 1910 as a prominent civil rights activist and attorney with an accomplished local and national record. Hawkins began his career as the Baltimore correspondent for T. Thomas Fortune's *New York Globe*. In 1885 Hawkins became a teacher while he put himself through law school. In 1892 he completed his law training at Howard University in Washington, DC, after being expelled from the Maryland law school when that institution decided to bar black students. With his degree in hand, Hawkins returned to a Baltimore where, thanks to the activism of Harvey Johnson, African Americans could now read for the bar.[28]

Hawkins's legal activities exemplify Baltimore's local history of grassroots activism and the new efforts taking hold in the national organizing for civil rights. Hawkins built on the tradition of black legal activism that

Figure 9. Attorney W. Ashbie Hawkins. Hawkins became one of the most prominent activists in the city in the early twentieth century, leading legal efforts against residential segregation. He was also an early member of the Niagara Movement and the NAACP. (Photograph date unknown.) Courtesy of Philip J. Merrill Nanny Jack & Co. Archives.

Johnson directed during the late nineteenth century. Although Hawkins had not participated in these cases, his work for the *New York Globe* during the period and his friendship with Johnson made him familiar with these successes. Johnson's persistence and deft use of the courts established a blueprint for successful civil rights activism. The lessons that Johnson's activism provided were further reinforced on the national level. Together with Johnson, Hawkins attended early meetings of W. E. B. DuBois's Niagara Movement, a forerunner of the NAACP. During the organization's brief existence, Hawkins gained legal experience challenging racial discrimination when he worked on the Barbara Pope case, the group's first test suit that contested segregation on Virginia's rail lines. The next year, 1907, Hawkins represented Harvey Johnson in a lawsuit against the Baltimore and Ohio Railroad, after Johnson refused to move to a separate car while en route to a Niagara Movement meeting. Hawkins also served as the NAACP's treasurer and worked on test case litigation in that organization's early years.[29]

Given Hawkins's track record, segregationists must have found his purchase especially discomforting, perhaps knowing that it portended another battle for civil rights. When Hawkins published an account of Baltimore's segregation battles in the November 1911 issue of the NAACP's *Crisis*, he omitted that he purchased the home on McCulloh and that his law partner moved into the house. Despite his silence, circumstantial evidence strongly indicates that Hawkins had political motivations. He bought and sold numerous properties (sometimes in conjunction with fellow attorney and activist William T. McCard) mainly in the city's northwest between 1909 and 1910. With a firsthand knowledge of the city's race relations and legal experience challenging Jim Crow, it is likely that Hawkins saw the spaces as crucial in the next battle against segregation.[30]

Hawkins's purchase opened a new front in the fight over integration as grassroots pressure from both African Americans and segregationists moved from the streets into City Hall and the courts. As an attorney with experience fighting inequality in the courtroom, Hawkins was well positioned to mount a legal challenge to residential segregation, but so were the white residents of Northwest Baltimore. When the neighborhood associations began to fight racial integration, they already had years of experience working with the city government.[31]

Segregationists had other important connections. Chief among them were two attorneys, Milton Dashiell and William L. Marbury, who became instrumental in bringing the concerns of citizens on the streets into the formal halls of power. Both Dashiell and Marbury lived in Northwest Baltimore. Dashiell resided seven blocks away from the home that Hawkins purchased on McCulloh Street and a block away from the predominantly black Biddle Alley district. Marbury lived on Lanvale Avenue, a few blocks east of McCulloh Street. Both men harbored personal reasons for wanting to keep African Americans from moving into the city's northwest and had fought to restrict black rights in the past. Hawkins singled out Dashiell as a "rampant negro hater," and Marbury helped support the failed disfranchisement effort of the early 1900s.[32]

Dashiell thought he had found a way to stop integration. He cited Baltimore's original charter, written in 1796, which enabled the city to use "police power" for "preserving order and securing property and persons from violence, danger and destruction." Since, according to Dashiell, African Americans who encroached on "white neighborhoods" both lowered property values and "tend[ed] to the disturbance and destruction of the peace to a marked degree," the city was fully justified in legalizing residential segregation. Using the city's charter as his foundation, Dashiell authored the West Segregation Ordinance. The proposed law became the first legal attempt in the United States to impose residential segregation. The legislation—which city councilman Samuel L. West introduced before the city council—forbade African Americans from moving into white-majority blocks and whites from moving into black-majority blocks. It also prescribed a hundred-dollar fine for African Americans who violated the law.[33]

Dashiell's reliance on "police power" has been overlooked in previous analyses of Baltimore's segregation effort. Its invocation, however, was telling. Over the course of the previous decade, segregationists had steadily built the specious case that African Americans were inherently criminal. They used this contention to justify efforts to disfranchise black voters, dole out harsher punishment to black defendants, and control African Americans in the city's public spaces. By relying on "police power," the West Ordinance effectively expanded the roles that the police played as foot soldiers in the fight against integration. In addition, the use of "police power" criminalized the presence of African Americans in "white blocks" and identified them as a threat to social order. The law essentially said that African Americans—not angry whites that attacked black families—caused disorder and violence by their very presence. This fallacious justification allowed

Baltimore's politicians and their supporters in the press to frame the proposed law "as an ordinance for preserving peace, preventing conflict and ill-feeling between the white and colored races."[34]

Other supporters of government-sponsored apartheid, however, belied the notion that the law was proposed out of altruistic concerns for racial harmony. From the outset, it was clear that racial prejudice fueled concerns over integration. As early as 1909, the *Baltimore Sun* reported that the Harlem Improvement Association declared "the negro a menace to the neighborhood and his encroachment one of the most potent forces in the deterioration of property values." Others demonstrated how entangled white privilege and property had become. As city solicitor Edgar Allan Poe, an ardent supporter of segregation, stated, "From my earliest recollection my feeling for the race has been one associated with affection; my old negro 'mammy,' my little nurse-girl playmate, all are among my happiest recollections. But the idea of their assuming to live next door to me," Poe continued, "is abhorrent."[35]

Letter writers to the *Baltimore Sun* similarly contradicted claims that the ordinance was proposed out of a spirit of beneficence. A writer who signed his name "1800 Block"—a reference to the site of the McCulloh Street attacks—claimed that African Americans were now becoming the favored people in the city even though they have "certainly cost this country an immense amount of money and blood." Another letter read, "Property in West Baltimore is not worth what it should be and solely on account of the negro invasion of white neighborhoods this time [in] the best of Baltimore." One writer vaguely hinted at violence if something was not done to prevent African Americans from "invading" the northwest section of the city. "The negro should know by this time that every attempt on his part to force himself into places where he is not wanted will surely react upon his race," the writer intoned, "and the more surely forge the fetters of doom which seem to be closing upon him."[36] Although government officials tried to sell the West Ordinance as a way to peacefully order the city, they could not control the message articulated by angry citizens living along the city's racial frontiers.

It should be noted that segregationists never desired strict racial separation but rather sought to control cross-racial interactions with the law. This can most clearly be seen in the clause (which appeared in all four versions of the ordinance) that allowed black servants to remain in "white" neighborhoods. At once a tacit admission of the importance of black labor in the functioning of the white household, the domestic exception also revealed white anxieties concerning the intersection of race and class. Domestic space was an important stage where whites constructed and transmitted ideas about race. The authors of the West Segregation Ordinances made certain that whites could continue to display and communicate their power over black employees. This also ensured that white children would continue to learn the lessons of race by witnessing the power dynamics at work in their parents' interactions with domestic laborers. The exception, inserted in other cities' attempts at imposing residential segregation, prompted an editorial in the *Crisis* to ask, "Are not servants colored? Is the objection, then, to colored people or to colored people who are not servants? In other words, is this race prejudice inborn antipathy or a social and economic caste?"[37]

When middle-class African Americans such as Hawkins, the Mc-Mechens, and Hamer moved into majority-white neighborhoods, they undermined the visual cues of supposed white superiority and complicated attempts to portray African Americans as an inferior race. All three men held steady employment. Hawkins and McMechen owned a private law practice while Hamer had been employed for sixteen years at the Baltimore post office. Hamer and McMechen also expressed a desire for more comfortable living quarters. Hamer had been living on Druid Hill Avenue but decided to rent on McCulloh Street because he thought it was a better neighborhood. McMechen expressed similar sentiments when he noted, "We merely desired to live in more commodious and comfortable quarters." When asked about her family's move, Anne McMechen, George McMechen's wife, universalized their aspirations by proclaiming, "We wanted to be more comfortable—a right I think everyone has to exercise."[38] The class and professional background of Hawkins, the McMechens, and Hamer, along with their desire for a middle-class life, made it difficult for segregationists to fall back on their time-honored tropes of black inferiority, difference, and disorder.

From the outset African Americans were not fooled by attempts to sell segregation as a benefit to both races. The inaugural issue of the *Crisis*, published in November 1910, devoted numerous articles to the proposed ordinance, terming it "an inevitable step forward in anti-Negro prejudice." After several segregationists, including Dashiell, appeared before the First Branch City Council to discuss the West Ordinance, the *Afro-American* excoriated the law's supporters. The paper sarcastically described Dashiell as "apparently sicklied over with the pale cast of anti Negro thought" because "he was a man of peace, who had the highest regard for the Negro (when he stays back in the alleys)." The paper categorized the West Ordinance itself as the "great measure which is to relieve the city of the great 'scourge' caused by thrifty, intelligent, law-abiding colored people getting better homes."[39]

Activists also predicted dire consequences if the law passed. Rev. A. L. Gans, a representative of the Ministerial Alliance, thought that the law would exacerbate tensions between whites and blacks. Sharp Street Memorial Church's Rev.W. A. C. Hughes contended that the ordinance would do "incalculable harm," and Trinity Baptist Church's G. R. Waller invoked the horror of lynching. Finally, Dr. R. M. Hall, a prominent black physician, pointedly compared the law to Russia's treatment of Jews, asking West at one hearing if he approved of Jewish segregation. Hall was far from alone. Waller termed the law "a bold attempt to Russianize Baltimore."[40]

Black Baltimoreans knew that the West Ordinance, far from protecting both races, protected white power and endangered African Americans. An editorial cartoon published in the *Crisis* in 1911 directly commented on these pernicious aspects of the West Segregation Ordinance. In the cartoon, printed as a centerfold, the first image, labeled "1900," shows an African American couple discussing their finances. The caption reads, "The colored man that saves his money and buys a brick house will be universally respected by his white neighbors." In the second panel, on the opposite page, a well-dressed black man walks away from a bank teller while he places his bankbook in a coat pocket. This image, labeled "1910," demonstrates the prejudice that undergirded the law and the racial discourse it broadcast to the public. The editorial's caption sarcastically quips, "New and dangerous species of Negro criminal lately discovered in Baltimore. He will be segregated in order to avoid lynching." In the span of two pages, the *Crisis* delivered a devastating critique of how the law made criminals of black Baltimoreans who strove to improve their living conditions. The image also highlighted the violence that African Americans faced when moving to "white blocks."[41]

African Americans—and some white activists—immediately protested the proposed West Ordinances. At one city council meeting, Jacob M. Levy, who identified himself as a socialist, denounced the legislation for putting "property rights above human rights," while Charles Kemper, the secretary of the Socialist Party, argued that segregating African Americans opened the door for similar efforts against other minority groups. J. H. Murphy,

1900

"The colored man that saves his money and buys
a brick house will be universally respected by his
white neighbors."

Figures 10a and 10b. These cartoons, published in the February 1911 issue of the
Crisis, countered segregationists' claims that the West Segregation Ordinances
were designed to benefit African Americans. Courtesy of Manuscripts, Archives
and Rare Books Division, Schomburg Center for Research in Black Culture, The
New York Public Library.

1910

"New and dangerous species of Negro criminal lately discovered in Baltimore. He will be segregated in order to avoid lynching."

the publisher of the *Afro-American,* and Rev. G. R. Waller challenged segregationists' specious claims that blacks lowered property values. The *Afro-
American* denounced the proposed acts as "anti-American."[42]

In spite of the protests, Baltimore's mayor, J. Barry Mahool, signed the
West Segregation Ordinance, making it the first residential segregation
ordinance in the country. Throughout the 1910s, various cities and real
estate interests looked to Baltimore for guidance in crafting or maintaining their own forms of legalized segregation. Throughout the 1910s,
requests flowed into the mayor's office from Dallas; Roanoke, Virginia;
Greenville, South Carolina; and the National Democratic Association in
Washington, DC. Louisville, Saint Louis, and Richmond passed segregation ordinances after Baltimore paved the way with the West Ordinance.
Smaller towns, including Madisonville, Kentucky; Winston-Salem,
Mooresville, and Asheville, North Carolina; and (according to the *Crisis*)
"various cities of Texas and Oklahoma" made their own stabs at imposing
legalized segregation.[43]

For Hawkins, the measure naturally followed Baltimore's and Maryland's recent attempts to institute Jim Crow. In a fiery editorial published
in the *Afro-American Ledger,* Hawkins proclaimed the West Ordinance to
be "in line with the legislation in this State in the last dozen or so years
aimed at our humiliation." Yet Hawkins's knowledge of Baltimore's past
gave him comfort. "It is true," Hawkins wrote of the law, "that the author,
Mr. Milton [Dashiell], and its sponsor, Mr. [Samuel L.] West, believe in its
legality; that Mr. Poe, and the eminent Mr. Marbury have pronounced it
constitutional, and the city government and the political party behind it are
pledged to its enforcement." But, Hawkins pointed out, this was "not the
first time and it won't be the last when our enemies' idea of legality and
constitutionality, have not favorably impressed courts of justice, and when
the latter have blocked the enforcement of unfair and unjust measures
aimed at us." In Hawkins's estimation, the West Segregation Ordinance was
a call to arms: "It is high time we were letting our enemies understand that
we don't propose to be driven any further without vigorous protest, and in
that protest every man of us needs to be counted, and I beg to be in at the
count."[44]

Before Hawkins could even mount a legal challenge, the West Ordinance proved to be a headache for the police and the courts. Although
precedent-setting, the language of the law was confusing and ineffective. It

also faced stiff resistance and court challenges that hampered segregation-ists' efforts.[45] A mere three weeks after its passage, the police arrested six people for violating its mandates. By the end of January the *Baltimore Sun* reported that "about 20 cases of alleged violation of the ordinance have been sent to court and nearly every day the grand jury is acting on one or more of them." Weeks later the Board of Police Commissioners ordered their patrolmen, due to the large number of arrests, to stop apprehending people based on West Ordinance violations. Between 1910 and 1913, the law also met with resistance from real estate agents who owned property in mixed-race neighborhoods.[46]

Although legally ineffective, the West Ordinance did play an important role in ratcheting up racial tensions on the streets. By criminalizing the movement of African Americans into white neighborhoods, the law height-ened and created panic among whites. White Baltimoreans viewed the impending moves of African Americans as more than mere threats; they perceived them as invasions that foretold disorder. The city government validated this notion by passing the West Ordinance. This, above all else, would serve as the law's most notable impact. In their efforts to create a stable racial order, government officials confirmed segregationists' un-founded claims that African Americans caused neighborhood degradation, augured violence, and lowered property values. Paradoxically, then, the law helped create the violence it claimed it was trying to prevent. When the laws failed to stand up to legal challenges, racial tensions only increased. After Judge Thomas Elliott deemed the second version of the West Ordi-nance invalid in April 1913, alarmed white residents held a mass meeting to "protect their streets from what is thought to be a general invasion by negroes" and debate what actions could be taken to stop integration.[47]

As the city labored to create a legally valid version of the West Ordi-nance, segregationists fired off hostile letters to the *Baltimore Sun* and mes-sages to Baltimore's new mayor, James H. Preston. In these missives one can sense increasing desperation in the tone of the writers as the laws failed to halt integration. One indignant letter writer sarcastically exclaimed to the mayor, "If this thing keeps up we will have a beautiful city, a lovely city, a picturesque city indeed. It will be our pleasure, our pride to show strang-ers what an attractive city we have, with its increasing dark spots." In another letter, C. E. Stonebraker wrote to Preston, pleading with him to "lend your best efforts towards putting an end to this hideous negro inva-sion." Then, in July 1913, a writer named Donnelly reported to the *Baltimore*

Sun that the failure of the laws to halt the progress of black Baltimoreans
in the northwest led some to suggest that the city change its name to
"Negromore." Another Baltimore newspaper published a letter bringing
these fears to their zenith when the writer warned that the city was in
danger of becoming "a second Darkest Africa."[48]

In each of the letters it is apparent that segregationists had grown frustrated waiting for effective legislation. Although none of the missives
directly called for violence, the sense of indignation and anger was apparent. For instance, J. L. Blake, who signed his screed as "A Property Owner
and Sufferer," wrote, "Too much valuable time has already been lost 'waiting,' a la Mr. West, for the 'decision of the Court of Appeals.' "[49] There were
other signs that racial tensions were escalating to dangerous levels. White
Baltimoreans increasingly emphasized themes of invasion and doom when
describing integration. One Baltimorean wrote to Preston, asking if there
was anything to stop the city from being "engulfed by the moves of negroes
now pouring in upon her." A letter to the *Baltimore Sun* claimed that African Americans "are simply swarming over this city and country like the
black plague of old, and if we do not heed the signs of the times will soon
be in possession of this city and country." At a meeting of the Harlem
Improvement Association on 12 June 1913, the group proclaimed, "The time
has come when conditions are such as to result in disorders, breaches of
the peace, and riots."[50]

The *Baltimore Sun* also did its part to drum up racial antipathy. Because
the Maryland Court of Appeals did not release the text of their full judgment
against the second West Ordinance immediately, legislators decided to wait
so they could make the necessary corrections in accordance with the ruling.
In the interim, the *Sun* published multiple stories concerning racial integration. For example, the paper reported that a black caterer, Charles R. Shipley,
moved into a house on Madison Avenue in "what is regarded as a plain
attempt to defeat the principle of race segregation." In another story, it told
of an African American family moving into a house on Myrtle Avenue. When
they could not detail actual "invasions," the paper resorted to publishing
rumors. The *Sun* reported a "threatened negro invasion" on West Lexington
Street after one black family took possession of a house; another story followed Milton Dashiell as he personally "investigated" claims of racial integration.[51] All of these stories were in addition to the multiple sensationalist letters
that either told of "negro invasions" or predicted dire consequences if the
city did not implement a new segregation ordinance.[52]

These tensions soon reached a breaking point. September 1913 turned out to be a violent and bloody month in Northwest Baltimore. The *Sun* reported that since "there is no law under which they can prevent further inroads, the white people openly declared that they will use their own methods in disposing of the unwelcome neighbors. They said they were tired of standing idly by and seeing their property depreciate in value because of the advent of the blacks." On 18 September the first confrontation occurred when a group of "men and boys" pummeled a house on Stricker Street with a variety of brickbats. As in prior incidents, the attackers severely damaged the property before the police arrived.[53] It was an ominous sign of things to come.

On 25 September 1913 Mayor Preston hurriedly signed the third version of the segregation ordinance in the vain hope that it would quell the passions of segregationists. Instead, it precipitated the greatest outbreak of violence yet. The next day, whites arrived at Mosher Street to bombard a house occupied by African Americans. Despite the presence of a police officer, the gang managed to break every window in the front of the dwelling. As the cops dealt with the disturbance on Mosher, the *Baltimore Sun* reported that a group of young African Americans seized the opportunity for revenge and began to pummel the houses of white residents. Whether this happened—the *Afro-American* did not report such an event—is open to speculation. It is entirely possible that it did occur, but it is at least equally possible that the *Sun* fabricated the episode. What is certain is that African Americans in the neighborhood gathered to ensure that white youths would not continue their bombardment on Mosher Street. As the night wore on, the violence continued to spread over Northwest Baltimore. At midnight another gang of youths and young men returned to the house on Stricker Street and smashed several windows. By 12:45 A.M. African Americans in the neighborhood had seen enough. According to the *Baltimore Sun*, a large number of African Americans gathered and "out of their midst four pistol shots were fired." This finally caught the attention of the police, who dispatched twenty-five officers to quell the disturbances. In total they arrested three men, two white and one black, and reported that four people were injured. The *Baltimore Sun* claimed that African Americans caused all of the injuries, with the exception of one.[54]

As the week wore on, violence continued to spread across the city's northwest, leaving behind a trail of wounded. A black woman, Carrie Green, was shot in the knee, allegedly by a drunken African American who was among a group of blacks confronting hostile whites; another African American, George Stapleton, was stabbed by an unknown assailant who successfully alluded the police; then George Snyder, who was white, claimed that an unknown African American cut him with a beer bottle after the two had engaged in an argument over segregation. That same evening, the *Baltimore Sun* reported that white youths pummeled six houses occupied by African Americans. The paper stated that "at least eight more or less organized gangs of whites" had formulated a strategy to divide the attentions of the police. Among their intended targets was Lillian List, who, while holding her nine-month-old child, narrowly missed being struck in the head by a brick lobbed at her doorway.[55]

Following the outbreaks of violence, "a committee representing those who live in the vicinity" offered to pay blacks to leave the area. Segregationists also used anonymous letters to threaten their new neighbors. The "Committee of Decent White Citizens Against Negro Invasion" sent a letter to Charles Shipley, the caterer who had moved to Madison Avenue. The group threatened to "dynamite" Shipley's house. Because of the threats, the city dispatched two policemen and three other plainclothes officers to protect Shipley and his home.[56]

By 1913, segregationists had intensified their street-level campaign to stop integration. The failures of the law opened the floodgates, but waters in the city had been rising for some time. When the city government passed a new version of the West Ordinance in September 1913, it did little, if anything, to stem the oncoming deluge. In fact, it only precipitated more disorder by criminalizing black mobility and legitimizing the stigmatization of African Americans. This can clearly be seen in the near riot at George Howe's residence on Harford Avenue. Howe did nothing to provoke the attacks on his house other than move into a "white neighborhood." Howe was the victim in this case; as the *Afro-American* pointed out, it was only "after his windows had been broken and the brickbats showered against his house, [that] Howe pulled the trigger on a double barreled shotgun." According to the ordinance, however, Howe's actions were criminal from the moment he purchased his home. Fearing disorder as well as a loss of their property value, segregationists decided they could not rely on an ineffective law and took matters into their own hands.[57]

Throughout the 1910s, black Baltimoreans fought against segregation in numerous ways. Hawkins advocated a legal remedy. Beginning in 1910, he defended multiple clients who violated the segregation ordinances. Weeks after the law's passage, he successfully defended Catherine Dixon, who rented a house on a majority-white block. Early the next year, the Suffrage League and the Maryland Progressive League hired Hawkins and "other attorneys" to direct the legal fight against the West Ordinances.[58] Together with McMechen, Hawkins also successfully defended the Gurry family, who bought a house that they intended to use as a church. In 1911 police tried to stop Carrie Gurry, the church's minister, from holding services on an all-white block of Laurens Street. While awaiting the fate of an injunction Hawkins filed on their behalf, John Gurry, Carrie's husband, attempted to move into the home. Police arrested and charged him with violating the West Ordinance. Finally, in 1913, Hawkins defended George Howe in two separate trials in the aftermath of the race riot outside his home.[59]

The NAACP also monitored the fight against segregation in Baltimore. Like Hawkins, the organization favored legal action and peaceful protests. The previous year, the organization had retained Hawkins as legal counsel in the Baltimore segregation cases. Shortly after the violence of 1913, the NAACP held a rally in the city. Oswald Garrison Villard—the grandson of William Lloyd Garrison and editor of the *New York Evening Post*—and Mary White Ovington led a protest against segregation at Baltimore's Bethel AME Church. In front of an estimated 1,500 people, Villard called for a "peaceful rebellion" in the face of the violence of that summer.[60] The *Afro-American* championed Villard's plan. "Let us be careful to maintain peaceful lives and conduct," an editorialist urged, "that can not be impeached." Finally, at its 1913 board of directors meeting, a report from the "Maryland Committee" noted, "The new segregation ordinance just passed in Baltimore has been the cause of rioting and bloodshed. The Baltimore Branch intends to bring a test case under this new ordinance as soon as possible and the Association [NAACP] will cooperate."[61]

The events of September 1913 galvanized Baltimore's black community but also revealed a divergence in the strategies of middle-class black activists and those, such as Howe, on the front lines. Some black Baltimoreans refused to be intimidated, despite the risks to their well-being, and weathered the storm without striking back. Even months after repeated incidents at his house, McMechen remained at the same address. After segregationists stoned John Blanchard's house, he told the *Baltimore Sun* that he liked the neighborhood and planned on staying as long as his white landlord would pay for repairs. William B. Hamer, who was the victim of repeated bombardments and threats, declared, "I expect to live here permanently" and "won't move out for anybody." But it should also be noted that George Howe's decision to strike back at the mob was not unusual in Baltimore in the 1910s. In each of the 1913 confrontations, African Americans confronted segregationists in the streets, sometimes with arms.[62]

Despite these schisms, African Americans supported the fight against segregation in numerous ways. In 1911 black Baltimoreans boycotted businesses owned by white merchants who did not oppose the West Ordinances.[63] Many others attended rallies organized by city churches. Sharp Street Church, Grace Presbyterian Church, and Asbury ME Church held mass meetings as activists geared up to challenge the legality of the ordinances in 1914. Sharp Street Church collected money to help pay for legal counsel, and the Baltimore Branch of the NAACP solicited funds from the public on a number of occasions.[64] In 1913 the Baltimore Branch of the NAACP reported that they had raised more than $1,200 that year in membership fees and "miscellaneous collections," which they used to "fight all sorts of unjust measures from Jim-Crow Bills to Segregation."[65] Following the widespread outbreak of violence in 1913, Dr. Howard E. Young purchased a house on Myrtle Street in a "white block." Young volunteered to allow the NAACP to use the house to challenge the segregation ordinance if the community helped him pay the ten-dollar-a-day fine. Young noted, "The testing of the validity of the segregation law is a matter which vitally concerns all of the colored citizens, and they should feel as much responsibility as the citizen who makes the test for them."[66]

Many black Baltimoreans understood the battle against residential segregation as part of the wider fight for equality. This framing—especially by activists and the *Afro-American*—had roots in the first community efforts at housing reform in the early 1900s, which linked the home environment to problems of structural racism. In subsequent years, African Americans continued to speak of the importance of housing to full political and social rights. When the *Afro-American* interviewed scholars, political officials, and religious leaders in 1913, each explicitly linked housing segregation to inequality. As one of the interviewees, Dr. C. V. Roman, the editor of the *Journal of the National Medical Association,* asserted, "The fight against segregation is not only a fight for liberty but a fight for life." At a meeting in October 1913, Warner T. McGuinn, an activist and attorney in Baltimore, remarked, "Physical slavery has been abolished, but its subtler forms are still here. Disfranchisement, 'jim crowism' and segregation are but the subtler forms of race slavery."[67]

The *Afro-American* most clearly connected housing to civil rights in a series of illustrations published in 1913. In "Civilization as It Is Understood in America," the paper depicted a crowd of angry whites pelting the "home of a colored citizen" with rocks as police officers casually ignored the events. Although whites often blamed the riots on the machinations of disreputable youths, the paper markedly depicted the instigators as middle-aged, respectably dressed white men. Then the paper went a step further in its condemnation. Around the side of the home, a white man is seen shooting an African American man at point-blank range. On the other side of the building, the drawing illustrates another group of white males in the process of lynching a black man. This illustration was followed the next week by "They Will Want His Shirt Next; Five to One—Might Makes Right." The editorial cartoon portrayed a seated "colored citizen" surrounded by white Baltimoreans. In the illustration, Councilman West and two unnamed men pull away a house that represented property rights, a hat that depicted voting rights, and a streetcar that signified the right to travel. In the background, a man is about to club the "colored citizen." In the paper's next issue, "Advertising Baltimore by the New Ad Club—City Council and Police Department; Mr. Business Man Is This the Best Kind of Advertising for Baltimore?" showed a train, labeled "Jim Crowism Made in Baltimore," moving across a map of the United States. Near Baltimore, numerous signs read "Mob Law Made in Baltimore" and "Segregation Made in Baltimore." Then two weeks later, another cartoon, "He Will Eventually Break Loose and Reach the Top," depicted a white man (labeled "White Race") standing at the bottom of a set of stairs denoted as the "Pit of Ignorance—Mob Rule-Segregation." The white man is holding onto the jacket of a black man (labeled "Colored Race") as he struggles to ascend to the "Temple of Higher Intelligence."[68]

The *Afro-American*'s cartoons stripped the West Ordinances of the niceties that segregationists used to sell them to the public. By juxtaposing segregation with lynching, mob violence, the denial of equal rights, and oppression, the illustrations unequivocally shattered the notion that the city implemented the laws to protect African Americans or maintain racial harmony. Instead, the illustrations exposed the violence, oppression, and racial prejudice at the center of these efforts. They also undermined the

CIVILIZATION AS IT IS UNDERSTOOD IN AMERICA

Policeman Watching to Keep Negroes Away While the Mob Gets in its Work

Figure 11a. "Civilization as It Is Understood in America." Following the racial violence of September 1913, the *Afro-American Ledger* published a series of editorial cartoons examining the rising tide of Jim Crow in Maryland. This cartoon, published on 27 September 1913, connected racial violence, police neglect, and housing rights. It highlighted the racial animus at the heart of the legislation. Courtesy of the *Afro-American*.

popular discourse that depicted blacks as the cause of disorder. In each of the drawings, segregation was the font from which disorder spouted. Furthermore, in portraying whites as the sole violent aggressors, and the police department and city council as aiding and abetting their actions, the cartoons produced a counternarrative about the violence inherent in the actions of these supposedly respectable men.

It is notable that the *Afro-American* singled out the police for particular approbation. In many cases, the *Baltimore Sun* depicted the police as the arbiters of law and order; they either came to restore the peace or arrest the African American resident at the center of the controversy. The *Afro-American*'s cartoons painted a different picture. In "Civilization as It Is Understood in America," the police actively participated in the disorder.

Figure 11b. "They Will Want His Shirt Next." In this cartoon, published on 4 October 1913, the *Afro-American Ledger* connected various Jim Crow initiatives that Baltimore and Maryland politicians attempted to pass in the early twentieth century. Courtesy of the *Afro-American*.

The patrolman in the foreground is "watching to keep negroes away" while segregationists committed murder and vandalism. In "Advertising Baltimore by the New Ad Club" the *Afro-American* identified the police department as promoters of not only segregation but also "mob law" in Baltimore. Although the West Segregation Ordinances failed in the courts, the police played an active role in making sure segregation functioned on the streets of Baltimore's racial frontiers.

Together, these four illustrations underscored the ways that black activists framed the fight against housing segregation. African American reformers universalized the movement by demonstrating how it was intrinsically connected to other injustices. Even for blacks who could not afford to move to more affluent neighborhoods, the cause still warranted their support. It is difficult to precisely gauge the effectiveness of these messages, although some evidence suggests that the wider community was listening. For

Figure 11c. "Advertising Baltimore by the New Ad Club—City Council and
Police Department." In this cartoon, published on 11 October 1913, the *Afro-
American Ledger* drew attention to Baltimore's central role in creating Jim Crow
laws, including those that established residential segregation, in the twentieth
century. Courtesy of the *Afro-American*.

instance, the number of African Americans who gathered in defense of
black homeowners was disproportionate to the population of black residents in Northwest Baltimore neighborhoods and to those personally
affected by the ordinances. The importance of the measure to the wider
black community was further reflected in the size of the crowd attending
Villard's rally against segregation in October 1913. The approximately 1,500
people present far exceeded those who had run afoul of the ordinance.

In the years after 1913, Baltimore's black community continued to disregard the West Ordinance. While the ordinances failed to halt black mobility
on the streets, African American activists continued to ensure that they also
failed to gain legal traction. In April 1915 Thomas S. Jackson and Charles
Morton stood trial for violating the fourth version of the segregation law,
known as the Curtis Segregation Ordinance. Jackson, who was black, rented
a house from Morton, who was white. Hawkins represented Jackson in

Figure 11d. "He Will Eventually Break Through and Reach the Top." Segregationists in Baltimore publicly contended that segregation laws would benefit white and black citizens. In the final image of the series, published on 25 October 1913, the *Afro-American Ledger* pointedly argued that "Mob Rule-Segregation" served only to oppress African Americans. Courtesy of the *Afro-American*.

criminal court, where Judge Henry Arthur Stump upheld the legality of the Curtis Segregation Ordinance. Activists immediately appealed the verdict. In March 1916 the Maryland Court of Appeals could not render a unanimous decision, so it decided to wait on the expected ruling by the Supreme Court in *Buchanan v. Warley*, a case with multiple connections to Baltimore. *Buchanan v. Warley* involved a Louisville, Kentucky, segregation ordinance modeled after the Baltimore law. In addition, the NAACP based their challenge to the law on the work that Hawkins completed in Baltimore.[69]

In late 1917 housing segregation as a legal reality ended when the Supreme Court struck down Louisville's segregation ordinance. The ruling

provided the NAACP their second Supreme Court victory and its first dealing with segregation. Following the decision, the editors of the *Crisis* highlighted the work that Hawkins completed. "The National Association for
the Advancement of Colored People and *The Crisis*, in turn," the editorial
read, "pause to raise their hats to one man who bore the burden in the heat
of the day, initiated the fight against segregation, carried it victoriously up
through the state courts, and filed a brief in the Supreme Court case—
William Ashbie Hawkins, the attorney of our Baltimore Branch." Hawkins
clearly appreciated the gesture. Shortly after receiving his copy of the *Crisis*,
he expressed his gratitude to DuBois. "Without the encouraging words of
the *Crisis* under your editorial management, the moral support of the
National Association for the Advancement of Colored People, and the sympathy of a small number of personal friends," Hawkins wrote, "I might
have given up the fight long before its glorious end. Your kind words,"
Hawkins continued, "wipe out all recollection of the many discouragements
I had to encounter in the long drawn out fight."[70]

Even with the ruling, segregationists would not give up their dream of
legalized segregation. Baltimore's city solicitor, S. S. Field, announced that
the city would continue to enforce segregation since the Supreme Court
ruled on the Louisville law, not the Baltimore ordinance. Milton Dashiell
immediately began drafting a new version of the legislation. In the meantime, police arrested at least two African Americans for violating the Curtis
Ordinance.[71] After police arrested Dr. William T. Coleman, his attorney,
Warner T. McGuinn, submitted a petition for a habeas corpus hearing. In
December, a month after the Supreme Court decision, Judge John C. Rose
of the US District Court granted Coleman a writ of habeas corpus when he
deemed that the ruling in *Buchanan v. Warley* applied to Baltimore. Then,
in March 1918, the *Afro-American* reported that the "local segregation law
was given its last rites" after the Maryland Court of Appeals reversed the
verdict in the case of Thomas S. Jackson.[72] After seven years, various court
battles, outbreaks of violence, and numerous protests and arrests, African
Americans scored a legal victory over Jim Crow. Given the local power
structure and the city's persistence in enforcing residential segregation, this
was a stunning turn of events.

Although Baltimore's segregation ordinances died a legal death, their
impact outlasted their official life span. By pursuing legalized segregation,
the city government legitimized segregationists and the grievances of racist

neighborhood improvement associations. The years in Baltimore following the *Buchanan v. Warley* decision are instructive of how even unsuccessful campaigns to institute Jim Crow led to greater racial inequality. Throughout the early 1900s, newspapers, segregationists, and government officials linked African Americans with plummeting property values, disorder, and neighborhood declension. This ratcheted up racial tensions on the streets. Even if whites held no racial animus toward their black neighbors, they often feared losing their life's investment if an African American family moved onto their block. By criminalizing the movement of African Americans into majority-white neighborhoods, the ordinances validated these ideas and underwrote de facto racial segregation. These ideas also played a pivotal role in the racial violence in Baltimore's residential neighborhoods. Black successes in combating segregation led whites to redouble their resistance to integrated neighborhoods. This, above all else, served as the law's lasting impact.

Following the *Buchanan v. Warley* decision, segregationists shifted strategies with the approval of Mayor James H. Preston. On 22 June 1918 Northwest Baltimore resident Alice J. Reilly wrote Mayor Preston to vent her frustration over the continuing movement of African Americans into "white blocks." In times past the mayor had responded by either extolling the virtues of the segregation law or promising enforcement. But he could do neither on this occasion. Instead, Preston offered a different solution to Reilly. Preston urged "the white property-owners themselves" to formulate "restrictions on their property to protect it from negro occupancy." Nor was this advice only given in private. At a biracial conference to chart the city's plans in the wake of the failed ordinances, the mayor publicly suggested this course of action as his favored solution.[73]

In 1919 approximately three hundred residents took the mayor's advice by signing covenants that barred property owners from renting or selling their homes to African Americans. They also planned to "oust such as already have secured a foothold in the community." A year later, a group known as the Neighborhood Corporation won an injunction that forbade a black man from moving into a neighborhood dwelling.[74] This was not the only way that neighborhood associations guarded the color line. In 1920 a "white association" attempted to sell Rev. J. H. Green's home while he was on vacation. Green, an African American, had been living in the house for about a month. By encouraging white citizens to organize to "protect" their neighborhoods, Preston invested new power in citizens and the many "neighborhood improvement associations."[75]

The legal demise of the West Segregation Ordinances passed the burden of surveillance and enforcement from the police department to neighborhood residents. While the police were at times both overtly and tacitly guilty of corruption and brutality, they were also beholden to a stricter code of conduct. Their actions often attracted attention (sometimes a public outcry) and could bring unwanted attention to city officials. Now even that modicum of protection vanished, as neighborhood protective associations ascended to new positions of power. This shift in power would have important consequences in the coming years.

The cruel irony of the African American victory over the West Segregation Ordinances was apparent by the late 1910s. With the demise of the poorly designed laws, it became more difficult for African Americans to target real estate companies, neighborhood improvement associations, and citizens who refused to sell them property. Because there were no laws outlawing speculation, racism, or the racial ideologies of neighborhood associations, African Americans no longer had visible targets to attack. African Americans' success in challenging the formal implementation of Jim Crow in Baltimore proved to be only half the battle.

Yet the legacies of the failed West Segregation Ordinances were not apparent at the end of the 1910s. While problems continued, the activism and resistance of black Baltimoreans did more to reshape the city's racial geography than any efforts of white segregationists. Certainly, the housing market remained circumscribed, but African Americans pushed the boundaries of Baltimore's racial frontier. Baltimore's black activist community also left behind important legacies by scoring victories over segregationists who had sought to limit the franchise, circumscribe black mobility, and impose Jim Crow laws on the city's transportation system.

Conclusion

On 14 April 1919, 1,200 students lined up outside of Northwest Baltimore's Robert Brown Elliott School. That morning, the children marched in a "long and silent procession" to Sharon Baptist Church to pay their final respects to Rev. William M. Alexander. For older residents of the neighborhood, the sight of the students filing through the streets conjured memories of one of Alexander's earliest triumphs. In the late 1880s Alexander had campaigned to secure public schools for African Americans. At the time, the only school in the neighborhood open to black children was the private one that Alexander and his wife, Mary, along with a few assistants, conducted at Sharon Baptist. After years of protest, the city finally relented in 1889 when they opened the Number Nine School (which would eventually be renamed Robert Brown Elliott School) to black Baltimoreans. On the first day of classes, Alexander led a "triumphal march of two hundred school children" from Sharon Baptist to the first African American public school in the city's northwest. Thirty years later, the students paid tribute to Alexander's memory by embarking on the same journey, only this time they reversed the origin and destination.[1] It was a touching homage to a man who spent his life working to expand educational opportunities for black children and fighting for racial equality.

During the late 1910s and early 1920s, Baltimore's first generation of civil rights activists began to succumb to old age. A little less than a year after Alexander's death, Henry Jerome (H. J.) Brown died. Amelia E. Johnson died a year later, shortly followed by her husband, Rev. Harvey Johnson, who passed away in 1923 at the age of seventy-nine. Not surprisingly, the passing of these community leaders and activists elicited an array of tributes from black Baltimoreans. In addition to the children's homage, the *Afro-American* called for the community to name a school in Alexander's honor. The paper published two obituaries of Brown, each one recounting at length his many accomplishments and his work toward racial equality.[2]

For many, however, Harvey Johnson cast the longest shadow. As the editors of the *Afro-American* noted, "The decade following the Civil War produced a number of sterling characters who wrote their names in flaming letters in the hearts of Baltimore. Among them none was of nobler and finer stuff than Dr. Harvey Johnson."[3] For years after his passing, black Baltimoreans evoked Johnson's memory as the standard for community activism. When Dr. David E. Over, Johnson's successor at Union Baptist, attempted to move the congregation to a new building in 1928, the police were summoned to break up a "near riot." The *Afro-American* reported, "A noticeable aspect of the meeting Thursday night was the constant reference to the late Dr. Harvey Johnson, founder of the church. In almost every group discussion, his spirit came to life, many declaring that the present building was a shrine to their dead pastor and it should not be sold." Two weeks later, the congregants voted to dismiss Dr. Over.[4] In 1931 the *Afro-American* celebrated Johnson's legacy. The paper remarked that Johnson, "by his indomitable will, his strength of character and his illimitable vision, was to go down to bedrock in his pioneering efforts to raise a progressive urban life for the colored people of this city, that still rests on the piles he sank into a literally unchartered social, political, economic, and religious foundation."[5]

The popular memory of Baltimore's first civil rights activists, however, has not survived the passage of time or received widespread recognition. Baltimore's white community never acknowledged their accomplishments. The *Baltimore Sun* did not deem Alexander, Brown, or the Johnsons worthy of obituaries. Although the *Sun* had supported many of the causes they championed in the 1880s, times had most certainly changed, and so had the paper's editorial stance. By the 1910s, the *Sun* advocated segregationist causes, including efforts to disfranchise blacks and legalize housing segregation. Nevertheless, the death of the city's foremost African American activists should have garnered at least a brief obituary. Instead, Baltimore's activists, along with their many accomplishments in the period between 1860 and 1920, were erased by omission. The *Sun* was not the only culprit. Neither of the Johnsons, Alexander, Brown, or even W. Ashbie Hawkins appear on Baltimore's Enoch Pratt Free Public Library's list of "Prominent African American Marylanders." In the "Monumental City," there are no statues erected in honor of Baltimore's early civil rights activists.

The disappearance from public memory of Baltimore's activists is troubling. Between 1865 and 1920, black Baltimoreans made the city the starting point for civil rights activism in the United States. In part, circumstances determined the path these activists pursued. Because the state barred African Americans from participating in electoral politics, black Baltimoreans needed to find another way to address inequality. Although the state government tried to ensure that African Americans remained disfranchised, they could not stop changes at the federal level. With the passage of the 1866 Civil Rights Act, black Baltimoreans attacked many of the state's prejudicial laws by resorting to the courts. Less than two months after passage of the 1866 legislation, black Baltimoreans initiated lawsuits to test the strength of the new laws. They opened cases to challenge a state law that prohibited African Americans from testifying against whites in court. African American men and women refused to abide by early efforts to impose Jim Crow segregation on mass transportation. Instead, they engaged in civil disobedience and then filed suit to try to overturn segregation laws. Others worked to expand educational opportunities for black children and fought numerous battles for labor rights. In doing so, black Baltimoreans sustained a tradition of activism, begun in the antebellum era, which refused to accept racial inequality. Without the benefit of state, local, or federal aid, black Baltimoreans scored important victories against staggering odds.

In the 1880s a new generation built on this culture of protest and activism. Black Baltimoreans heeded the call of national activists to forge organizations that coordinated civil rights activism. Seeing the political process as a dead end, Rev. Harvey Johnson founded the Mutual United Brotherhood of Liberty to coordinate legal challenges to segregation. This organization, like the activists themselves, has receded from our collective memory. Yet for black Baltimoreans and activists throughout the country, the group's strategies were a revelation. After Johnson helped dismantle Maryland's ban on black attorneys, the Brotherhood used the courts to fight the state's remaining black laws and defend workers on Navassa Island. The latter case made it to the Supreme Court, where the organization's attorney, Everett J. Waring, became the first black attorney to argue before the highest court in the land. The Brotherhood also continued the work of antebellum activists in fighting for greater public education. The group organized protests, threatened lawsuits, and beseeched the city government to hire black teachers and improve school facilities. Activists across the country, including T. Thomas Fortune and W. E. B. DuBois, celebrated the group's accomplishments and incorporated Baltimoreans' strategies in their own organizations.

Black Baltimoreans' notable achievements also caught the attention of segregationists. Beginning in the 1890s, segregationists exploited Progressive Era anxieties over crime and public order to roll back the gains that black Baltimoreans had made since the 1860s. Scholars have had trouble explaining how Jim Crow segregation arose alongside progressive ideas. The evidence suggests that, in many respects, progressives did not hold progressive views in regards to race. When segregationists added race to concerns about urban disorder, crime, and political corruption, they used the language of progressivism to marginalize African Americans. Through newspapers and speeches, segregationists wove racial prejudice into the fabric of everyday life, transforming quotidian street interactions into signs that black political power was ascendant. Once back in power, politicians made racial prejudice an operating principle for institutions, including the police and the courts, as they tried to undermine democracy to cement their triumphs. Segregationists in Baltimore targeted African Americans for arrest and marked them as a disorderly presence in streets, leisure spaces, and residential neighborhoods. In the early 1900s they further exploited concerns over race and crime to sell the public on black disfranchisement.

The events of the Progressive Era in Baltimore ultimately went a long way toward stalling the advance of civil rights in the city. Even though African American activists won legal victories, Baltimore was a city plagued by outbursts of racial violence and divided along racial lines. Activists' battles against criminalization, disfranchisement, and legalized housing segregation—all orchestrated by segregationists in the name of progressive reform—forced black Baltimoreans into a defensive battle. Activists devoted considerable time, money, and energy to maintaining their right to vote and live in a neighborhood of their own choosing. Although they stopped the advance of Jim Crow, they could not combat the ways in which its racial justifications further embedded racism in politics, culture, and the legal system.

Although segregationists were able to slow activists' momentum, they could not undo black Baltimoreans' accomplishments. Activists and black citizens rallied to defeat three separate disfranchisement bills at the beginning of the twentieth century. The black community also opened multiple fronts in their efforts to defeat legalized segregation. Black Baltimoreans refused to follow the law, struck back at segregationists who threatened or committed violence against them, and initiated lawsuits to challenge the ordinances' legality. Jim Crow did not cross the Maryland border because of the steadfast activism of black Baltimoreans who fought these attempts each step of the way.

Just as black Baltimoreans authored their own self-reconstruction of Maryland, they similarly articulated a black progressivism. By most measures, the goals of black Baltimoreans placed them squarely within the mainstream of the progressive reform agenda. There was, however, a key difference: African Americans insisted on racial justice. While segregationists used the concerns of the Progressive Era to promote a racially unjust vision of society, African Americans sought solutions that placed true racial equality at the center of their efforts. Black Baltimoreans pushed to open educational opportunities to all children, campaigned for a more equitable justice system, advocated for greater labor rights, implored city officials to tackle crime in their neighborhoods, supported efforts to end political corruption, and fought to preserve democracy in Maryland.

Black Baltimoreans recognized that racial inequality was at the heart of the disorder that many white progressives claimed they were fighting to end. Activists saw within segregated neighborhoods the fruits of racism and the problems caused by official neglect. They contended that the segregation ordinances, far from preventing racial strife as white progressives claimed, precipitated the violence that plagued Baltimore by ratcheting up racial tensions. As W. Ashbie Hawkins noted in a report he filed to the NAACP, the white attacks on George Howe's home in 1913 were "the direct consequence of the new Segregation Legislation, and the inflamed state of the public mind produced thereby."[6]

At the beginning of the twentieth century, black Baltimoreans also knew all too well that the resilience of white supremacy posed a grave danger to democracy. They recognized, for instance, disfranchisement as the cause of political corruption, pointing to the problems of American apartheid in the South. In leading the fight against disfranchisement, black Baltimoreans not only preserved their own right to vote but also saved Maryland's democracy. Although versions of the legislation were nominally targeted at African Americans, contemporaries recognized that state Democrats hoped to make Maryland a one-party state. If they had been successful, the city's substantial immigrant population, along with white Republicans, would have been effectively stripped of their franchise.

While African Americans did not enjoy access to political power or command the ears of most politicians, we should not exclude them from discussions of progressivism. In fact, despite the considerable roadblocks they encountered, black Baltimoreans notched notable accomplishments throughout the Progressive Era. Their efforts demonstrated that democracy works when everyone has a voice and a place within it. They have a lot to teach our current and future generations about the importance of fighting for equality and freedom even in the face of insurmountable odds. But we can only learn from Baltimore's black activists when we know what they did and how they did it.

These lessons were not lost on black Baltimoreans who lived between 1865 and 1920. Black Baltimoreans after the Civil War built an activist tradition that they passed from generation to generation. Their work furthered the legacy of earlier generations and helped bridge the divide between Reconstruction and the civil rights era. This legacy would be in turn picked up by a new generation of activists beginning in the 1930s. Black Baltimoreans, including Thurgood Marshall, Juanita Jackson, William P. Carter, and Clarence Mitchell, would lead the next stage of the struggle in the post–World War II era by combining community protests and litigation to defeat Jim Crow. By this time, these strategies were well established in Baltimore.

NOTES

Introduction

1. "The Fifteenth Amendment," *Baltimore Sun*, 20 May 1870, p. 1; "The Fifteenth Amendment," *Baltimore American and Commercial Advertiser*, 20 May 1870, p. 1.

2. "The Fifteenth Amendment," *New York Times*, 20 May 1870, p. 5.

3. "The Fifteenth Amendment," *Baltimore American and Commercial Advertiser*, 20 May 1870, p. 1; "The Fifteenth Amendment," *Baltimore Sun*, 20 May 1870, p. 1.

4. "The Fifteenth Amendment," *Baltimore Sun*, 20 May 1870, p. 1; "The Fifteenth Amendment," *Baltimore American and Commercial Advertiser*, 20 May 1870, p. 1.

5. Campbell King and Kay Jung, "Historical Census Statistics on Population Totals by Race, 1790 to 1990, and by Hispanic Origin, 1970 to 1990, for Large Cities and Other Urban Places in the United States," Washington, D.C., U.S. Census Bureau, February 2005, Table 21, https://www.census.gov/population/www/documentation/twps0076/twps0076.pdf.

6. Alfred J. Pairpoint, *Uncle Sam and His Country; or Sketches of America in 1854–55–56* (London: Simpkin, Marshall, 1857), p. 219. For Maryland and Baltimore prior to the Civil War, see Seth Rockman, *Scraping By: Wage Labor, Slavery, and Survival in Early Baltimore* (Baltimore: Johns Hopkins University Press, 2009); Barbara Jeanne Fields, *Slavery and Freedom on the Middle Ground: Maryland During the Nineteenth Century* (New Haven, CT: Yale University Press, 1984); Robert J. Brugger, *Maryland, a Middle Temperament: 1634–1980* (Baltimore: Johns Hopkins University Press, 1996); Christopher Phillips, *Freedom's Port: The African American Community of Baltimore, 1790–1860* (Urbana: University of Illinois Press, 1997); Martha S. Jones, *Birthright Citizens: A History of Race and Rights in Antebellum America* (Cambridge: Cambridge University Press, 2018).

7. For Reconstruction, see Steven Hahn, *A Nation Under Our Feet: Black Political Struggles in the Rural South from Slavery to the Great Migration* (Cambridge, MA: Belknap Press, 2003); Eric Foner, *Reconstruction: America's Unfinished Revolution, 1863–1877* (New York: Harper Perennial Modern Classics, 2014).

8. There are a number of important analyses of the Border States during Reconstruction. See Anne E. Marshall, *Creating a Confederate Kentucky: The Lost Cause and Civil War Memory in a Border State* (Chapel Hill: University of North Carolina Press, 2013); Aaron Astor, *Rebels on the Border: Civil War, Emancipation, and the Reconstruction of Kentucky and Missouri* (Baton Rouge: Louisiana State University Press, 2012); Adam Arenson, *The Great Heart of the Republic: St. Louis and the Cultural Civil War* (Columbia: University of Missouri Press, 2015).

9. T. W. C., "Impressions of Baltimore—Number 1," *Christian Recorder*, 13 October 1866.

10. "Suffrage in Missouri—Forward Steps," *New York Times*, 11 January 1870, p. 4.

11. For the political climate in Maryland during the war, see Brugger, *Maryland*; Charles L. Wagandt, *The Mighty Revolution: Negro Emancipation in Maryland, 1862–1864* (Baltimore: Maryland Historical Society, 2004); William Starr Myers, *The Maryland Constitution of 1864* (Baltimore: Johns Hopkins Press, 1901).

12. Judge H. L. Bond, "Civilization in Maryland," *Zion's Herald and Wesleyan Journal* 38, no. 26 (26 June 1867): p. 0_1.

13. William Starr Myers, *The Self-Reconstruction of Maryland, 1864–1877* (Baltimore: Johns Hopkins Press, 1909).

14. See, for example, Shawn Leigh Alexander, *An Army of Lions: The Civil Rights Struggle Before the NAACP* (Philadelphia: University of Pennsylvania Press, 2012).

15. See, for instance, Michael McGerr, *A Fierce Discontent: The Rise and Fall of the Progressive Movement, 1870–1920* (New York: Oxford University Press, 2003).

16. On the Progressive Era, see Khalil Gibran Muhammad, *The Condemnation of Blackness: Race, Crime, and the Making of Modern Urban America* (Cambridge, MA: Harvard University Press, 2011).

Chapter 1

1. "Inauguration of Douglass Institute: Lecture of Fred'k Douglass, Esq." *Liberator* 35, no. 41 (13 October 1865): 162; J. Thomas Scharf, *The Chronicles of Baltimore: Being a Complete History of Baltimore Town and Baltimore City from the Earliest Period to the Present Time* (Baltimore: Turnbill Brothers, 1874), p. 661.

2. "Inauguration of Douglass Institute," p. 162; Phillip S. Foner, ed., "Address of Frederick Douglass at the Inauguration of Douglass Institute, Baltimore, October 1, 1865," *Journal of Negro History* 54, no. 2 (April 1969): 174–183.

3. This study builds on the recent work that has foregrounded African Americans' protest and resistance as a constant throughout the Reconstruction and Jim Crow eras. See Jane Elizabeth Dailey, Glenda Elizabeth Gilmore, and Bryant Simon, eds., *Jumpin' Jim Crow: Southern Politics from Civil War to Civil Rights* (Princeton, NJ: Princeton University Press, 2000); Stephanie Cole and Natalie Ring, eds., *The Folly of Jim Crow: Rethinking the Segregated South* (College Station: Texas A&M University Press, 2012). See also Charles Payne, *"I Got the Light of Freedom": The Organizing Tradition in the Mississippi Freedom Struggle* (Berkeley: University of California Press, 2007).

4. Christopher Phillips, *Freedom's Port: The African American Community of Baltimore, 1790–1860* (Urbana: University of Illinois Press, 1997).

5. Phillips, *Freedom's Port*, ch. 8; A Colored Baltimorean, "Maryland Colonization Society," *Liberator* 4, no. 4 (25 January 1834): 14.

6. Phillips, *Freedom's Port*, p. 227.

7. Phillips, *Freedom's Port*, ch. 5; Bettye Gardner, "Ante-Bellum Black Education in Baltimore," *Maryland Historical Magazine* 71, no. 3 (Fall 1976): 360–366.

8. Gardner, "Ante-Bellum Black Education in Baltimore"; Charles Varle, *A Complete View of Baltimore* (Baltimore: Samuel Young, 1833), p. 33.

9. Gardner, "Ante-Bellum Black Education in Baltimore"; James M. Wright, *The Free Negro in Maryland, 1634–1860* (New York: Columbia University, 1921), pp. 198–206; Richard Paul Fuke, "The Baltimore Association for the Moral and Educational Improvement of the Colored People, 1864–1870," *Maryland Historical Magazine* 66, no. 4 (Winter 1971): 369–371; Phillips, *Freedom's Port*, pp. 163–169, 228.

10. Phillips, *Freedom's Port*, esp. ch. 7; Bettye C. Thomas, "A Nineteenth Century Black Operated Shipyard, 1866–1884: Reflections upon Its Inception and Ownership," *Journal of Negro History* 59, no. 1 (January 1974): 1–12.

11. Campbell J. Gibson and Emily Lennon, "Historical Census Statistics on the Foreign-Born Population of the United States: 1850–1990," Population Division Working Paper No. 29 (Washington, DC: US Bureau of the Census, 1999). For a detailed look at the city's changing demographics, see M. Ray Della, Jr., "An Analysis of Baltimore's Population in the 1850s," *Maryland Historical Magazine* 68, no. 1 (1973): 20–35.

12. "Local Matters," *Baltimore Sun*, 10 June 1858, p. 1; "Local Matters," *Baltimore Sun*, 11 June 1858, p. 1. For an account of the racial violence, see Phillips, *Freedom's Port*, pp. 200–202.

13. "Local Matters," *Baltimore Sun*, 14 December 1859, p. 1; "Local Matters," *Baltimore Sun*, 1 March 1864, p. 1; "Local Matters," *Baltimore Sun*, 2 April 1864, p. 1; Journeyman Caulker, "The Trouble Among the Mechanics," *Baltimore Sun*, 7 October 1865, p. 2.

14. Phillips, *Freedom's Port*, 208–210, 232–234.

15. The quotation about conditions on the waterfront appears in Richard Paul Fuke, *Imperfect Equality: African Americans and the Confines of White Racial Attitudes in Post-Emancipation Maryland* (New York: Fordham University Press, 1999), p. 132. For the state convention meetings, see "Local Matters," *Baltimore Sun*, 29 December 1865, p. 1; "Local Matters," *Baltimore Sun*, 30 December 1865, p. 1; "Local Matters," *Baltimore Sun*, 1 January 1866, p. 1.

16. Fuke, *Imperfect Equality*, pp. 112–113. On census figures, see Campbell Gibson and Kay Jung, "Historical Census Statistics on Population Totals by Race, 1790 to 1990, and by Hispanic Origin, 1790 to 1990, for Large Cities and Other Urban Places," Washington, DC: US Census Bureau, February 2005, https://www.census.gov/population/www/documentation/twps0076/twps0076.pdf.

17. Robert J. Brugger, *Maryland, a Middle Temperament: 1634–1980* (Baltimore: Johns Hopkins University Press, 1988), esp. ch. 6 and 7; William Starr Myers, *The Self-Reconstruction of Maryland, 1864–1877* (Baltimore: Johns Hopkins Press, 1909).

18. "Maryland," *Chicago Tribune*, 24 October 1866, p. 2.

19. The *Philadelphia Press* article was reprinted in "An Administration Plot," *Chicago Daily Tribune*, 22 October 1866, p. 1. See also "Maryland," *Chicago Daily Tribune*, 24 October 1866, p. 2.

20. Maryland had much in common with the other Border States. See Richard O'Curry, ed., *Radicalism, Racism, and Party Realignment: The Border States During Reconstruction* (Baltimore: Johns Hopkins University Press, 1969); Anne E. Marshall, *Creating a Confederate Kentucky: The Lost Cause and Civil War Memory in a Border State* (Chapel Hill: University of North Carolina Press, 2013); Aaron Astor, *Rebels on the Border: Civil War, Emancipation, and the Reconstruction of Kentucky and Missouri* (Baton Rouge: Louisiana State University Press, 2012); Adam Arenson, *The Great Heart of the Republic: St. Louis and the Cultural Civil War* (Columbia: University of Missouri Press, 2015).

21. Black Baltimoreans and Marylanders' experience in Reconstruction differed markedly with their counterparts farther south. For accounts that focus mainly on the Deep South, see W. E. B. DuBois, *Black Reconstruction in America, 1860–1880* (New York: Free Press, 1998); Steven Hahn, *A Nation Under Our Feet: Black Political Struggles in the Rural South from Slavery to the Great Migration* (Cambridge, MA: Belknap Press, 2005); Eric Foner, *Reconstruction:*

America's Unfinished Revolution (New York: Harper Perennial Modern Classics, 2014); Paul Ortiz, *Emancipation Betrayed: The Hidden History of Black Organizing and White Violence in Florida from Reconstruction to the Bloody Election of 1920* (Berkeley: University of California Press, 2006).

22. See, for instance, "Memorial from the Mayor and Members of City Council of Baltimore," *The Journal of the House of Representatives of the United States Being the First Session of the Fortieth Congress; Begun and Held at the City of Washington, March 4, 1867* (Washington: Government Printing Office, 1867), p. 151; "A Bill to Territorialize Maryland," *Baltimore Sun*, 19 December 1866, p. 1; "Local Matters," *Baltimore Sun*, 24 January 1867, p. 1; Myers, *Self-Reconstruction of Maryland*, pp. 103–104; J. Thomas Scharf, *History of Maryland: From the Earliest Period to the Present Day*, vol. 3 (Baltimore: John B. Piet, 1879), p. 701.

23. "The Civil Rights Bill and Its Consequences," *Baltimore Sun*, 9 April 1866, p. 2.

24. Historians have uncovered a long history of black protest centering on public transportation stretching beyond the Civil War. See Elizabeth Stordeur Pryor, *Colored Travelers: Mobility and the Fight for Citizenship Before the Civil War* (Chapel Hill: University of North Carolina Press, 2016); Barbara Young Welke, *Recasting American Liberty: Gender, Race, Law, and the Railroad Revolution, 1865–1920* (Cambridge: Cambridge University Press, 2001). For restrictions on Marylanders, see Phillips, *Freedom's Port*, p. 194.

25. "Local Matters," *Baltimore Sun*, 17 May 1866, p. 1; "Proceedings of the Courts," *Baltimore Sun*, 21 May 1866, p. 1. For more background on the case, see David Skillen Bogen, "Precursors of Rosa Parks: Maryland Transportation Cases Between the Civil War and the Beginning of World War I," *Maryland Law Review* 63, no. 4 (2004).

26. "Released on Parole," *Baltimore Sun*, 5 January 1866, p. 1; E. Merton Coulter, "Aaron Alpeoria Bradley, Georgia Negro Politician During Reconstruction Times," *Georgia Historical Quarterly* 51, no. 1 (March 1967): 15–41. For information on African American protest of Jim Crow cars in Massachusetts, see Pryor, *Colored Travelers*, ch. 3.

27. "Local Matters," *Baltimore Sun*, 23 May 1866, p. 1; "Local Matters," *Baltimore Sun*, 24 May 1866, p. 4; "Local Matters," *Baltimore Sun*, 25 May 1866, p. 1; "Local Matters," *Baltimore Sun*, 26 May 1866, p. 1. Employment of Hutt and Davis found in *Woods' Baltimore City Directory*, 1867–1868 (Baltimore: John W. Woods).

28. Barbara Y. Welke, "When All the Women Were White, and All the Blacks Were Men: Gender, Class, Race, and the Road to *Plessy*, 1855–1914," *Law and History Review* 13, no. 2 (Autumn 1995): 273.

29. "Local Matters," *Baltimore Sun*, 23 May 1866, p. 1; "Local Matters," *Baltimore Sun*, 24 May 1866, p. 4; "Local Matters," *Baltimore Sun*, 25 May 1866, p. 1; "Local Matters," *Baltimore Sun*, 26 May 1866, p. 1. For the history of segregation on the passenger rail, see "Local Matters," *Baltimore Sun*, 24 May 1866, p. 4.

30. "Local Matters," *Baltimore Sun*, 10 July 1866, p. 1. For information on Jakes's background, see Jennifer Harris, "Black Canadian Contexts: The Case of Amelia E. Johnson," *African American Review* 49, no. 3 (Fall 2016): 243.

31. "Local Matters," *Baltimore Sun*, 23 April 1866, p. 1; "The Civil Rights Bill," *New York Times*, 7 July 1866, p. 4; "Decision Under the Civil Rights Bill," *Baltimore Sun*, 9 July 1866, p. 1; "Chief Justice Bowie's Opinion," *Baltimore Sun*, 9 July 1866, p. 2.

32. For an examination of the system of gradual emancipation, see James J. Gigantino III, *The Ragged Road to Abolition: Slavery and Freedom in New Jersey, 1775–1865* (Philadelphia: University of Pennsylvania Press, 2016).

33. "Maryland," *New York Times*, 17 October 1867, p. 8; Jeffrey R. Brackett, *Notes on the Progress of the Colored People of Maryland Since the War* (Baltimore: Johns Hopkins University, 1890), p. 62. For an extended look at the Turner case, see Harold M. Hyman, *The Reconstruction Justice of Salmon P. Chase: In Re Turner & Texas v. White* (Lawrence: University Press of Kansas, 1997).

34. "Rights of Colored Persons," *Baltimore Sun*, 30 April 1870, p. 1. Giles based his decision on the 1867 case of *Westchester and Philadelphia Railroad Company v. Mary E. Miles*, a case later cited by the Supreme Court in *Plessy v. Ferguson*, which ruled that railroads could separate passengers by race if the accommodations were equal. Giles's quotation is taken from "Rights of Passengers," *Baltimore Sun*, 30 April 1870, p. 1.

35. "Local Matters," *Baltimore Sun*, 2 May 1870, p. 1; "Local Matters," *Baltimore Sun*, 3 May 1870, p. 4; "Local Matters," *Baltimore Sun*, 10 May 1870, p. 1; "Local Matters," *Baltimore Sun*, 15 July 1870. Weaver's occupation determined from *Woods' Baltimore City Directory, 1870* (Baltimore: John W. Woods), p. 754.

36. "Local Matters," *Baltimore Sun*, 11 November 1871, p. 4; "The City," *Baltimore American and Commercial Advertiser*, 11 November 1871; "The Street Car Case," *Baltimore American and Commercial Advertiser*, 13 November 1871.

37. "Local Matters," *Baltimore Sun*, 13 November 1871, p. 4; "The Colored Passenger Question in Baltimore," *New York Times*, 15 November 1871, p. 8; "Local Matters," *Baltimore Sun*, 14 November 1871, p. 4.

38. "Local Matters," *Baltimore Sun*, 27 September 1865, p. 1; "Local Matters," *Baltimore Sun*, 28 September 1865, p. 1; Justice, "The Strike on Negro Caulkers," *Baltimore Sun*, 30 September 1865, p. 2.

39. 400 Colored Caulkers, "Appeal of the Colored Caulkers of Baltimore to the Merchants and Business Men of Baltimore City and State of Maryland," *Baltimore Sun*, 2 October 1865, p. 2, emphasis in original.

40. "Advertisement," *Baltimore Sun*, 6 October 1865, p. 2. For information on the Journeymen's shipyard, see "Local Matters," *Baltimore Sun*, 25 October 1865, p. 1. On the strike's conclusion, see "Local Matters," *Baltimore Sun*, 28 October 1865, p. 1; "Local Matters," *Baltimore Sun*, 6 November 1865, p. 1. For the job figures, see Brackett, *Colored People of Maryland*, 37–38.

41. "Political Condition of the Colored People," *New York Tribune*, 1 September 1870, p. 2; Fuke, *Imperfect Equality*, pp. 132, 135; Brackett, *Colored People of Maryland*, 29, 32–33.

42. For a detailed examination of Myers's biography, see William George Paul, "The Shadow of Equality: The Negro in Baltimore, 1864–1911" (PhD diss., University of Wisconsin, 1972), pp. 93–94.

43. "Enterprise of Colored Baltimoreans," *Christian Recorder*, 7 April 1866. For a comprehensive history of the shipyard, see Thomas, "Nineteenth Century Black Operated Shipyard," pp. 1–12; "(Communicated) The Chesapeake Marine Railway and Dry Dock Company of Baltimore, Maryland," *Christian Recorder*, 7 November 1868, p. 125; Matthew A. Crenson, *Baltimore: A Political History* (Baltimore: Johns Hopkins University Press, 2017), p. 278.

44. "Enterprise of Colored Baltimoreans," *Christian Recorder*, 7 April 1866, p. 54.

45. Thomas, "Nineteenth Century Black Operated Shipyard," pp. 1–12. Business figures taken from "(Communicated) The Chesapeake Marine Railway and Dry Dock Company of Baltimore, Maryland," *Christian Recorder*, 7 November 1868. See also Crenshon, *Baltimore*, p. 278.

46. Fuke, *Imperfect Equality*, pp. 124–125; Brackett, *Colored People of Maryland*, p. 30.

47. Fuke, *Imperfect Equality*, pp. 124–125; Brackett, *Colored People of Maryland*, pp. 29–30. For the coal yard, see "Baltimore Letter," *People's Advocate*, 16 August 1879, p. 2; "Baltimore Notes," *People's Advocate*, 24 July 1880, p. 2.

48. Brackett, *Colored People of Maryland*, pp. 29–31.

49. "Local Matters," *Baltimore Sun*, 20 July 1869, p. 1. Quotations from "Convention of Colored Mechanics," *Christian Recorder*, 14 August 1869, p. 4.

50. "The Colored People's National Labor Convention," *Baltimore Sun*, 10 December 1869; "Proceedings of the Colored National Labor Convention Held in Washington, D.C. on December 6th, 7th, 8th, 9th, and 10th, 1869" (Washington, DC: Printed at the Office of the New Era, 1870), pp. 10–12. Quotation from "Proceedings of the Colored National Labor Convention" (Washington, DC: Office of the New Era, 1870), p. 3.

51. Paul D. Moreno, *Black Americans and Organized Labor: A New History* (Baton Rouge: Louisiana State University, 2006), pp. 28–32. For the quotation, see "The National Labor Convention," *New National Era*, 19 January 1871, p. 2.

52. John Mercer Langston, *Freedom and Citizenship* (Washington, DC: Rufus H. Darby, 1883), pp. 259–261.

53. *Proceedings and Debates of the 1864 Constitutional Convention* (Annapolis, MD: Richard P. Bayly, Printer, 1864), pp. 761–763.

54. Fuke, "Baltimore Association," pp. 369–371.

55. The Gailbraith Lyceum is briefly mentioned in William J. Simmons, *Men of Mark: Eminent, Progressive and Rising* (Cleveland: Geo. M. Rewell, 1887), p. 246.

56. Baltimore Association for the Moral and Education Improvement of the Colored People, Second Annual Report (Baltimore: J. B. Rose & Co., 1866), pp. 10–11.

57. "Local Matters," *Baltimore Sun*, 1 February 1865, p. 1; "First Annual Report of the Baltimore Association for the Moral and Educational Improvement of the Colored People, 1865," pp. 8, 10–12, https://archive.org/stream/ASPC0001939000. "Second Annual Report of the Baltimore Association for the Moral and Educational Improvement of the Colored People, November 1866," p. 4.

58. "Local Matters," *Baltimore Sun*, 28 November 1866, p. 1; "The Colored Schools," *Baltimore Sun*, 10 January 1868, p. 2. See also "First Annual Report of the Baltimore Association, 1865"; "Second Annual Report of the Baltimore Association for the Moral and Educational Improvement of the Colored People, November 1866"; "Third Annual Report of the Baltimore Association for the Moral and Educational Improvement of the Colored People, December 1867" (Baltimore: John W. Woods, Printer, 1868).

59. "First Annual Report of the Baltimore Association, 1865," pp. 4–5. Quotation taken from "Second Annual Report of the Baltimore Association, November 1865," p. 9.

60. "Local Matters," *Baltimore Sun*, 15 February 1867, p. 1. Financial information found in Baltimore Association for the Moral and Educational Improvement of the Colored People, "Baltimore. December 15th, 1864," Library of Congress, Printed Ephemera Collection, Portfolio 31, Folder 19; "Local Matters," *Baltimore Sun*, 15 February 1867, p. 1; "Second Annual Report of the Baltimore Association, November 1866," p. 8; "Third Annual Report of the Baltimore Association, December 1867," p. 8.

61. Information pulled from T. W. C., "Impressions of Baltimore, No. 5," *Christian Recorder*, 8 December 1866; *Woods' Baltimore City Directory*, 1867, pp. 584, 622. Quotation

taken from George F. Bragg, *Men of Maryland* (Baltimore: Church Advocate Press, 1914), p. 123.

62. T. W. C., "Impressions of Baltimore, No. 5."

63. T. W. C., "Impressions of Baltimore, No. 5."

64. "Local Matters," *Baltimore Sun*, 24 November 1866, p. 1; "Third Annual Report of the Baltimore Association," pp. 1–5.

65. "Local Matters," *Baltimore Sun*, 10 June 1868, p. 1; "John F. W. Ware, and His Work for the Freedmen," *Unitarian Review and Religious Magazine* 15, no. 5 (May 1881): 435; J. Thomas Scharf, *History of Baltimore City and County from the Earliest Period to the Present Day Including Biographical Sketches of Their Representative Men* (Philadelphia: Louis H. Everts, 1881), p. 228.

66. "Local Matters," *Baltimore Sun*, 29 March 1871, p. 4.

67. John R. Slattery, "Twenty Years' Growth of the Colored People in Baltimore, MD," *Catholic World* 66, no. 394 (January 1898): 521. Biographical information about the Berry sisters culled from 1860 United States Federal Census, p. 215; *Woods' Baltimore City Directory, 1865–1866* (Baltimore: John W. Woods), p. 470; *Woods' Baltimore City Directory, 1881* (Baltimore: John W. Woods), p. 940.

68. Calbraith B. Perry, *Twelve Years among the Colored People* (New York: James Pott, 1884), p. 94; "A Brilliant Reception," *Baltimore Sun*, 21 April 1879, p. 1.

69. For an account of the Oblate Sisters of Providence, see Diane Batts Morrow, *Persons of Color and Religious at the Same Time: The Oblate Sisters of Providence, 1828–1860* (Chapel Hill: University of North Carolina Press, 2002); Gardner, "Ante-Bellum Black Education in Baltimore," pp. 360–366; "Local Matters," *Baltimore Sun*, 27 July 1872, p. 1.

70. Perry, *Twelve Years among the Colored People*, ch. 4.

71. "Forty-First Annual Report of the Board of Commissioner of Public Schools to the Mayor and City Council of Baltimore" (Baltimore: Kelly, Piet & Co., City Printers, 1870), p. xxiv.

72. See "Colored People's Educational Meeting—Demand for Colored Teachers &c," *Baltimore Sun*, 10 April 1879; Brackett, *Colored People of Maryland*, 84–88.

73. For more on the conventions, see Gabrielle P. Foreman, "The Colored Conventions Project and the Changing Same," *Common-place* 16, no. 1 (Fall 2015), http://common-place.org/book/the-colored-conventions-project-and-the-changing-same. See also Susan D. Carle, *Defining the Struggle: National Organizing for Racial Justice, 1880–1915* (New York: Oxford University Press, 2013), p. 55.

74. "Address of the Colored Men's Border State Convention," *National Anti-Slavery Standard*, 30 January 1968, http://coloredconventions.org/items/show/568; "Colored Border State Convention," *Baltimore Sun*, 6 August 1868, p. 1.

75. *Woods' City Directory, 1867*, p. 571; "Colored Border State Convention," *Baltimore Sun*, 5 August 1868, p. 1.

76. "Proceedings of the National Convention of Colored Men of America," Washington, DC, 1869, http://coloredconventions.org/items/show/452.

77. "Local Matters," *Baltimore Sun*, 5 April 1870, p. 4.

78. Paul, "Shadow of Equality," pp. 96–101. See also "Local Matters," *Baltimore Sun*, 14 June 1873, p. 1; "Mass Meeting of Colored Man," *Baltimore Sun*, 4 September 1873, p. 4.

79. "Local Matters," *Baltimore Sun*, 23 February 1870, p. 4.

80. "Local Matters," *Baltimore Sun*, 13 June 1873, p. 1. For black support of Greeley, see "Local Matters," *Baltimore Sun*, 20 April 1872, p. 1; "The Grand Torchlight Procession," *Baltimore Sun*, 11 October 1872, p. 1; Paul, "Shadow of Equality," p. 98. On the separate party, see "Advertisement," *Baltimore Sun*, 26 August 1873, p. 2; "Mass Meeting of Colored Man," *Baltimore Sun*, 4 September 1873, p. 4. For an overview of the fights between Myers and more radical voices, see Paul, "Shadow of Equality," pp. 94–100.

81. Frank Richardson Kent, *The Story of Maryland Politics* (Baltimore: Thomas and Evans Printing Co., 1911), p. 33. The best source of information about African Americans' relationships to the Republican and Democratic Parties can be found in Paul, *Shadow of Equality*, esp. ch. 5 and 6, and Margaret Law Callcott, "The Negro in Maryland Politics, 1870–1912" (PhD diss., University of North Carolina, 1967).

82. "State Democratic Convention," *Baltimore Sun*, 22 July 1875, p. 1; "Municipal Political Movements," *Baltimore Sun*, 26 August 1875, p. 1. For an examination of the campaign, see Crenson, *Baltimore*, pp. 297–299.

83. "Baltimore Municipal Election," *New York Times*, 28 October 1875, p. 1; "Miscellaneous," *Chicago Daily Tribune*, 29 October 1875, p. 2; "Untitled," *Chicago Daily Tribune*, 31 October 1875, p. 4.

84. "City Council Contested Election," *Baltimore Sun*, 18 December 1875, p. 4; "Tuesday's Elections," *Chicago Daily Tribune*, 4 November 1875, p. 2; "The Late Elections," *Chicago Daily Tribune*, 5 November 1875, p. 1; "Maryland: The Republican and Reform Ticket Defeated by Fraud and Terrorism in Baltimore," *New York Times*, 3 November 1875, p. 5.

85. "Maryland: Republican and Reform Ticket Defeated by Fraud and Terrorism in Baltimore," *New York Times*, 3 November 1875, p. 5.

86. "The Late Elections," *Chicago Daily Tribune*, 5 November 1875, p. 1.

87. "Guns Used in Maryland's State Election of 1875," *Afro-American*, 15 October 1932, p. 22; "Baltimore Election Contests," *Baltimore Sun*, 13 January 1876, p. 4; "City Election Contests," *Baltimore Sun*, 18 January 1876, p. 4; "City Election Contests," *Baltimore Sun*, 19 January 1876, p. 4. Brown quotation from "Colored Republicans in Mass Meeting," *Baltimore Sun*, 26 August 1876, p. 1.

88. "Tumultuous Crowds of Democratic Roughs Blockading the Streets of Baltimore," *New York Times*, 11 November 1876, p. 1; "Baltimore," *Chicago Daily Tribune*, 18 January 1877, p. 3.

89. "The South," *Chicago Daily Tribune*, 24 October 1879, p. 1; "Maryland," *New York Times*, 5 November 1879, p. 5.

90. "Colored Voters Mass Meeting," *Baltimore Sun*, 28 October 1879, p. 4.

91. "The National Labor Convention," *New National Era*, 19 January 1871, p. 2.

Chapter 2

1. "Revolt of Colored Voters," *Baltimore Sun*, 1 October 1885, p. 6. For background on the Colored Advisory Council and Briscoe, see "Local Matters," *Baltimore Sun*, 25 March 1881, p. 1; "The Colored Independents," *Baltimore Sun*, 16 August 1883, p. 1; William George Paul, "The Shadow of Equality: The Negro in Baltimore, 1864–1911" (PhD diss., University of Wisconsin, 1972), ch. 6.

2. "Republican Primaries," *Baltimore Sun*, 22 September 1885, p. 4; "Extract: From a Speech Delivered by Isaac Myers," *Baltimore Sun*, 26 October 1885, p. 1.

3. "Revolt of Colored Voters: The Advisory Council Repudiates the Republican Primaries," *Baltimore Sun*, 1 October 1885, p. 6. For Myers, see "Extract: From a Speech Delivered by Isaac Myers," *Baltimore Sun*, 26 October 1885, p. 1. For background on African Americans in the Maryland Republican Party, see Paul, "Shadow of Equality," pp. 186–188.

4. See, for instance, Evelyn Brooks Higginbotham, *Righteous Discontent: The Women's Movement in the Black Baptist Church, 1880–1920* (Cambridge, MA: Harvard University Press, 1993); Glenda Elizabeth Gilmore, *Gender and Jim Crow: Women and the Politics of White Supremacy in North Carolina, 1896–1920* (Chapel Hill: University of North Carolina Press, 1996); Steven Hahn, *A Nation Under Our Feet: Black Political Struggles in the Rural South from Slavery to the Great Migration* (Cambridge, MA: Belknap Press, 2005); Paul Ortiz, *Emancipation Betrayed: The Hidden History of Black Organizing and Violence in Florida from Reconstruction to the Bloody Election of 1920* (Berkeley: University of California Press, 2005); Leslie Brown, *Upbuilding Black Durham: Gender, Class, and Black Community Development in the Jim Crow South* (Chapel Hill: University of North Carolina Press, 2008).

5. In particular, see Shawn Leigh Alexander, *An Army of Lions: The Civil Rights Struggle Before the NAACP* (Philadelphia: University of Pennsylvania Press, 2012); Susan D. Carle, *Defining the Struggle: National Organizing for Racial Justice, 1880–1915* (New York: Oxford University Press, 2013); Blair L. M. Kelley, *Right to Ride: Streetcar Boycotts and African American Citizenship in the Era of* Plessy v. Ferguson (Chapel Hill: University of North Carolina Press, 2010); Ortiz, *Emancipation Betrayed.*

6. For more on Delany's campaign, see Thomas Holt, *Black over White: Negro Political Leadership in South Carolina During Reconstruction* (Urbana: University of Illinois Press, 1979).

7. "Movement of Colored People," *Baltimore Sun*, 25 April 1882, p. 1.

8. George F. Adams, *Baptist Churches of Maryland* (Baltimore: J. F. Weishampel, Jr., 1885), pp. 130–132; A. W. Pegues, *Our Baptist Ministers and Schools* (Springfield, MA: Willey, 1892), pp. 89, 291; Kenneth M. Hamilton, *Booker T. Washington in American Memory* (Urbana: University of Illinois Press, 2017).

9. "Movement of Colored People," *Baltimore Sun*, 25 April 1882, p. 1.

10. On the Readjuster Movement, see Jane Dailey, *Before Jim Crow: The Politics of Race in Postemancipation Virginia* (Chapel Hill: University of North Carolina Press, 2000). For the Independent Party, see Ortiz, *Emancipation Betrayed*, pp. 41–45.

11. Paul, "Shadow of Equality," p. 197; "The Colored Independents," *Baltimore Sun*, 16 August 1883, p. 1. Paul claimed that four African Americans ran for city council, but the *Baltimore Sun* only lists three: "Baltimore Municipal Election," *Baltimore Sun*, 28 October 1880, p. 1.

12. "Development of the Colored Race," *Baltimore Sun*, 23 May 1882, p. 1; "Local Matters," *Baltimore Sun*, 13 June 1882, p. 4.

13. "Colored Republican Meetings," *Baltimore Sun*, 18 August 1882, p. 1; "Baltimore Politics," *Baltimore Sun*, 28 September 1885, p. 1; "The Fusion Ticket," *Baltimore Sun*, 4 October 1885, p. 4.

14. Clayton Colman Hall, ed., *Baltimore: Its History and Its People*, vol. 1 (New York: Lewis Historical Publishing, 1912), p. 258; "The Committee of One Hundred and the Judiciary Question," *Baltimore Sun*, 17 August 1882; "To the People of Baltimore," *Baltimore Sun*, 14 October 1882, p. 1. For more information on the independent judiciary movement, see "A New Judiciary Ticket," *Baltimore Sun*, 9 October 1882, p. 1; "To the People of Baltimore,"

Baltimore Sun, 14 October 1882, p. 1; "Independent Judges," *Baltimore Sun*, 19 October 1882, p. 1.

15. "The Colored Advisory Council," *Baltimore Sun*, 31 October 1882, p. 1; "Colored Citizens on the Issues," *Baltimore Sun*, 4 November 1882, p. 4; "Mass-Meeting of Colored Citizens," *Baltimore Sun*, 2 November 1882, p. 1.

16. "Independent Judiciary Ticket," *Baltimore Sun*, 28 October 1882, p. 1; "Mass-Meeting of Colored Citizens," *Baltimore Sun*, 28 October 1882, p. 1.

17. "Views of Colored Clergymen," *Baltimore Sun*, 6 November 1882, p. 4; "Mass-Meeting of Colored Citizens," *Baltimore Sun*, 2 November 1882, p. 1; "The Colored Advisory Council," *Baltimore Sun*, 31 October 1882, p. 1. For election results, see "The Elections," *Baltimore Sun*, 8 November 1882, p. 1.

18. Joseph E. Briscoe, "To Colored Republicans," *Baltimore Sun*, 6 November 1882, p. 1.

19. Accounts of the *Steamer Sue* case taken from the *Sue* 22 F. 843 (D. Md. 1885); A. Briscoe Koger, "Dr. Harvey Johnson: Minister and Pioneer Civic Leader," The A. B. Koger Collection, Maryland State Archives, 9–10; "Colored Passengers," *Baltimore Sun*, 3 February 1885, p. 6; David S. Bogen, "Precursors of Rosa Parks: Maryland Transportation Cases Between the Civil War and the Beginning of World War I," *Maryland Law Review* 63, no. 4 (2004): 721–751. Martha Stewart quotation found in Testimony of Martha Stewart (libellant), *Martha Stewart et al. v. The Steamer Sue* (29 January 1885), p. 2, District of Maryland Records, Admiralty Cases 90–93, National Archives and Record Administration, Philadelphia.

20. See, for instance, Jeffrey R. Brackett, *Notes on the Progress of the Colored People of Maryland since the War: A Supplement to the Negro in Maryland: A Study of the Institution of Slavery* (Baltimore: Publication Agency of the Johns Hopkins University, 1890), pp. 70–71; Koger, "Dr. Harvey Johnson," pp. 9–10; Paul, "Shadow of Equality," pp. 205–207.

21. W. Ashbie Hawkins, "Harvey Johnson's Contribution to the Life of Baltimore," Trustees of Union Baptist Church, November 1922, The A. B. Koger Collection, Maryland State Archives, p. 6; W. M. Alexander, "The Brotherhood of Liberty or Our Day in Court: Including the Navassa Case" (Baltimore: Printing Office of J. F. Weishampel, 1891), p. 47.

22. For the national context, see Carle, *Defining the Struggle*.

23. See, for instance, Ronald M. Labbe and Jonathan Luire, *The Slaughterhouse Cases: Regulation, Reconstruction, and the Fourteenth Amendment* (Lawrence: University of Kansas Press, 2005).

24. Joseph R. Palmore, "The Not-So-Strange Career of Interstate Jim Crow: Race, Transportation, and the Dormant Commerce Clause, 1878–1946," *Virginia Law Review* 83, no. 8 (November 1997): 1773–1817. See also Barbara Young Welke, *Recasting American Liberty: Gender, Race, Law, and the Railroad Revolution, 1865–1920* (Cambridge: Cambridge University Press, 2001), pp. 337–342; Thomas J. Davis, "Race, Identity, and the Law," in Annette Gordon-Reed, ed., *Race on Trial: Law and Justice in American History* (New York: Oxford University Press, 2002), pp. 64–65.

25. Alexander, "Brotherhood of Liberty," p. 6; Koger, "Dr. Harvey Johnson," pp. 9–10; Davis, "Race, Identity, and the Law," pp. 64–65. For Clifford quotation, see William T. Otto, *United States Reports, Supreme Court*, vol. 95 (Boston: Little, Brown, 1878), p. 501. For more on the 1883 decision, see Carle, *Defining the Struggle*.

26. The Brotherhood of Liberty, *Justice and Jurisprudence: An Inquiry Concerning the Constitutional Limitations of the Thirteenth, Fourteenth, and Fifteenth Amendments* (Philadelphia: J. B. Lippincott Company, 1889), pp. 10, 192, 487.

27. Kelley, *Right to Ride*; Barbara Y. Welke, "When All the Women Were White, and All the Blacks Were Men: Gender, Class, Race, and the Road to *Plessy*, 1855–1914," *Law and History Review* 13, no. 2 (Autumn 1995): 261–316; Carle, *Defining the Struggle*, p. 34.

28. Wendy Wagner, "Black Separatism in the Periodical Writings of Mrs. A. E. (Amelia) Johnson," in Todd Vogel, ed., *The Black Press: New Literary and Historical Essays* (New Brunswick, NJ: Rutgers University Press, 2001), p. 93; Jennifer Harris, "Black Canadian Contexts: The Case of Amelia E. Johnson," *African American Review* 49, no. 3 (Fall 2016): 241–259.

29. Koger, "Dr. Harvey Johnson," 23. For the most complete account of Amelia Johnson's life and activism, see Gabrielle Foreman, *Activist Sentiments: Reading Black Women in the Nineteenth Century* (Urbana: University of Illinois Press, 2009), p. 146. Jennifer Harris has completed a much-needed examination of Amelia Johnson's family history. See Harris, "Black Canadian Contexts." See also Hawkins, "Harvey Johnson's Contribution," pp. 3, 6.

30. "Local Matters," *Baltimore Sun*, 10 July 1866, p. 1; Harris, "Black Canadian Contexts," p. 243.

31. Harris, "Black Canadian Contexts," p. 243; "Stenographer Receipt," District of Maryland Records, Admiralty Cases 90–93, National Archives and Record Administration, Philadelphia. For biographical information on Dennis Johnson, see Testimony of Dennis Johnson (witness for libellant), *Martha Stewart et al. v. The Steamer Sue* (29 January 1885), pp. 47–48, District of Maryland Records, Admiralty Cases 90–93, National Archives and Record Administration, Philadelphia. Biographical information for Andrew J. Reed taken from Testimony of Andrew J. Reed (witness for libellant), *Martha Stewart et al. v. The Steamer Sue* (29 January 1885), pp. 60–61, District of Maryland Records, Admiralty Cases 90–93, National Archives and Record Administration, Philadelphia; *Woods' Baltimore City Directory* (Baltimore: John W. Woods, 1885), p. 1067. For Dennis Gaskins, see Testimony of Dennis Gaskins (witness for libellant), *Martha Stewart et al. v. The Steamer Sue* (29 January 1885), pp. 39–40, District of Maryland Records, Admiralty Cases 90–93, National Archives and Record Administration, Philadelphia. Membership in the Brotherhood was determined by cross-referencing the witness testimonies with Alexander, "Brotherhood of Liberty," pp. 2, 43–44.

32. The *Sue*, 22 F. 843 (D. Md. 1885); Koger, "Dr. Harvey Johnson," pp. 9–10; "Colored Passengers," *Baltimore Sun*, 3 February 1885, p. 6; Testimony of Martha Stewart (libellant), p. 12, Testimony of Winnie Stewart (libellant), *Martha Stewart et al. v. The Steamer Sue* (29 January 1885), p. 20, District of Maryland Records, Admiralty Cases 90–93, National Archives and Record Administration, Philadelphia; Testimony of Pauline Braxton (witness for libellant), *Martha Stewart et al. v. The Steamer Sue* (29 January 1885), pp. 33–34, District of Maryland Records, Admiralty Cases 90–93, National Archives and Record Administration, Philadelphia.

33. The *Sue*, 22 F. 843 (D. Md. 1885); Koger, "Dr. Harvey Johnson," pp. 9–10; "Colored Passengers," *Baltimore Sun*, 3 February 1885, p. 6; "Local Matters," *Baltimore Sun*, 19 September 1884, p. 4; Testimony of Lucy Jones (libellant), *Martha Stewart et al. v. The Steamer Sue* (29 January 1885), p. 28, District of Maryland Records, Admiralty Cases 90–93, National Archives and Record Administration, Philadelphia.

34. Welke, "When All the Women Were White," p. 266.

35. Testimony of Martha Stewart (libellant), p. 5; Testimony of Winnie Stewart (libellant), p. 15. See also Record in the *Sue*, 22 F. 843 (D. Md. 1885).

36. The *Sue*, 22 F. 843 (D. Md. 1885); Welke, "When All the Women Were White," p. 266.

37. Brotherhood of Liberty, *Justice and Jurisprudence*, pp. 297–298, emphasis in original.

38. The *Sue*, 22 F. 843 (D. Md. 1885); "Colored Passengers," *Baltimore Sun*, 3 February 1885, p. 6. For Bond's decision, see "Rights of Colored People," *New York Times*, 8 July 1885, p. 3.

39. Hawkins, "Harvey Johnson's Contribution," p. 6. William M. Alexander agreed with this assessment. He remembered that activists, "encouraged by this decision of the Court . . . agreed to test the law prohibiting colored lawyers from practicing at the Maryland Bar." Alexander, "Brotherhood of Liberty," p. 6.

40. Hawkins, "Harvey Johnson's Contribution," p. 8.

41. "Can Colored Men Be Lawyers," *Baltimore Sun*, 16 February 1885, p. 6; F. Johnson, "Legal Lights of Baltimore," *Afro-American Ledger*, 26 March 1910, p. 6.

42. *Proceedings and Acts of the General Assembly, 1872*, vol. 190 (Annapolis: Wm. Thompson of R., Printer, 1872), p. 2713. Not much is known about this case. Occasionally it is referenced in the *Afro-American*, but only in broad outlines of Johnson's life and work. After the case, Wolff left to practice in Massachusetts and Taylor in New York City. See "Forty Years Pastor of Union Bapt. Church," *Afro-American Ledger*, 19 October 1912, p. 7; F. Johnson, "Legal Lights of Baltimore," *Afro-American Ledger*, 26 March 1910, p. 6. It does seem that Wolff at least kept up with Johnson's activities. Ten years later, when Johnson helped successfully challenge the Maryland law prohibiting black attorneys, Wolff wrote him a letter of congratulations. See Harvey Johnson, *Nations from a New Point of View* (Nashville, TN: National Baptist Publishing Board, 1903), p. 22.

43. "Colored Man at the Bar," *Baltimore Sun*, 23 June 1877, p. 4; "Right of Colored Citizens to Practice Law in Maryland Courts," *Baltimore Sun*, 22 December 1877, p. 1. On Bradwell, see Richard L. Aynes, "*Bradwell v. Illinois*: Chief Justice Chase's Dissent and the 'Sphere of Women's Work,'" *Louisiana Law Review* 59, no. 2 (Winter 1999): 520–541.

44. For information on King's background, see "Baltimore Topics," *New York Globe*, 10 April 1884, p. 1. Hawkins's quotation from Wm. A. Hawkins, "Baltimore Topics," *New York Globe*, 5 April 1884, p. 1.

45. For King's effort before the Senate, see *Congressional Record*, "Memorial of Richard King complaining that law regarding admission to bar is a violation of Constitution," 15 (1884): 4312. For the *Sun*'s coverage, see "Colored Men as Lawyers," *Baltimore Sun*, 12 March 1884, p. 5; "From Washington," *Baltimore Sun*, 21 May 1884, p. 1. For the *Globe*'s coverage, see Hawkins, "Baltimore Topics," *New York Globe*, 5 April 1884, p. 1; "Baltimore Topics," *New York Globe*, 19 April 1884, p. 1.

46. Alexander, "Brotherhood of Liberty," p. 6.

47. "Admitted to the Bar," *Baltimore Sun*, 20 March 1885, p. 1; "Admission of Colored Lawyers to the Bar," *Baltimore Sun*, 20 March 1885, p. 2.

48. Brackett, *Colored People of Maryland*, p. 76.

49. Hawkins, "Harvey Johnson's Contribution," p. 7.

50. "Can Colored Men Be Lawyers," *Baltimore Sun*, 16 February 1885, p. 6; Brackett, *Colored People of Maryland*, p. 76. For Alexander's quote, see Alexander, "Brotherhood of Liberty," p. 6.

51. "Miss Gray's Brave Struggle," *Baltimore Sun*, 3 April 1885, p. 4. On Cooper's capture, see "Telegraphic Summary, Etc.," *Baltimore Sun*, 7 April 1885, p. 1; "Howard Cooper's Crime," *Baltimore Sun*, 21 May 1885, p. 1.

52. "A Talk with Cooper," *Baltimore Sun*, 8 April 1885, p. 5; "Cooper's Case and Other Matters," *Baltimore Sun*, 14 April 1885, p. 6; "Howard Cooper's Crime," *Baltimore Sun*, 21 May 1885, p. 1.

53. "Howard Cooper's Case," *Baltimore Sun*, 5 May 1885, p. 4. On Hoblitzell, see "Telegraphic Summary, Etc.," *Baltimore Sun*, 12 May 1885, p. 1; "Cooper's Counsel," *Baltimore Sun*, 13 May 1885, p. 4.

54. "Counsel for Cooper," *Baltimore Sun*, 15 May 1885, p. 4. For White, see Henry Elliot Shepherd, ed., *History of Baltimore, Maryland, from its Founding as a Town to the Current Year, 1729–1898* (n.p.: S. B. Nelson, 1898), pp. 854–855. For Weld, see Conway Whittle Sams and Elihu Samuel Riley, *The Bench and Bar of Maryland: A History, 1634 to 1901* (Chicago: Lewis, 1901), p. 430; "Obituary," *Baltimore Sun*, 1 January 1907, p. 9.

55. Brackett, *Colored People of Maryland*, p. 68; "Howard Cooper to Be Tried Today," *Baltimore Sun*, 20 May 1885, p. 4; "The Howard Cooper Case," *Baltimore Sun*, 29 May 1885, p. 4.

56. "Howard Cooper's Crime," *Baltimore Sun*, 21 May 1885, p. 1.

57. "Court of Appeals Decisions," *Baltimore Sun*, 24 June 1885, p. 5; "The Law's Delay," *Baltimore Sun*, 26 June 1985, p. 2. Quotations from "The Howard Cooper Case," *Baltimore Sun*, 29 May 1865, p. 4.

58. "Cooper's Death Warrant Signed," *Baltimore Sun*, 30 June 1885, p. 6; "Howard Cooper Taken to Towson," *Baltimore Sun*, 1 July 1885, p. 4.

59. "Howard Cooper's Case," *Baltimore Sun*, 25 June 1885, p. 4; "The Cooper Case in the Court of Appeals," *Baltimore County Union*, 27 June 1885, p. 3.

60. "Howard Cooper Hanged," *Baltimore Sun*, 13 July 1885, p. 1; "A New Point in the Howard Cooper Case," *Baltimore Sun*, 4 July 1885, p. 4; "Cooper's Backers," *Baltimore Sun*, 11 July 1885, p. 4.

61. "Howard Cooper's Appeal," *Baltimore Sun*, 9 July 1885, p. 4; "Cooper and His Counsel," *Baltimore Sun*, 10 July 1885, p. 4; "Cooper's Backers," *Baltimore Sun*, 11 July 1885, p. 4; "A New Point on the Howard Cooper Case," *Baltimore Sun*, 4 July 1885, p. 4; "Cooper's Counsel and Friends," *Baltimore Sun*, 14 July 1885, p. 1.

62. "Howard Cooper's Appeal," *Baltimore Sun*, 9 July 1885, p. 4; "Howard Cooper Hanged," *Baltimore Sun*, 13 July 1885, p. 1.

63. "Howard Cooper Hanged," *Baltimore Sun*, 13 July 1885, p. 1.

64. For instance, see Grace Elizabeth Hale, *Making Whiteness: The Culture of Segregation in the South, 1890–1940* (New York: Vintage, 1998), esp. ch. 5; W. Fitzhugh Brundage, *Lynching in the New South: Georgia and Virginia, 1880–1930* (Urbana: University of Illinois Press, 1993); Jacquelyn Dowd Hall, "The Mind That Burns in Each Body," in Ann Snitow, Christine Stansell, and Sharon Thompson, eds., *Powers of Desire: The Politics of Sexuality* (New York: Monthly Review Press, 1983), pp. 328–349.

65. "The Lynching of Cooper," *Baltimore Sun*, 14 July 1885, p. 1; "The Story of a Lyncher," *Baltimore Sun*, 14 July 1885, p. 1.

66. "Howard Cooper's Fate," *Chicago Daily Tribune*, 14 July 1885, p. 3.

67. "Untitled," *Baltimore County Union*, 18 July 1885, p. 2.

68. "The Sentence of Howard Cooper," *Baltimore Sun*, 22 May 1885, p. 2; "The Law's Delay," *Baltimore Sun*, 26 June 1885, p. 2.

69. "The Lynching of Howard Cooper," *Baltimore Sun*, 14 July 1885, p. 2.

70. "Maryland Press on the Cooper Lynching," *Baltimore Sun*, 15 June 1885, p. 5; "Lynched Him," *Rising Sun Journal*, 18 July 1885.

71. "The Lynching of Howard Cooper," *Baltimore Sun*, 14 July 1885, p. 2.

72. "Condemning the Cooper Lynching," *Cleveland Gazette*, 1 August 1885, p. 2.

73. "Cooper's Counsel and Friends," *Baltimore Sun*, 14 July 1885, p. 1.

74. Alexander, "Brotherhood of Liberty," p. 6.

Chapter 3

1. W. M. Alexander, "The Brotherhood of Liberty or Our Day in Court: Including the Navassa Case" (Baltimore: Printing Office of J. F. Weishampel, 1891), p. 6.

2. Other civil rights activists in this period shared this belief. See Susan D. Carle, *Defining the Struggle: National Organizing for Racial Justice, 1880–1915* (New York: Oxford University Press, 2013).

3. For more information on the early stages of the black freedom struggle in the United States, see Carle, *Defining the Struggle*; Shawn Leigh Alexander, *An Army of Lions: The Civil Rights Struggle Before the NAACP* (Philadelphia: University of Pennsylvania Press, 2012).

4. See "Baltimore Notes," *People's Advocate*, 24 July 1880, p. 2. For an examination of Fortune during these years, see Alexander, *Army of Lions*, esp. ch. 1.

5. A brief description of the short-lived black newspapers can be found in Jeffrey R. Brackett, *Notes on the Progress of the Colored People of Maryland Since the War: A Supplement to the Negro in Maryland: A Study of the Institution of Slavery* (Baltimore: Publication Agency of the Johns Hopkins University, 1890), pp. 241–242.

6. Unfortunately, no copies of these early black papers exist. The *Christian Recorder* reported the founding of the *Baltimore Beacon*. See "Baltimore Is to Have a New Paper, Published in the Interest of Her Colored Citizens," *Christian Recorder*, 12 January 1882. On the *Colored Citizen*, see "The Colored Citizen of Baltimore, Isaac Myers, Editor-in-Chief," *Christian Recorder*, 13 September 1883. See also "Gossip About Newspapers and Editors," *New York Globe*, 8 September 1883, p. 2; *Geo. P. Rowell's American Newspaper Directory* (Geo. P. Rowell & Co., 1884), p. 1136.

7. Evelyn Brooks Higginbotham, *Righteous Discontent: The Women's Movement in the Black Baptist Church, 1880–1920* (Cambridge, MA: Harvard University Press, 1993); James Melvin Washington, *Frustrated Fellowship: The Black Baptist Quest for Social Power* (Macon, GA: Mercer University Press, 1985).

8. George F. Adams, *History of Baptist Churches of Maryland* (Baltimore: J. F. Weishampel, Jr., 1885), p. 175.

9. Adams, *History of Baptist Churches of Maryland*, p. 175.

10. "Funeral of Reverend Wm. M. Alexander on Monday," *Afro-American Ledger*, 11 April 1919, p. A1; "Sharon Baptist Church," *Afro-American Ledger*, 17 February 1912, p. 7; A. Briscoe Koger, "Dr. Harvey Johnson—Pioneer Civic Leader" (Baltimore: self-published, 1957), p. 3; Howard Young, "Macedonia Baptist Begins in Horse Stable Soon to Enter $100,000 Marble Church," *Afro-American*, 4 April 1925, p. 18.

11. William J. Simmons, *Men of Mark: Eminent, Progressive and Rising* (Cleveland: Press of W. W. Williams, 1887), pp. 1049–1050; Adams, *History of Baptist Churches in Maryland*, p. 188; Brackett, *Colored People of Maryland*, p. 44.

12. Biographical information about Waller from "Rev. Waller, 84 Dies in Balto," *Afro-American Ledger*, 15 March 1941, p. 18; Angela Jones, *African American Civil Rights: Early*

Activism and the Niagara Movement (Denver: Praeger, 2011), p. 233. On the formation of the Baltimore NAACP, see "Untitled," *Crisis* 4, no. 1 (May 1912): 23.

13. "Sharon Baptist Church," *Afro-American Ledger*, 17 February 1912, p. 7; "Church to Observe 25th Anniversary," *Afro-American Ledger*, 11 February 1911, p. 5. Quotation from "Sharon Baptist Church Rounds Thirtieth Year," *Afro-American Ledger*, 13 February 1915, p. 6.

14. The churches in Baltimore confirmed Evelyn Brooks Higginbotham's contention that the "black church . . . came to signify public space." Higginbotham, *Righteous Discontent*, p. 7. On the Douglass Institute, see Karen Olson, "Old West Baltimore: Segregation, African-American Culture, and the Struggle for Equality," in Elizabeth Fee, Linda Shopes, and Linda Zeidman, eds., *The Baltimore Book: New Views on Local History* (Philadelphia: Temple University Press, 1991), pp. 63–64. On black churches' multiple uses, see, for instance, "For Prohibition," *Baltimore Sun*, 14 July 1886, p. 6; "Rights of Colored People," *Baltimore Sun*, 29 November 1887, p. 6; "City News in Brief," *Baltimore Sun*, 21 June 1889, p. 4. For Sharon Baptist, see Wanda L. Dobson, "Sharon Baptist Church: A Hub of Black Cultural Heritage in Baltimore," *Baltimore Sun*, 16 January 1977, p. SM5. For Calvary Baptist, see "The Colored People," *Baltimore Sun*, 27 May 1887, p. 6; "A Political Sermon: What a Colored Minister Has to Say on Government and Parties," *Baltimore Sun*, 29 August 1887, p. 6; "Women's Home Mission Society," *Baltimore Sun*, 16 May 1888, p. 1.

15. Alexander, "Brotherhood of Liberty," p. 7.

16. "Supreme Bench and a Colored Lawyer," *Baltimore Sun*, 12 October 1885, p. 4; "Everett James Waring, Esq.," *Christian Recorder*, 5 January 1893, p. 1; Plebeian, "Progress of the Emancipated Race," *Phrenological Journal of Science of Health* 84, no. 2 (February 1887): 85.

17. "The Bastardy Law Sustained," *Baltimore Sun*, 3 July 1886, p. 4; Alexander, "Brotherhood of Liberty," p. 11. For more information on the history of the Bastardy Act, see Henry J. McGuinn, "Equal Protection of the Law and Fair Trials in Maryland," *Journal of Negro History* 24, no. 2 (April 1939): 146–147; William George Paul, "The Shadow of Equality: The Negro in Baltimore, 1864–1911" (PhD diss., University of Wisconsin, 1972), ch. 6.

18. "An Unjust Law," *Baltimore Sun*, 8 May 1886, p. 2.

19. Quotation from "The Bastardy Law," *Baltimore Sun*, 2 July 1886, p. 4. For information about the law and its application, see "To Protect Colored Women," *Baltimore Sun*, 7 June 1886, p. 6; "Plunkard v. State," *Atlantic Reporter* 10 (July 27–November 23, 1887): 225–231.

20. "An Unjust Law," *Baltimore Sun*, 8 May 1886, p. 2; Alexander, "Brotherhood of Liberty," pp. 14–15; "A Bastardy Law Sustained," *Baltimore Sun*, 3 July 1886, p. 4.

21. "Maryland's Bastardy Law," *New York Freeman*, 23 January 1886; Brackett, *Colored People of Maryland*, p. 80; Alexander, "Brotherhood of Liberty," 11. Waring's partial testimony was reprinted in "Maryland's Unjust Law," *New York Freeman*, 12 June 1886, p. 2.

22. "A Bourbon Law Blasted," *New York Freeman*, 12 November 1886, p. 1.

23. "Telegraphic Summary, etc.," *Baltimore Sun*, 6 December 1886, p. 1; Alexander, "Brotherhood of Liberty," p. 15; "Items from Hagerstown," *Baltimore Sun*, 16 December 1886, p. 6; "Judge Syester on the Bastardy Law," *Baltimore Sun*, 20 December 1886, p. 6.

24. "Court of Appeals Decisions," *Baltimore Sun*, 23 June 1887, p. 6.

25. See Alexander, "Brotherhood of Liberty," pp. 15–16; "Our Baltimore Budget," *New York Age*, 7 April 1888.

26. "Bishop Wayman Agreeably Surprised," *Baltimore Sun*, 1 May 1888, p. 4. Information about the women and the other protests are also gleaned from Brackett, *Colored People of Maryland*, pp. 79–80.

27. Alexander, "Brotherhood of Liberty," p. 16; Brackett, *Colored People of Maryland*, p. 79; Gabrielle Foreman, *Activist Sentiments: Reading Black Women in the Nineteenth Century* (Urbana: University of Illinois Press, 2009), pp. 153–154.

28. "Bishop Wayman Agreeably Surprised," *Baltimore Sun*, 1 May 1888, p. 4; Alexander, "Brotherhood of Liberty," p. 16. On Poe's tenure as dean of the Maryland law school, see David S. Bogen, "The First Integration of the University of Maryland School of Law," *Maryland Historical Magazine* 84, no. 1 (Spring 1989): 39–49.

29. Paul, "Shadow of Equality," p. 303; "Some Race Doings," *Cleveland Gazette*, 5 February 1887, p. 1; "Baltimore Colored Schools," *New York Freeman*, 20 February 1886, p. 1. For conditions in 1885, see Brackett, *Colored People of Maryland*, p. 88; Alexander, "Brotherhood of Liberty," p. 16; Paul, "Shadow of Equality," pp. 238–240. The fight for black education after the Civil War had roots reaching back into the 1860s. See Leroy Graham, *Baltimore: The Nineteenth Century Black Capital* (New York: University Press of America, 1982), pp. 208–223; Paul, "Shadow of Equality."

30. Brackett, *Colored People of Maryland*, p. 84.

31. "Colored Educational Work," *Baltimore Sun*, 6 July 1887, p. 4; Alexander, "Brotherhood of Liberty," p. 17.

32. "The School Before the War," *Afro-American*, 5 December 1914, p. 1; Brackett, *Colored People of Maryland*, 89. For the information on Davis and the numbers of black children attending private schools, see "The Colored People," *Baltimore Sun*, 27 May 1887, p. 6.

33. Brackett, *Colored People of Maryland*, p. 84; "What Baltimore City Was Like When Morgan Was Founded Here 100 Years Ago," *Afro-American*, 3 June 1967, p. 12. For the lists of graduating classes, see "The Colored Normal School," *Baltimore Sun*, 24 June 1887, p. 6; "Normal School Exhibition," *Baltimore Sun*, 17 December 1886, p. 4; "School Commencements," *Baltimore Sun*, 24 June 1887, p. 6.

34. "Colored Teachers," *Baltimore Sun*, 9 February 1886, p. 3; "The City School Board," *Baltimore Sun*, 17 February 1886, p. 3; Alexander, "Brotherhood of Liberty," pp. 16–17.

35. "A Baltimore Issue," *New York Freeman*, 12 March 1887, p. 4; "Intermarriage Discussed," *Baltimore Sun*, 16 February 1887, p. 5.

36. Bettye C. Thomas, "Public Education and Black Protest in Baltimore, 1865–1900," *Maryland Historical Magazine* 71, no. 3 (Fall 1976): 381–391; "Colored Teachers," *Baltimore Sun*, 6 April 1887, p. 6; "Colored Teachers," *Baltimore Sun*, 20 April 1887, p. 4.

37. "Colored School Teachers," *Baltimore Sun*, 4 May 1887, p. 4; "Colored Teachers," *Baltimore Sun*, 6 April 1887, p. 6; "Colored Teachers," *Baltimore Sun*, 20 April 1887, p. 4. For the meeting, see "The Colored People," *Baltimore Sun*, 27 May 1887, p. 6.

38. There were multiple teachers' associations in Maryland that met to discuss teaching. The Maryland State Progressive Teachers' Association appears to be a separate organization that had more political intent. See "Colored Teachers and the City Council," *Baltimore Sun*, 7 July 1887, p. 4; "Colored Educational Work," *Baltimore Sun*, 6 July 1887, p. 4.

39. Brackett, *Colored People of Maryland*, p. 88.

40. "They Mean Business," *Baltimore Sun*, 20 July 1887, p. 6; "Colored Teachers," *Baltimore Sun*, 20 April 1887, p. 4. Historian William George Paul contends that the threat of legal action compelled the city council to cave. However, he does not provide attribution, and the extant evidence is similarly silent about a direct correlation. See Paul, "Shadow of Equality," pp. 238–239. For the Brotherhood, see Alexander, "Brotherhood of Liberty," p. 18.

41. "The School Before the War," *Afro-American Ledger*, 5 December 1914, p. 1.

42. Brackett, *Colored People of Maryland*, p. 90; "Approved by the Mayor," *Baltimore Sun*, 4 May 1888, p. 4.

43. "The School Before the War," *Afro-American Ledger*, 5 December 1914, p. 1; "Colored High School," *Baltimore Sun*, 11 October 1888, p. 6. On the efforts of whites to block the school, see Alexander, "Brotherhood of Liberty," p. 18.

44. Alexander, "Brotherhood of Liberty," p. 19. Expenditures appear in Paul, "Shadow of Equality," p. 247. For information on the 1890s battles, see Paul, "Shadow of Equality," esp. ch. 9.

45. "Driven to Desperation," *New York Times*, 21 October 1889, p. 2. Background information also taken from "Americans Slain at Navassa," *Washington Post*, 20 September 1889, p. 7.

46. Alexander, "Brotherhood of Liberty," p. 28. The contract is reprinted in *Jones v. U.S.*, 11 S. Ct. 80 (1890).

47. "Driven to Desperation," *New York Times*, 21 October 1889, p. 2; Alexander, "Brotherhood of Liberty," p. 28.

48. Alexander, "Brotherhood of Liberty," p. 28.

49. "The Navassa Murders," *Baltimore Sun*, 27 November 1889, p. 6; "Hunted Down by Negroes," *New York Times*, 2 October 1889, p. 9; "The Defense Begins," *Baltimore Sun*, 26 November 1889, p. 6; "Story of Wm. James," *Baltimore Sun*, 21 November 1889, p. 6. See also Alexander, "Brotherhood of Liberty," p. 38; "Roby's Great Pluck," *Baltimore Sun*, 23 November 1889, p. 8.

50. "The Navassa Rioters," *Baltimore Sun*, 18 October 1889, p. 1; "That Is the Man!" *Baltimore Sun*, 22 November 1889, p. 6; Alexander, "Brotherhood of Liberty," p. 40; "Story of Wm. James," *Baltimore Sun*, 21 November 1889, p. 6.

51. Alexander, "Brotherhood of Liberty," p. 43; National Grand Tabernacle, Order of Galilean Fisherman, Baltimore, Md., "The Navassa Island Riot" (Baltimore: American Job Office, 1889), p. 6. In effect, the prosecution named one to three of the men as principals in each of the five murders; the remaining men were then charged as accessories. "Navassa Rioters Confess," *Baltimore Sun*, 8 November 1889, p. 4; "Navassa Rioters Indicted," *Washington Post*, 11 November 1889, p. 7; "The Navassa Rioters' Trial Postponed," *Baltimore Sun*, 12 November 1889, p. 5; "Indicted on Five Separate Charges," *Baltimore Sun*, 15 November 1889, p. 4. For unknown reasons, the courts consolidated the four remaining counts into two separate trials. See "Their Third Fight for Life," *Washington Post*, 6 February 1890, p. 1; "Key Guilty of Murder," *Baltimore Sun*, 3 December 1889, p. 3.

52. "Hunted Down by Negroes," *New York Times*, 2 October 1889, p. 9; "A Horrible Butchery," *Washington Post*, 2 October 1889, p. 1; "The Navassa Riot," *New Orleans Daily Picayune*, 19 October 1889, p. 2; "The Black Butchers," *Galveston Daily News*, 11 October 1889, p. 1; "Mob Without Mercy," *Milwaukee Daily Journal*, 1 October 1889, p. 4; "Who the Butchered Men Were," *Baltimore Sun*, 11 October 1889, p. 1; "The Navassa Rioters," *Baltimore Sun*, 18 October 1889, p. 1.

53. "Untitled," *(Detroit) Plaindealer*, 8 November 1889, p. 4; "Untitled," *Cleveland Gazette*, 9 November 1889, p. 2; "The Race's Doings," *Cleveland Gazette*, 16 November 1889, p. 1; "Untitled," *(Detroit) Plaindealer*, 4 October 1889, p. 4; "The Navassa Riot," *(Detroit) Plaindealer*, 25 October 1889, p. 6.

54. "Driven to Desperation," *New York Times*, 21 October 1889, p. 2; Alexander, "Brotherhood of Liberty," pp. 23–43.

55. "Saturday's City News," *Baltimore Sun*, 4 November 1889, p. 6; "Navassa Rioters Confess," *Baltimore Sun*, 8 November 1889, p. 4. For a history of the dispute over the island, see *Jones v. U.S.*, 11 S. Ct. 80 (1890). For the defense team, see "All Said 'Not Guilty,'" *Baltimore Sun*, 16 November 1889, p. 5.

56. "Untitled," *Washington Bee*, 14 December 1889, p. 2; "The Baltimore Letter," *Indianapolis Freeman*, 12 July 1890, p. 1. For other efforts, see "To Relieve Colored People," *Washington Post*, 25 October 1889, p. 2; "Aid for the Negroes from Navassa," *Washington Post*, 1 November 1889, p. 2; "Central Bureau of Relief," *Washington Post*, 8 November 1889, p. 4; "Central Bureau of Relief," *Washington Post*, 12 November 1889, p. 2; "The Baltimore Federation of Labor," *Baltimore Sun*, 23 April 1891, p. 6.

57. For conditions precipitating the riot, see "The Navassa Murders," *Baltimore Sun*, 27 November 1889, p. 6.

58. "Navassa Rioters Confess," *Baltimore Sun*, 8 November 1889, p. 4; "Story of Wm. James," *Baltimore Sun*, 21 November 1889, p. 6; "The Defense Begins," *Baltimore Sun*, 26 November 1889, p. 6.

59. Alexander, "Brotherhood of Liberty," p. 25; National Grand Tabernacle, Order of Galilean Fisherman, "The Navassa Island Riot," pp. 12–13; "Saturday's City News," *Baltimore Sun*, 23 December 1889, p. 4.

60. "Fate of Navassa Rioters," *Baltimore Sun*, 21 February 1890, p. 5; Alexander, "Brotherhood of Liberty," p. 26.

61. "Navassa Rioters Confess," *Baltimore Sun*, 8 November 1889, p. 4; "To Relieve Colored People," *Washington Post*, 25 October 1889, p. 2; "Aid for the Negroes from Navassa," *Washington Post*, 1 November 1889, p. 2; "Central Bureau of Relief," *Washington Post*, 8 November 1889, p. 4; "Central Bureau of Relief," *Washington Post*, 12 November 1889, p. 2.

62. "The Navassa Trials," *Baltimore Sun*, 30 October 1890, p. 6; "Navassa Rioters to Hang," *Baltimore Sun*, 25 November 1890, p. 4. On the efforts to obtain a presidential pardon, see Alexander, "Brotherhood of Liberty," pp. 36–37; "An Appeal from Bishop Wayman," *Washington Post*, 2 April 1891, p. 11. For Waring's quotation, see "The Navassa Murder Cases," *New York Age*, 19 April 1890, p. 4.

63. "An Historical Event," *New York Age*, 15 November 1890, p. 2.

64. "To Relieve Colored People," *Washington Post*, 25 October 1889, p. 2. The group soon decided to support the Navassa defendants. See "Aid for the Negroes from Navassa," *Washington Post*, 1 November 1889, p. 2; "Central Bureau of Relief," *Washington Post*, 8 November 1889, p. 4; "Central Bureau of Relief," *Washington Post*, 12 November 1889, p. 2; "The Baltimore Federation of Labor," *Baltimore Sun*, 23 April 1891, p. 6.

65. "A Good Case for Clemency," *Washington Post*, 17 March 1891, p. 4.

66. The jurors and Ensor's letter are mentioned in Alexander, "Brotherhood of Liberty," pp. 37–41, and "The Baltimore Federation of Labor," *Baltimore Sun*, 23 April 1891, p. 6.

67. "Imprisonment for Life," *Washington Post*, 19 May 1891, p. 7.

68. "Slaves Under Our Flag," *New York Times*, 14 May 1891, p. 9. See also "All Quiet at Navassa," *New York Times*, 1 July 1891, p. 9; "They Would Not Eat Salt Horse," *Chicago Daily Tribune*, 12 July 1891, p. 1; "Tortured, Starved, and Defrauded," *Chicago Daily Tribune*, 15 July 1891, p. 7; "Outrages on Navassa Island," *Washington Post*, 6 January 1885, p. 13.

69. For more background information on the women, see Foreman, *Activist Sentiments*, pp. 151–152. See also Alexander, "Brotherhood of Liberty," pp. 4, 43–44.

70. "Colored Men Divided," *Baltimore Sun*, 29 October 1891, p. 6; Paul, "Shadow of Equality," pp. 253–254.

71. Alexander, "Brotherhood of Liberty," pp. 43–44.

72. "Death Comes to Harry S. Cummings," *Afro-American*, 8 September 1917, p. 1. Cummings was listed as a contributor in Alexander, "Brotherhood of Liberty," p. 43.

73. For information on the publishing history of the *Afro-American*, see Hayward Farrar, *The Baltimore* Afro-American, *1892–1950* (Westport, CT: Greenwood, 1998).

74. Joseph S. Davis, "A Baltimore Lawyer's View of the Case," *New York Freeman*, 16 July 1887, p. 1. I found this letter through Carle, *Defining the Struggle*, p. 56.

Chapter 4

1. "Is Gorman Night," *Baltimore Sun*, 31 October 1903, p. 12; "Senator Gorman's Speech," *Baltimore Sun*, 31 October 1903, p. 12.

2. Historians have recently begun to expand the chronology of the Reconstruction era beyond 1877. See, for instance, Heather Cox Richardson, *West from Appomattox: The Reconstruction of America After the Civil War* (New Haven, CT: Yale University Press, 2008); Steven Hahn, *A Nation Under Our Feet: Black Political Struggles in the Rural South from Slavery to the Great Migration* (Cambridge, MA: Belknap Press, 2003).

3. The history of the carceral state has received renewed attention in recent years. In 2015 the *Journal of American History* published an issue dedicated to the building of the carceral state (vol. 102, no. 1). Other historians have produced book-length examinations. See especially Khalil Gibran Muhammad, *The Condemnation of Blackness: Race, Crime, and the Making of Modern Urban America* (Cambridge, MA: Harvard University Press, 2010); Rebecca M. McLennan, *The Crisis of Imprisonment: Protest, Politics, and the Making of the American Penal State, 1776–1941* (Cambridge: Cambridge University Press, 2008). For the late twentieth and early twenty-first centuries, see Michelle Alexander, *The New Jim Crow: Mass Incarceration in the Age of Color Blindness* (New York: New Press, 2012); Heather Ann Thompson, *Blood in the Water: The Attica Prison Uprising of 1971 and Its Legacy* (New York: Vintage, 2017). On Reconstruction, see Eric Foner, *Reconstruction: America's Unfinished Revolution, 1863–1877* (New York: Harper Perennial Modern Classics, 2014). For white supremacy as an ongoing reactive process, see Michael Perman, *Struggle for Mastery: Disfranchisement in the South, 1888–1908* (Chapel Hill: University of North Carolina Press, 2001); Jane Dailey, Glenda Elizabeth Gilmore, and Bryant Simon, eds., *Jumpin' Jim Crow: Southern Politics from Civil War to Civil Rights* (Princeton, NJ: Princeton University Press, 2000).

4. Ideas about black criminality long circulated in the city. See Richard Paul Fuke, *Imperfect Equality: African Americans and the Confines of White Racial Attitudes in Post-Emancipation Maryland* (New York: Fordham University Press, 1999), p. 127; Adam Malka, *The Men of Mobtown: Policing Baltimore in the Age of Slavery and Emancipation* (Chapel Hill: University of North Carolina Press, 2018). On the wider urban North, see Muhammad, *Condemnation of Blackness*.

5. "Young Ladies Insulted," *Baltimore Sun*, 30 March 1898, p. 10; "'Sporty Niggers,'" *Baltimore Sun*, 31 March 1898, p. 10.

6. Carroll D. Wright, *The Slums of Baltimore, Chicago, New York, and Philadelphia* (Washington, DC: Government Printing Office, 1894), pp. 15–17.

7. H. L. Mencken, *Newspaper Days* (Baltimore: Johns Hopkins University Press, 2006), pp. 21–23; "Justice Eugene Grannan: The Man and His Work," *Baltimore Sun*, 18 August 1907, p. 13; "Tenderloin Justice as Dan Loden Dispenses It," *Baltimore Sun*, 28 October 1906, p. 14.

8. *The New Charter of Baltimore City*, rev. ed. (Baltimore: Press of the Sun Printing Office, 1900), p. 246. For a list of crimes tried in the police courts, see Poe, *Supplement to the Code of Public General Laws of Maryland, 1898* (Baltimore: King Brothers, 1898), pp. 145–149.

9. "Aging Sergeant Sad at Closing," *Baltimore Sun*, 9 September 1951, p. 30; "Tenderloin Justice as Dan Loden Dispenses It," *Baltimore Sun*, 28 October 1906, p. 14.

10. "Justice Eugene Grannan: The Man and His Work," *Baltimore Sun*, 18 August 1907, p. 13.

11. *New Charter of Baltimore City*, p. 246.

12. "'Sporty Niggers,'" *Baltimore Sun*, 31 March 1898, p. 10.

13. "Negro Rowdyism," *Baltimore Sun*, 31 March 1898, p. 4; "Agree with Justice Grannan," *Baltimore Sun*, 14 April 1898, p. 7.

14. Quotation taken from "Let 'Er Zip!" *Baltimore World*, 13 April 1898, p. 1. For other stories, see "Threw a Brick," *Baltimore World*, 12 April 1898, p. 1; "City's Safety," *Baltimore World*, 14 April 1898, p. 1; "Tough Crowd," *Baltimore World*, 18 April 1898, p. 1.

15. See, for instance, "The Police Know It," *Baltimore News*, 4 April 1898, p. 12; "Rampant Rowdyism," *Baltimore News*, 12 April 1898, p. 12; "Negroes Crowd the Court," *Baltimore News*, 13 April 1898, p. 12.

16. For the sentencing guideline, see Poe, *Supplement*, p. 159. On Brown's conviction, see "Negro Rowdyism," *Baltimore Sun*, 15 April 1898, p. 10.

17. "Recent Rowdyism," *Baltimore News*, 14 April 1898, p. 12. Also see letters published in the *Baltimore News* between 14 and 16 April 1898. For the *Sun*, see "Agree with Justice Grannan," *Baltimore Sun*, 14 April 1898, p. 7; "A Police Inquiry," *Baltimore Sun*, 16 April 1898, p. 12; "Negro Rowdyism Again," *Baltimore Sun*, 14 April 1898, p. 4; "'Sporty Niggers,'" *Baltimore Sun*, 31 March 1898, p. 10; "A Police Inquiry," *Baltimore Sun*, 16 April 1898, p. 12; "Poverty and Crime," *Baltimore Sun*, 9 August 1898, p. 10; "Responsibility for Rowdyism," *Baltimore Sun*, 18 April 1898, p. 4. On the lack of statistics, see "Need for Repression of Crime," *Baltimore Sun*, 9 September 1898, p. 4.

18. "A Police Inquiry," *Baltimore Sun*, 16 April 1898, p. 2; "Is for Vindication," *Baltimore News*, 15 April 1898, p. 12. The *Baltimore World* presented the most detailed accounting of the eyewitness testimony. See "No Charges to Be Made," *Baltimore World*, 15 April 1898, p. 1.

19. "A Police Inquiry," *Baltimore Sun*, 16 April 1898, p. 2; W. E. B. DuBois, *Some Notes on Negro Crime, Particularly in Georgia* (Atlanta: Atlanta University Press, 1904), pp. 23–25.

20. "No Charges to Be Made," *Baltimore World*, 15 April 1898, p. 1.

21. "An Inquiry into Negro Rowdyism," *Baltimore American*, 16 April 1898.

22. "The Race Cry," *Baltimore World*, 13 April 1899.

23. For a complete account of the Danville race riot, see Jane Dailey, *Before Jim Crow: The Politics of Race in Postemancipation Virginia* (Chapel Hill: University of North Carolina Press, 2000). Street altercations also preceded the Wilmington race riot. See Glenda Elizabeth Gilmore, *Gender and Jim Crow: Women and the Politics of White Supremacy in North Carolina, 1896–1920* (Chapel Hill: University of North Carolina Press, 1996).

24. "No Charges to Be Made," *Baltimore World*, 15 April 1898, p. 1; "More Disorderly Negroes," *Baltimore News*, 19 April 1898, p. 6; "Rampant Rowdyism," *Baltimore News*, 12 April

1898, p. 12; "Negroes Crowd the Court," *Baltimore News*, 13 April 1898, p. 12. For examinations of everyday resistance, see James C. Scott, *Weapons of the Weak: Everyday Forms of Peasant Resistance* (New Haven, CT: Yale University Press, 1987); Robin D. G. Kelley, " 'We Are Not What We Seem': Rethinking Black Working-Class Opposition in the Jim Crow South," *Journal of American History* 80, no. 1 (June 1993): 75–112.

25. "Rowdyism in Baltimore," *Baltimore News*, 19 April 1898, p. 6; "Is Literally True," *Baltimore News*, 20 April 1898, p. 6; "If the Police Were Not Afraid," *Baltimore News*, 20 April 1898, p. 6.

26. "No Charges to Be Made," *Baltimore World*, 15 April 1898, p. 1; "Responsibility for Rowdyism," *Baltimore Sun*, 18 April 1898, p. 4; "An Instant Remedy Wanted for the Black Plague," *Baltimore Sun*, 18 May 1898, p. 4; "Recent Rowdyism," *Baltimore News*, 14 April 1898, p. 12. Also see letters published in the *Baltimore News* between 14 and 16 April 1898. On Heddinger, see "A Police Inquiry," *Baltimore Sun*, 16 April 1898, p. 12.

27. "A Serious Condition," *Baltimore Sun*, 3 November 1898, p. 1.

28. Guy Carleton Lee, "Evils of Negro Rule," *Baltimore Sun*, 16 November 1898, p. 1. See also Guy Carleton Lee, "The Northern Negro," *Baltimore Sun*, 7 November 1898, p. 7; Guy Carleton Lee, "The Negro Problem," *Baltimore Sun*, 12 November 1898, p. 2; Guy Carleton Lee, "Placing the Blame," *Baltimore Sun*, 17 November 1898, p. 1.

29. "Lilly Whiteism at the Bottom of It," *Afro-American Ledger*, 23 April 1898, p. 2.

30. "A Colored Man's Views," *Baltimore News*, 15 April 1898, p. 12.

31. For background on the election and the Democratic Ring, see Robert J. Brugger, *Maryland, a Middle Temperament: 1634–1980* (Baltimore: Johns Hopkins University Press, 1988), esp. ch. 8; James B. Crooks, *Politics and Progress: The Rise of Urban Progressivism in Baltimore 1895 to 1911* (Baton Rouge: Louisiana State University Press, 1968), esp. ch. 2. On the origins and usage of the phrase "negro domination," see Perman, *Struggle for Mastery*, pp. 24–31.

32. "Cheers for the Sun," *Baltimore Sun*, 18 April 1899, p. 12. A similar phenomenon occurred throughout this period in other locales. See Muhammad, *Condemnation of Blackness*. This suggests, as historian Kevin Mumford argues, that "Progressivism ought to be understood as a deeply racial movement." See Kevin J. Mumford, *Interzones: Black/White Sex Districts in Chicago and New York in the Early Twentieth Century* (New York: Columbia University Press, 1997), pp. xxii–xxiii.

33. "A Mighty Host," *Baltimore Sun*, 6 April 1899, p. 10; "Ladies Interested," *Baltimore Sun*, 7 April 1899, p. 10; "A Great Meeting," *Baltimore Sun*, 14 April 1899, p. 10; "Negro Domination," *Baltimore Sun*, 20 April 1899, p. 10.

34. On Miles, see "A Sea of Faces," *Baltimore Sun*, 21 April 1899, p. 10; Clayton Colman Hall, ed., *Baltimore: Its History and Its People*, vol. 3 (New York: Lewis Historical Publishing Company, 1912), p. 719; "Malster and the Negroes," *Baltimore Sun*, 21 April 1899, p. 10; "Mr. Hayes' Neighbors," *Baltimore Sun*, 14 March 1899, p. 10; "Encouraged Rowdyism," *Baltimore Sun*, 20 April 1899, p. 10; "Wants the Independents," *Baltimore Sun*, 25 April 1899, p. 7.

35. "How Negro Rowdy Cases Are Made Up by the Sunpaper in Order to Keep Up the Race War Cry," *Baltimore Sun*, 26 April 1899, p. 1.

36. "Colored Ministers," *Baltimore Sun*, 29 April 1899, p. 1.

37. "The Mayor Elect," *Afro-American Ledger*, 6 May 1899, p. 2.

38. "The Republican Record," *Baltimore Sun*, 31 October 1899, p. 2.

39. "Col. Smith in Harford," *Baltimore Sun*, 1 November 1899, p. 10; "Col. Smith and the Negro," *Afro-American Ledger*, 30 September 1899, p. 2.

40. "A. P. Gorman Letter," 31 October 1931, pp. 2–3, Arthur Pue Gorman Papers, Maryland Historical Society, Baltimore.

41. Harvey Johnson, "The White Man's Failure in Government" (Baltimore: Press of Afro-American Co., 1900), p. 6, in Daniel A. P. Murray Pamphlet Collection, Library of Congress, Washington, DC.

42. "White Gentleman—Black Criminal," *Afro-American Ledger*, 10 November 1906, p. 4.

43. "Exercising Patience," *Afro-American Ledger*, 13 August 1904, p. 4.

44. "Exercising Patience," *Afro-American Ledger*, 13 August 1904, p. 4; J. H. N. Waring, "Some Causes of Criminality Among Colored People," *Charities*, 7 October 1905, p. 47; "The Police Department and the Negroes," *Afro-American Ledger*, 31 May 1902, p. 4.

45. "Negro Rowdyism," *Baltimore Sun*, 24 June 1899, p. 12; Poe, *Supplement*, p. 159; "Say Negro Spoke to Them," *Baltimore Sun*, 13 February 1905, p. 12.

46. "A Negro Insults Miss Sarah Owens," *Baltimore Sun*, 4 May 1898, p. 12; "Negro Rowdyism Again," *Baltimore Sun*, 14 April 1898, p. 4; "Agree with Justice Grannan," *Baltimore Sun*, 14 April 1898, p. 7; "Adopts Sterner Method," *Baltimore Sun*, 18 November 1907, p. 14; "Negro Rowdyism," *Baltimore Sun*, 15 April 1898, p. 10; "A Police Inquiry," *Baltimore Sun*, 16 April 1898, p. 12; "Riotous Negroes," *Baltimore Sun*, 26 May 1898, p. 10.

47. "The Grand Jury's Report," *Afro-American Ledger*, 5 September 1908, p. 5.

48. "Negroes' Heavy Sentences," *Baltimore Sun*, 15 October 1904, p. 7; "Justice Loden Is Nonplussed," *Baltimore Sun*, 25 July 1907, p. 9; "Adopts Sterner Method," *Baltimore Sun*, 18 November 1907, p. 14; "To Repress Negro Crime," *Baltimore Sun*, 15 November 1907, p. 9. For Llewellyn, see " '$25' Llewellyn Takes a Day Off," *Baltimore News*, 17 October 1909, p. 14.

49. "Gets Ten-Year Sentence," *Baltimore Sun*, 30 July 1908, p. 8.

50. "Opposes Long Jail Terms," *Baltimore Sun*, 10 July 1909, p. 7.

51. "Manufacturing Criminals," *Afro-American Ledger*, 23 September 1906, p. 4; Eugene O'Dunne, *Report of Maryland Penitentiary Penal Commission* [Baltimore, 1913]), pp. 311–312, Maryland Historical Society; W. E. B. DuBois, *The Philadelphia Negro: A Social Study* (New York: Schocken, 1899).

52. Booker T. Washington, "Law and Order and the Negro," *Outlook* 93 (September–December 1909): 548.

53. James H. N. Waring, "Work of the Colored Law and Order League: Baltimore, MD" (Cheney, PA: Committee of Twelve for the Advancement of the Interests of the Negro Race), pp. 27–28; Washington, "Law and Order and the Negro," pp. 549–550. Quotations reprinted in the "Work of the Colored Law and Order League," p. 28.

54. "Baltimore Negroes Are in the Thrall of Cocaine," *Baltimore Sun*, 16 December 1906, p. 15.

55. "Four Suspended," *Baltimore Sun*, 27 May 1908, p. 12; "Dr. Dull Again Accused," *Baltimore Sun*, 28 May 1908, p. 14.

56. "Abrupt Close to the Cocaine Investigation," *Baltimore News*, 9 June 1908.

57. "The 'Cocaine Pot' Challenges the Police," *Baltimore World*, 10 June 1908.

58. "War to Be Waged on Cocaine's Sale," *Baltimore News*, 9 June 1908, p. 1; " 'The Pot' Frothing Over," *Baltimore World*, 9 June 1908; "Severe on 'Pot' and 'Jungle,' " *Baltimore Sun*, 10 June 1908, p. 14.

59. "The Police Department and Negroes," *Afro-American Ledger*, 31 May 1902, p. 4. See also "Let the Law Take Its Course," *Afro-American Ledger*, 8 August 1903, p. 4.

60. See "Still Harping on the Negro," *Afro-American Ledger,* 25 July 1908, p. 4; "Hiding Criminals," *Afro-American Ledger,* 29 December 1906, p. 4; "White Folks' Way of Doing Things," *Afro-American Ledger,* 8 August 1908, p. 4; "Judge Us by Our Best," *Afro-American Ledger,* 23 September 1906, p. 4.

61. "An Instant Remedy Wanted for the Black Plague," *Baltimore Sun,* 18 May 1898, p. 4.

62. "Negro Rowdyism," *Baltimore Sun,* 31 March 1898, p. 4; "Agree with Justice Grannan," *Baltimore Sun,* 14 April 1898, p. 7; "Negro Rowdyism," *Baltimore Sun,* 15 April 1898, p. 10. For Grannan's comments, see "Disorder Rampant," *Baltimore News,* 13 April 1898, p. 12. See Muhammad, *Condemnation of Blackness.*

63. "Exercising Patience," *Afro-American Ledger,* 13 August 1904, p. 4.

64. "Colored Patriots and the Police Court," *Afro-American Ledger,* 11 July 1903, p. 4; "White Gentleman—Black Criminal," *Afro-American Ledger,* 10 November 1906, p. 4; "A Brutal Policeman," *Afro-American Ledger,* 30 June 1906, p. 4; "That Police Drag Net," *Afro-American Ledger,* 17 April 1909, p. 4.

65. "Cheltenham Again," *Afro-American Ledger,* 25 August 1901, p. 4; "The Reformatory for Colored Boys," *Afro-American Ledger,* 17 May 1902, p. 4.

66. "489 Prisoners," *Baltimore Sun,* 4 January 1897, p. 10; "Scurvy in Prison," *Baltimore Sun,* 14 July 1900, p. 8.

67. See "Peril at Jessup," *Baltimore Sun,* 16 December 1911, p. 14; "Blame Economy at 'Cut,'" *Baltimore Sun,* 17 December 1911, p. 9. For Whitin, see "Would Clean Up Cut," *Baltimore Sun,* 29 December 1911, p. 12; "A Maryland Demand for Cleaning Up," *Journal of the Switchmen's Union* 14 (July 1912): 421.

68. O'Dunne, *Report of Maryland Penitentiary Penal Commission,* 4 February 1913, pp. 15–16, 21.

69. "Indefinite Sentences," *Baltimore Sun,* 14 January 1906, p. 16.

70. O'Dunne, *Report of Maryland Penitentiary Penal Commission,* pp. 49, 52–55, 59, 61.

71. "Justice Llewellyn Cuts Off One Vote Against His Party," *Baltimore News,* 15 October 1909, p. 1; "Llewellyn Sends More Negroes Up; They'll Not Vote," *Baltimore News,* 16 October 1909, p. 1.

72. "Negro White May Yet Get Freedom," *Baltimore News,* 18 October 1909, p. 12; "Justice Llewellyn Cuts Off One Vote Against His Party," *Baltimore News,* 15 October 1909, p. 1; "Llewellyn Sends More Negroes Up; They'll Not Vote," *Baltimore News,* 16 October 1909, p. 1.

73. "Justice Llewellyn Cuts Off One Vote Against His Party," *Baltimore News,* 15 October 1909, p. 1; "Llewellyn Sends More Negroes Up; They'll Not Vote," *Baltimore News,* 16 October 1909, p. 1.

74. "Justice Llewellyn Cuts Off One Vote Against His Party," *Baltimore News,* 15 October 1909, p. 1; "Llewellyn Sends More Negroes Up; They'll Not Vote," *Baltimore News,* 16 October 1909, p. 1.

75. "White Set Free, Then Rearrested," *Baltimore News,* 29 October 1909; "Negro White Free Second Time," *Baltimore News,* 1 November 1909, p. 10.

76. "Keep Out," *Afro-American Ledger,* 23 October 1909, p. 7.

Chapter 5

1. "Shall We Surrender the Franchise," *Afro-American Ledger,* 23 January 1904, p. 4.

2. Many historians have examined Maryland's disfranchisement movement, but few have foregrounded black resistance. For political histories, see James B. Crooks, *Politics and Progress: The Rise of Urban Progressivism in Baltimore, 1895 to 1911* (Baton Rouge: Louisiana State

University Press, 1968); Robert J. Brugger, *Maryland, A Middle Temperament: 1634–1980* (Baltimore: Johns Hopkins University Press, 1988). For disfranchisement and Baltimore's immigrant communities, see Gordon H. Shufelt, "Jim Crow Among Strangers: The Growth of Baltimore's Little Italy and Maryland's Disfranchisement Campaigns," *Journal of American Ethnic History* 19, no. 4 (Summer 2004): 49–78. For a notable exception, see Margaret L. Calcott, *The Negro in Maryland Politics, 1870–1912* (Baltimore: Johns Hopkins University Press, 1969).

3. "Niagara Movement Declaration of Principles, 1905," W. E. B. DuBois Papers (MS 312), Special Collections and University Archives, University of Massachusetts Amherst Libraries (hereafter DuBois Papers). For early examinations of African American civil rights organizations, see Shawn Leigh Alexander, *An Army of Lions: The Civil Rights Struggle Before the NAACP* (Philadelphia: University of Pennsylvania Press, 2012); Susan D. Carle, *Defining the Struggle: National Organizing for Racial Justice, 1880–1915* (New York: Oxford University Press, 2013).

4. Historians have frequently described the years between the 1880s and World War I as a period of accommodation. Recently, however, scholars have begun to question these assumptions, telling a story of vigorous resistance. Evelyn Brooks Higginbotham, *Righteous Discontent: The Women's Movement in the Black Baptist Church, 1880–1920* (Cambridge, MA: Harvard University Press, 1994); Paul Ortiz, *Emancipation Betrayed: The Hidden History of Black Organizing and White Violence in Florida from Reconstruction to the Bloody Election of 1920* (Berkeley: University of California Press, 2006); Glenda Elizabeth Gilmore, *Gender and Jim Crow: Women and the Politics of White Supremacy in North Carolina, 1896–1920* (Chapel Hill: University of North Carolina Press, 1996); Blair L. M. Kelley, *Right to Ride: Streetcar Boycotts and African American Citizenship in the Era of* Plessy v. Ferguson (Chapel Hill: University of North Carolina Press, 2010). For organization histories, see Alexander, *Army of Lions*; Carle, *Defining the Struggle*.

5. For a national look at disfranchisement, see Michael Perman, *Struggle for Mastery: Disfranchisement in the South, 1888–1908* (Chapel Hill: University of North Carolina Press, 2001). For Maryland and Baltimore specifically, see Crooks, *Politics and Progress*; Brugger, *Maryland*; Calcott, *Negro in Maryland Politics*.

6. "'A Citizens' Movement,'" *Baltimore Sun*, 27 April 1899, p. 10.

7. Pippa Holloway, "'A Chicken-Stealer Shall Lose His Vote': Disfranchisement for Larceny in the South, 1874–1890," *Journal of Southern History* 75, no. 4 (November 2009): 931–962. For an examination of the fears of "negro domination," see Perman, *Struggle for Mastery*, pp. 24–31.

8. "Not Doing Much Now," *Afro-American Ledger*, 12 October 1901, p. 4; "Keep Away from the Police Stations," *Afro-American Ledger*, 2 October 1909, p. 4. See also "Will They Stand It," *Afro-American Ledger*, 28 September 1901, p. 4. For Llewellyn, see "Llewellyn Sends More Negroes Up; They'll Not Vote," *Baltimore News*, 16 October 1909, p. 1; "'25' Llewellyn Takes a Day Off," *Baltimore News*, 17 October 1909, p. 14.

9. Crooks, *Politics and Progress*, pp. 56–57. For the Reform League's report, see Baltimore Reform League, "Reject the Amendment," Papers of the Baltimore Reform League, Maryland Historical Society, Baltimore.

10. For Warfield's comments, see "Mr. Warfield Accepts," *Baltimore Sun*, 27 September 1903, p. 14.

11. Perman, *Struggle for Mastery*, esp. ch. 2.

12. Proceedings of the House, 1904, *Journal of Proceedings* (Annapolis: Wm. J. Dulany Co., State Printers, 1904), pp. 5–6. See also Frank Richardson Kent, *The Story of Maryland Politics* (Baltimore: Thomas & Evans Printing Co., 1911), p. 330.

13. "To Eliminate the Negro," *Baltimore Sun*, 4 January 1907, p. 7; Arthur Pue Gorman, "A. P. Gorman Diary," 1–16 January 1904, Maryland Historical Society, Baltimore. For Poe's objections, see Kent, *Story of Maryland Politics*, pp. 331–332. For a general discussion of the Poe Amendment, see Crooks, *Politics and Progress*, pp. 59, 62–65; Jeffrey R. Brackett, *Notes on the Progress of the Colored People of Maryland Since the War: A Supplement to the Negro in Maryland: A Study of the Institution of Slavery* (Baltimore: John Murphy & Co., Printers, 1890), pp. 16–17; Perman, *Struggle for Mastery*, pp. 231–234.

14. "Not the Negro but His Vote," *Afro-American Ledger*, 9 September 1899, p. 2; "A Republican Split Is Narrowly Averted," *Baltimore Sunday Herald*, 10 September 1905.

15. "The Colored Voter's Side," *Baltimore Sun*, 26 January 1901, p. 12.

16. According to the 1880 census, at least a thousand African Americans lived in each of the twenty wards of the city with the exceptions of the First, Second, Fourth, and Seventeenth. See J. Thomas Scharf, A.M., *History of Baltimore City and County from the Earliest Period to the Present Day: Including Biographical Sketches of Representative Men* (Philadelphia: Louis H. Everts, 1881), p. 185.

17. Population information taken from "Census: Population of Baltimore City, November 1910," Baltimore Police Department, 28 November 1910, Baltimore City Archives. Church locations were found by cross-referencing city directories with a map of the city. See *Baltimore City Directory* (Baltimore: R. L. Polk & Company, 1905), and Map of Baltimore, 1905, Johns Hopkins University, http://jhir.library.jhu.edu/handle/1774.2/32606.

18. "Maryland's Backward Step," *Afro-American Ledger*, 5 March 1904, p. 1.

19. "The Negro Press," *Afro-American Ledger*, 15 February 1902, p. 4; Karen Olson, "Old West Baltimore," in Elizabeth Fee, Linda Shopes, and Linda Zeidman, eds., *The Baltimore Book: New Views of Local History* (Philadelphia: Temple University Press, 1991), p. 67. For a broad history of the paper, see Hayward Farrar, *The Baltimore Afro-American: 1892–1950* (Westport, CT: Greenwood Press, 1998).

20. "The Suffrage Matter," *Afro-American Ledger*, 3 June 1905, p. 4; "The Duty of the Hour," *Afro-American Ledger*, 16 September 1905, p. 3; "The Suffrage Matter," *Afro-American Ledger*, 3 June 1905, p. 4. For Alexander, see W. M. Alexander, "The Forum: Our Suffrage Question," *Afro-American Ledger*, 6 February 1904, p. 4; W. M. Alexander, "The Suffrage League of Maryland," *Afro-American Ledger*, 27 May 1904, p. 4.

21. "The State of Maryland," *Afro-American Ledger*, 12 March 1904, p. 1; "The State of Maryland," *Afro-American Ledger*, 30 January 1904, p. 1; "Suffrage League State Conference," *Afro-American Ledger*, 10 June 1905, p. 4.

22. W. Alexander, "Our Suffrage League," *Afro-American Ledger*, 11 June 1904, p. 4; "The Suffrage League," *Afro-American Ledger*, 30 July 1904, p. 8. For the *Afro-American*'s editorial, see "Excursions," *Afro-American Ledger*, 23 April 1904, p. 4. For Hawkins's plea, see W. Ashbie Hawkins, "Special Notice," *Afro-American Ledger*, 16 July 1904, p. 4.

23. "The State of Maryland," *Afro-American Ledger*, 2 July 1904, p. 1; "James Crow," *Afro-American Ledger*, 16 July 1904, p. 4; "Rev. Hughes Feels Hurt," *Afro-American Ledger*, 27 August 1904, p. 4; "Excursion Business Dull," *Afro-American Ledger*, 20 August 1904, p. 8. For

an example of the advertisement, see "To Colored Excursionists to Round Bay," *Afro-American Ledger*, 16 July 1904, p. 8.

24. "The Governor Says No!" *Baltimore Sun*, 23 November 1904, p. 1; "Ready to Be Filed," *Baltimore Sun*, 30 November 1904, p. 12; "People to Decide," *Baltimore Sun*, 24 March 1905, p. 1.

25. Niagara Movement (Organization), "Report on the Committee on Organization of the Niagara Movement, ca. 1905," and "Niagara Movement Declaration of Principles, 1905," DuBois Papers.

26. Niagara Movement (Organization), "Niagara Movement First Annual Meeting Attendance List, ca. 1905," DuBois Papers. For membership, see George H. Jackson, "Niagara Movement List of Dues Paid by Member, ca. August 15, 1906," and "Niagara Movement 1906 Treasurer's Report, ca. August 18, 1906," DuBois Papers. For the *Afro-American*'s sentiments, see "The Niagara Movement," *Afro-American Ledger*, 29 July 1905, p. 4.

27. "Niagara Movement Declaration of Principles, 1905," DuBois Papers.

28. "Carry Your Politics into Your Business," *Afro-American Ledger*, 12 August 1905, p. 4.

29. "Negro Women Play a Part in Campaign," *Baltimore Sunday Herald*, 5 November 1905, p. 1.

30. "Negro Women Play a Part in Campaign," *Baltimore Sunday Herald*, 5 November 1905, p. 1. Also see: "Untitled," *Afro-American Ledger*, 11 November 1905, p. 4; "Untitled," *Afro-American Ledger*, 28 October 1905, p. 4.

31. "They Maul the Amendment," *Baltimore Sun*, 24 October 1905, p. 12; "Pray De Good Lawd for Gorman to Die," *Baltimore World*, 24 October 1905, pp. 1, 10.

32. "Letter to the Editor," *Afro-American Ledger*, 14 October 1905, p. 4; "Special Notice," *Afro-American Ledger*, 3 June 1905, p. 4. For a thorough examination of the Niagara Movement and women, see Carle, *Defining the Struggle*.

33. W. M. Alexander, "The Suffrage League of Maryland," *Afro-American Ledger*, 27 May 1905, p. 4; "The Suffrage League of Maryland," *Afro-American Ledger*, 22 July 1905, p. 8.

34. "Registration Books Closed," *Baltimore Sun*, 11 October 1905, p. 12; "Democrats Suspicious," *Baltimore Sun*, 12 October 1905, p. 7. On Alexander's thoughts, see W. Alexander, "Letter to the Editor," *Afro-American Ledger*, 14 October 1905, p. 4.

35. "Registration Books Closed," *Baltimore Sun*, 11 October 1905, p. 12; "119,691 May Vote Nov. 7," *Baltimore Sun*, 22 October 1905, p. 16; "White 102,005 Colored 17,686," *Baltimore American*, 22 October 1905, p. 8.

36. "Foreign-Born Voters Protest," *Baltimore American*, 15 October 1905, p. 8. See Crooks, *Politics and Progress*, pp. 61–62. For others opposed to the amendment, see "Poe's Plan Under Fire," *Baltimore American*, 1 November 1905, p. 16; "Crescent Club Opposes," *Baltimore Sun*, 22 July 1905, p. 12; "Freedom of Speech Throttled," *Baltimore Sun*, 28 September 1905, p. 1.

37. Isidor Rayner, "The Constitutional Amendment," *Baltimore Sun*, 18 October 1905, p. 1.

38. "Baltimore, October 28, 1905," *Afro-American Ledger*, 28 October 1905, p. 4; "Untitled," *Afro-American Ledger*, 28 October 1905, p. 4; "Untitled," *Afro-American Ledger*, November 1905, p. 4; "The Last Chance," *Afro-American Ledger*, 4 November 1905, p. 4.

39. "Election Results," *Baltimore Sun*, 27 November 1905, p. 10.

40. "How Amendment Met Its Defeat," *Baltimore American*, 9 November 1905, p. 16.

41. "Republicans in a Joyful Mood," *Baltimore American*, 9 November 1905, p. 16; "Maryland Beats Poe Amendment," *Philadelphia Inquirer*, 8 November 1905, p. 4; "Untitled," *Afro-American Ledger*, 18 November 1905, p. 4.

42. "'Twas a Glorious Victory," *Afro-American Ledger*, 11 November 1905, p. 1; "The Vanished Year," *Voice of the Negro* 3, no. 1 (January 1906): 24; "'Maryland, My Maryland,'" *Voice of the Negro* 2, no. 12 (December 1905): 33.

43. "Maryland's Grapple with the Demagogue," *Voice of the Negro* 2, no. 11 (November 1905): 748; "Death of Senator Gorman," *Baltimore Sun*, 5 June 1906, p. 4; Crooks, *Politics and Progress*, p. 64.

44. "Governor's Message," *Baltimore Sun*, 1 January 1908, p. 2; "Message of Edwin Warfield, Governor of Maryland to the General Assembly at Its Regular Session, January 1908" (Baltimore: Geo. W. King Printing Co., 1908), pp. 25–26; "Mr. Straus Names 8," *Baltimore Sun*, 19 December 1907, p. 14; "Voting Test Discussed," *Baltimore Sun*, 24 December 1907, p. 12. For a list of those serving on the committee, see Kent, *Story of Maryland Politics*, p. 382.

45. "Suffrage Amendment," *Baltimore Sun*, 29 January 1908, p. 9; "Protested Vigorously," *Afro-American Ledger*, 15 February 1908, p. 1; Crooks, *Politics and Progress*, p. 64; Kent, *Story of Maryland Politics*, p. 382.

46. For general overviews, see Carle, *Defining the Struggle*, p. 119; Alexander, *Army of Lions*, pp. 284–294. On the Atlanta race riot, see David Fort Godshalk, *Veiled Visions: The 1906 Atlanta Race Riot and the Reshaping of American Race Relations* (Chapel Hill: University of North Carolina Press, 2005); Rebecca Burns, *Rage in the Gate City: The Story of the 1906 Atlanta Race Riot* (Athens: University of Georgia Press, 2009).

47. For more information on these two movements, see Alexander, *Army of Lions*.

48. J. Max Barber, "The Niagara Movement at Harpers Ferry," *Voice of the Negro* 3, no. 10 (October 1906): 404; George H. Jackson, "Niagara Movement List of Dues Paid by Member, ca. August 15, 1906," DuBois Papers. For the Baltimore chapter meeting of the Niagara Movement, see Niagara Movement (Organization), "Maryland Branch. Niagara Movement-Maryland Branch Annual Meeting Program, ca. February 1908," DuBois Papers.

49. On the founding of the DuBois Circle, see Minutes of the DuBois Circle, 22 January 1907. On school conditions, see Minutes of the DuBois Circle, 21 May 1907. On working as ushers, see Minutes of the DuBois Circle, 21 April 1908. On the lawsuit against the Pullman Company, see Minutes of the DuBois Circle, 19 May 1908. The Minutes of the DuBois Circle are courtesy of Beverly Carter and the DuBois Circle. It is most likely that this was the challenge spearheaded by Fredrick McGhee, a Niagara Movement attorney practicing in Saint Paul, Minnesota. Apparently, the case never went to court. See Paul D. Nelson, *Fredrick L. McGhee: A Life on the Color Line* (Saint Paul: Minnesota Historical Society, 2002), p. 164. For background on Foraker's statements, see Emma Lou Thornbrough, "The Brownsville Episode and the Negro Vote," *Mississippi Valley Historical Review* 44, no. 3 (December 1957): 469–493.

50. Richard Weightman, "Negro Vote in Maryland Issue in Campaign," *Chicago Daily Tribune*, 16 September 1905, p. 8. For the plank barring African Americans, see "Mr. Stone in Control," *Baltimore Sun*, 10 September 1905, p. 16; J. A., "Negro Ballot Issue," *Washington Post*, 5 November 1905, p. 3; Graham, "Can the Negro Settle It?" *Outlook* 84, no. 7 (13 October 1906): 365. On the Suffrage League meeting, see "Suffrage League Is Reorganized," *Afro-American Ledger*, 21 March 1908, p. 5.

51. "Constitution League Meets," *Afro-American Ledger*, 21 March 1908, p. 4.

52. "Uplifting the Afro-American," *Afro-American Ledger*, 2 October 1909, p. 4.

53. "About the City," *Afro-American Ledger*, 19 December 1908, p. 8. For the Colored Baptist Conventions, see "Minutes of the Eighth Annual Session of the Maryland Cooperative

Baptist State Convention," 16–19 June 1908, A. B. Koger Collection, Maryland State Archives (Baltimore: Press of the Guide Printing Co., 1909), pp. 20–21; "Minutes of the Twelfth Annual Session of the Colored Baptist Convention of the State of Maryland," 9–11 July 1909, A. B. Koger Collection, Maryland State Archives (Baltimore: Owl Printery, 1909), pp. 7–8.

54. "Bethel A.M.E. Church," *Afro-American Ledger*, 23 October 1909, p. 8; "Waters A.M.E. Church," *Afro-American Ledger*, 30 October 1909, p. 8. For the young men's meetings, see "Young Men to Hold Mass Meeting," *Afro-American Ledger*, 9 October 1909, p. 5; "Mass Meeting for Young Men by Young Men," *Afro-American Ledger*, 9 October 1905, p. 8. See also "Asbury M.E. Church," *Afro-American Ledger*, 16 October 1909, p. 8; "Come! Great Mass Meeting by Young Men," *Afro-American Ledger*, 23 October 1909, p. 4.

55. On Murphy, see "Y.W.C.A. Head Passes Away," *Afro-American Ledger*, 13 February 1915, p. 1. For Cummings, see "A Testimonial for Mrs. Eliza Cummings," *Afro-American Ledger*, 22 March 1913, p. 1. For Truxon, see "Old Normal Grad Is Buried," *Afro-American Ledger*, 2 May 1924, p. A8. For the quotation, see "What You Can Do," *Afro-American Ledger*, 16 October 1909, p. 4. For the practice of reading to illiterates, see Farrar, *Baltimore Afro-American*, p. 6.

56. "Mass Meeting and Call to Prayer," *Afro-American Ledger*, 25 September 1909; "Women in Fight Against Amendment," *Afro-American Ledger*, 2 October 1909, p. 4; "Third Mass Meeting and Call to Prayer by Women of Baltimore," *Afro-American Ledger*, 16 October 1909, p. 8; "Fifth Call to Prayer and Mass Meeting by Women of Baltimore," *Afro-American Ledger*, 23 October 1909, p. 4; Wm. Alexander, "Will We Let the Ballott [*sic*] Taken from Us," *Afro-American Ledger*, 15 July 1911, p. 4; "Women Hold Praise Service," *Afro-American Ledger*, 13 November 1909, p. 8. For the DuBois Circle, see Minutes of the DuBois Circle, 18 January 1910.

57. For the meetings, see "Suffrage League Holds Meeting," *Afro-American Ledger*, 18 September 1909, p. 8; "A Rousing Meeting at Sharp St. Church," *Afro-American Ledger*, 18 September 1909, p. 4. For the ad, see "To the Colored Men of Baltimore and the State of Maryland," *Afro-American Ledger*, 18 September 1909, p. 4.

58. The information on the school locations was found by cross-referencing "Suffrage League Open Voters Schools," *Afro-American Ledger*, 23 October 1909, p. 4, with the *Baltimore City Directory* for the Year Commencing April 1, 1909 (Baltimore: R. L. Polk & Co., 1909), pp. 209, 726, 856, 1027, 1054, 2111, and 2328. For the operating expenses associated with the schools, see "Suffrage League Accounts of the Campaign Audited," *Afro-American Ledger*, 20 November 1909, p. 4.

59. "96,246 Votes Counted," *Baltimore Sun*, 12 November 1909, p. 14; "Democrats Have Cause for Joy," *Baltimore Sun*, 4 November 1909, p. 1; "Untitled," *Afro-American Ledger*, 6 November 1909, p. 4.

60. "Five Laws Enacted," *Baltimore Sun*, 7 April 1910, p. 2.

61. "May Amend Digges Plan," *Baltimore Sun*, 31 March 1910, p. 1.

62. "Warning from South," *Baltimore Sun*, 8 April 1910, p. 1. For some of the views against the amendment, see "Senators Against It," *Baltimore Sun*, 28 March 1910, p. 5; "Mr. Baker Thinks It Foolish," *Baltimore Sun*, 8 April 1910, p. 1; "Democrats Deplore Action in Maryland," *New York Times*, 4 April 1910, p. 18; " 'Will Upset Government and Cause Chaos,' " *Baltimore Sun*, 7 April 1910, p. 1.

63. "Will Veto Digges Bill," *Washington Post*, 9 April 1910, p. 3.

64. "Ministers Waging Hot War on Amendment," *Afro-American Ledger*, 28 October 1911, p. 4. For the other meetings, see "Colored Men to the Front to Attend Mass Meetings," *Afro-American Ledger*, 28 October 1911, p. 4.

65. "A Blundering Policy," *Afro-American Ledger*, 14 October 1911, p. 4. On Lyon, see "Goldsborough and Victory the Slogan," *Afro-American Ledger*, 21 October 1911, p. 4. For the Colored Republican Auxiliary, see "Advertisement," *Afro-American Ledger*, 21 October 1911, p. 6.

66. "Women Will Help to Get Out Voters," *Afro-American Ledger*, 28 October 1911, p. 4; Franklin P. Johnson, "Voters Fight to Retain Ballot," *Broad Axe*, 11 November 1911, p. 3; "Along the Color Line," *Crisis* 3, no. 2 (December 1911): 53; "Untitled," *Afro-American Ledger*, 11 November 1911, p. 4.

67. "Have You Registered?" *Afro-American Ledger*, 7 October 1911, p. 4; "Three Amendments," *Afro-American Ledger*, 3 November 1911, p. 8.

68. "A Party of Progress," *Baltimore Sun*, 20 September 1907, p. 7.

69. See, for instance, "Not to Be Trusted," *Afro-American Ledger*, 9 September 1905, p. 3; "Untitled," *Afro-American Ledger*, 2 October 1909, p. 4; "Getting Together," *Afro-American Ledger*, 4 September 1909, p. 6. W. Ashbie Hawkins also made this contention. See W. Ashbie Hawkins, "The Forum," *Afro-American Ledger*, 2 October 1909, p. 4.

70. "Last Chance," *Afro-American Ledger*, 4 November 1905, p. 4; "Maryland's Grapple with the Demagogue," *Voice of the Negro* 2, no. 2 (November 1905): 748; "Three Times and Out," *Afro-American Ledger*, 11 November 1911, p. 4.

71. "Views of the Colored Suffrage League," *Baltimore Sun*, 20 April 1904, p. 7.

72. For women's suffrage, see "Ladies Discuss Suffrage," *Afro-American Ledger*, 25 November 1911, p. 4; Cynthia Neverdon-Morton, *Afro-American Women of the South and the Advancement of the Race, 1895–1925* (Knoxville: University of Tennessee Press, 1989), p. 177. For McGuinn, see "W. T. M'Guinn for Woman Suffrage," *Afro-American Ledger*, 2 December 1911, p. 4.

73. Farrar, *Baltimore Afro-American*, p. 5.

74. Baltimore Reform League, "Special Report of the Executive Committee to the Baltimore Reform League on the Poe Amendment," 19 April 1905, Maryland Historical Society, Baltimore; Baltimore Reform League, "Reject the Amendment," 1909, Maryland Historical Society; "Should Have Known Better," *Afro-American Ledger*, 11 November 1911, p. 4.

75. "Amendment Campaign," *Baltimore Sun*, 1 November 1909, p. 13; "An Opportune Moment," *Afro-American Ledger*, 2 December 1905, p. 4.

76. "The Way the Amendment Would 'Work,'" *Baltimore American*, 28 October 1905, p. 20.

77. "Colored Men Protest," *Baltimore Sun*, 29 March 1910, p. 10.

78. "Untitled," *Afro-American Ledger*, 11 September 1909, p. 4.

79. "Negroes Encroaching," *Baltimore Sun*, 27 October 1909, p. 9.

80. "Aid to Negro Invasion," *Baltimore Sun*, 30 October 1909, p. 15.

Chapter 6

1. The descriptions of events were culled from various reports. See "4 Shot in Race War," *Washington Post*, 1 October 1913, p. 1; "Negro Wounds 4 Boys," *Baltimore Sun*, 1 October 1913, p. 14; "Gets Jail Sentence for Defending His Home," *Afro-American Ledger*, 4 October 1913, p. 1; "Branches," *Crisis* 7, no. 3 (January 1914): 140.

2. "4 Shot in Race War," *Washington Post*, 1 October 1913, p. 1.

3. The literature dealing with early twentieth-century housing segregation is continually growing. See David M. Freund, *Colored Property: State Policy and White Racial Politics in Suburban America* (Chicago: University of Chicago Press, 2007); Joe William Trotter, Jr., *Black Milwaukee: The Making of an Industrial Proletariat, 1915–1945* (Urbana: University of Illinois Press, 2006); Douglass Massey and Nancy Denton, *American Apartheid: Segregation and the Making of the Underclass* (Cambridge, MA: Harvard University Press, 1993); David Delaney, *Race, Place, and the Law, 1836–1948* (Austin: University of Texas Press, 1998); Michael McGerr, *A Fierce Discontent: The Rise and Fall of the Progressive Movement in America, 1870–1920* (New York: Free Press, 2003).

4. For the most thorough overview of the segregation ordinances in Baltimore, see Garrett Power, "Apartheid Baltimore Style: The Residential Segregation Ordinances of 1910–1913," *Maryland Law Review* 42 (1983): 289–328; Gretchen Boger, "The Meaning of Neighborhood in the Modern City: Baltimore's Residential Segregation Ordinances, 1910–1913," *Journal of Urban History* 35, no. 2 (January 2009): 236–258. On the transnational dimensions, see Carl H. Nightingale, "The Transnational Contexts of Early Twentieth-Century American Urban Segregation," *Journal of Social History* 39, no. 3 (Spring 2006): 667–702. For a look at the segregation ordinances in Baltimore and other locations throughout the South, see Roger L. Rice, "Residential Segregation by Law, 1910–1917," *Journal of Southern History* 179 (1968): 179–199. A recent study by a former journalist for the *Baltimore Sun*, Antero Pietila, provides a longer history of race-based segregation in Baltimore. See Antero Pietila, *Not in My Neighborhood: How Bigotry Shaped a Great American City* (Chicago: Ivan R. Dee, 2010).

5. McGerr, *Fierce Discontent*, 183. While Garrett Power did not focus on the violence surrounding the passage of the West Ordinance, he correctly highlights the racism that underpinned the legislation. See Power, "Apartheid Baltimore Style," p. 289.

6. See McGerr, *Fierce Discontent*, pp. 182–184. Historians of Baltimore have not ignored the violence, but it has not been at the center of their analyses. See Pietila, *Not in My Neighborhood*; Power, "Apartheid Baltimore Style." For an examination of how many of these issues survived into the post–World War II United States, see Kevin M. Kruse, *White Flight: Atlanta and the Making of Modern Conservatism* (Princeton, NJ: Princeton University Press, 2007).

7. Paul A. Groves and Edward K. Muller, "The Evolution of Black Residential Areas in Late Nineteenth-Century Cities," *Journal of Historical Geography* 1, no. 2 (1975): 169–191.

8. W. Ashbie Hawkins, "A Year of Segregation in Baltimore," *Crisis* 3, no. 1 (November 1911): 27; Rhonda Y. Williams, *The Politics of Public Housing: Black Women's Struggles Against Urban Inequality* (New York: Oxford University Press, 2005), pp. 23–24.

9. Groves and Muller, "Evolution of Black Residential Areas"; Hawkins, "Year of Segregation in Baltimore," p. 27. Quotation from "A Social Problem in Baltimore," *Nation* 77, no. 2008 (24 December 1903): 497–498.

10. "A Social Problem in Baltimore."

11. Very Rev. John R. Slattery, "20 Years' Growth of the Colored People in Baltimore, MD," *Catholic World* 66, no. 394 (January 1898): 520–521.

12. "Colored Family Scared: Claim That Their House, on Druid Hill Avenue, Is Bombarded," *Baltimore Sun*, 1 September 1899, p. 7.

13. On Union Baptist, see "Fear for the School Girls," *Baltimore Sun*, 12 January 1901, p. 12. For Fannie Williams, see "Colored Family Unwelcome," *Baltimore Sun*, 5 May 1902,

p. 12. For Saint Paul's, see "Appreciate the Color Line," *Baltimore Sun*, 8 June 1903, p. 12; "Object to Colored School," *Baltimore Sun*, 10 September 1903, p. 6. Other incidents include "Indignant at School Board," *Baltimore Sun*, 15 July 1903, p. 6; "Section Is Up in Arms," *Baltimore Sun*, 16 July 1903, p. 12; "Will Hear Protests," *Baltimore Sun*, 17 July 1903, p. 12.

14. "Sale Raises a Storm," *Baltimore Sun*, 15 March 1906, p. 14; "Mr. Morton Annuls Sale," *Baltimore Sun*, 16 March 1906, p. 14.

15. "Will Oppose Negroes," *Baltimore Sun*, 6 April 1906, p. 12.

16. For a history of Baltimore's neighborhood improvement associations, see Joseph L. Arnold, "The Neighborhood and City Hall: The Origin of Neighborhood Associations in Baltimore, 1880–1911," *Journal of Urban History* 6, no. 1 (November 1979): 3–30; "Feared Negro Influx," *Baltimore Sun*, 1 November 1909, p. 12.

17. See Janet E. Kemp, *Housing Conditions in Baltimore* (New York: Arno Press, 1974), pp. 43–44. Other investigations offered similar observations, without deeper reflection of the root causes of these problems. Also see Helen B. Pendleton, "Negro Dependence in Baltimore," *Charities* 7, no. 1 (October 1905): 50–58. For a critical review of Kemp's research that has influenced my own reading, see Samuel Kelton Roberts, Jr., *Infectious Fear: Politics, Disease, and the Health Effects of Segregation* (Chapel Hill: University of North Carolina Press, 2009), pp. 128–130; Power, "Apartheid Baltimore Style," 292–297.

18. J. H. N. Waring, "Some Causes of Criminality Among Colored People," *Charities*, 7 October 1905, pp. 46–47; Booker T. Washington, "Law and Order and the Negro," *Outlook*, 6 November 1909, pp. 547–548; James H. N. Waring, "Work of the Colored Law and Order League: Baltimore, MD" (Cheney, PA: Committee of Twelve for the Advancement of the Interests of the Negro Race), p. 7.

19. Washington, "Law and Order and the Negro," p. 548.

20. Information culled from "Men of the Month," *Crisis* 8, no. 3 (July 1914): 117; Monroe N. Work, ed., *Negro Year Book: An Encyclopedia of the Negro, 1916–1917* (Tuskegee, AL: Negro Year Book Publishing Company, 1916), p. 4; "Hugh Burkett," *Afro-American Ledger*, 1 September 1922, p. 3.

21. "To Check Negro Invasion," *Baltimore Sun*, 27 September 1907, p. 9. In the early 1900s Weber was secretary of the Northwest Improvement Association and president of the Business Men's Association of Northwest Baltimore. The 1909 Baltimore city directory listed him as the secretary-treasurer of Peters Publishing and Printing Company. Biographical information on Weber culled from "Mr. F. C. Weber President," *Baltimore Sun*, 16 December 1908; *1909–1910 Baltimore Business Directory* (Baltimore: R. L. Polk & Co., 1909), p. 1298. My thinking on this has been influenced by Grace Elizabeth Hale, *Making Whiteness: The Culture of Segregation in the South, 1890–1940* (New York: Vintage, 1998). See also Robert H. Wiebe, *The Search for Order, 1877–1920* (New York: Hill & Wang, 1967).

22. "To Check Negro Invasion," *Baltimore Sun*, 27 September 1907, p. 9; "To Keep Out Negroes," *Baltimore Sun*, 8 November 1907, p. 9. For a brief history of the Harlem Improvement Association, see "Feared Negro Influx," *Baltimore Sun*, 1 November 1909, p. 12. Weber's arguments can be found in Frederick C. Weber, "The Negro Invasion in Northwest Baltimore," *Baltimore Sun*, 24 October 1907, p. 7.

23. "To Keep Out Negroes," *Baltimore Sun*, 8 November 1907, p. 9. For more on discourses of civilization in the late nineteenth and early twentieth centuries, see Gail Bederman, *Manliness and Civilization: A Cultural History of Gender and Race in the United States, 1880–1917* (Chicago: University of Chicago Press, 1996).

24. Colonel Peters is quoted in "Called Blacks Undesirables," *Baltimore Sun*, 25 October 1907, p. 14. Biographical information from "Winfield Peters Dead," *Baltimore Sun*, 19 July 1918, p. 14. Quotation from Bracken in W. J. Bracken, "Negro Invasion of Northwest Baltimore," *Baltimore Sun*, 3 October 1907, p. 7. See also Weber, "Negro Invasion in Northwest Baltimore," p. 7.

25. For instance, see Weber, "Negro Invasion in Northwest Baltimore," p. 7; "To Keep Out Negroes," p. 9; "Restricted Residence Area for Colored Families," *Baltimore Sun*, 14 November 1907, p. 7; "Bar Against Negroes," *Baltimore Sun*, 5 February 1909, p. 12.

26. Hawkins, "Year of Segregation in Baltimore," p. 27; "Baltimore Tries Drastic Plan of Race Segregation," *New York Times*, 25 December 1910, p. SM2. Historian Carl H. Nightingale points out that the Hawkins house sat in one of Baltimore's more exclusive neighborhoods. Nightingale, "Transnational Contexts," p. 673.

27. "Baltimore Tries Drastic Plan of Race Segregation," *New York Times*, 25 December 1910, p. SM2; "Negro Homes Stoned," *Baltimore Sun*, 9 September 1910, p. 14.

28. Biographical information about Hawkins can be found in "Ashbie Hawkins, Attorney for 50 Years, Dies at 78," *Afro-American*, 12 April 1941, p. 18. On Hawkins's expulsion from the Maryland law school, see "Drawing the Color Line," *Daily Inter Ocean*, 15 September 1890, p. 2.

29. For a longer look at the Pope case, see Susan D. Carle, *Defining the Struggle: National Organizing for Racial Justice, 1880–1915* (New York: Oxford University Press, 2013). For Hawkins's involvement in the case, see W. E. B. (William Edward Burghardt) DuBois, 1868–1963, "Niagara Movement Membership Letter No. 4, April 10, 1907," W. E. B. DuBois Papers (MS 312), Special Collections and University Archives, University of Massachusetts Amherst Libraries (hereafter DuBois Papers). On the Johnson suit, see "About the City," *Afro-American Ledger*, 19 January 1907, p. 8. For mention of Hawkins's early work with the NAACP, see Mary White Ovington, "How the National Association for the Advancement of Colored People Began," *Crisis* 8, no. 4 (1914): 184–188; Carle, *Defining the Struggle*, p. 264.

30. For some of Hawkins's transactions, see Baltimore City Superior Court, Land Records, Grantee Index 1909, H–O, pp. 12, 14; Baltimore City Superior Court, Land Records, Grantee Index 1910, H–O, pp. 3, 14, 16, 26; Baltimore City Superior Court, Land Records, Grantor Index 1910, H–O, pp. 2, 3, 16, 18, 30, all available at Maryland State Archives, Annapolis. Quotation taken from "Baltimore," *Crisis* 1, no. 1 (November 1910): 11.

31. See Arnold, "The Neighborhood and City Hall." In years previous, Mahool spoke at the Northwestern Improvement Association's banquets, in addition to those of other improvement associations. See, for instance, "Northwesterners Feast," *Baltimore Sun*, 12 February 1908; "Mayor for Bay Bridge," *Baltimore Sun*, 10 February 1909, p. 12.

32. Information culled from Power, "Apartheid Baltimore Style," pp. 299–301; Boger, "Meaning of Neighborhood," pp. 237–238; Nightingale, "Transnational Contexts," pp. 672–673.

33. Hawkins, "Year of Segregation in Baltimore," p. 28; "Baltimore Tries Drastic Plan of Race Segregation," *New York Times*, 25 December 1910, p. SM2. See also Power, "Apartheid Baltimore Style," 299.

34. Boger, "Meaning of Neighborhood," p. 238; *The Ordinances of the Mayor and City Council of Baltimore* (Baltimore: Meyer & Thalheimer, 1911), p. 294; "A New York View of the West Ordinance," *Baltimore Sun*, 28 November 1910, 6.

35. For the Harlem Improvement Association, see "Bar Against Negroes," *Baltimore Sun*, 5 February 1909, p. 12. For Poe, see "Baltimore Tries Drastic Plan of Race Segregation," *New York Times*, 25 December 1910, p. SM2.

36. 1800 Block, "Plea for the West Ordinance with Some Remarks on the 'White Man's Burden,'" *Baltimore Sun*, 2 October 1910, p. 6; Harvey H. Wilson, "Negro Invasion of White Neighborhoods Has Direct Influence on the Tax Rate," *Baltimore Sun*, 10 September 1910, p. 6; Republican, "From the People," *Baltimore Sun*, 31 August 1910, p. 6.

37. This was the only exemption written into the four versions of the law. See *Ordinances and Resolutions of the Mayor and City Council of Baltimore*, "Ordinance 654" (Baltimore: Meyer & Thalheimer, 1911), p. 294. "Baltimore Tries Drastic Plan of Race Segregation," *New York Times*, 25 December 1910, p. SM2; "Except Servants," *Crisis* 1, no. 3 (January 1911): 21. My thoughts on the nature of segregation have been influenced by Hale, *Making Whiteness*, and Jennifer Ritterhouse, *Growing Up Jim Crow: How Black and White Children Learned Race* (Chapel Hill: University of North Carolina Press, 2006). See also Robin D. G. Kelley, "'We Are Not What We Seem': Rethinking Black Working-Class Opposition in the Jim Crow South," *Journal of American History* 80, no. 1 (June 1993): 75–112; Tera W. Hunter, *To 'Joy My Freedom: Southern Black Women's Lives and Labors After the Civil War* (Cambridge, MA: Harvard University Press, 1997).

38. Hawkins, "Year of Segregation in Baltimore," pp. 27–30. On Hamer, see "Negro Homes Stoned," *Baltimore Sun*, 9 September 1910, p. 14. For the McMechens' quotations, see "Baltimore Tries Drastic Plan of Race Segregation," *New York Times*, 25 December 1910, p. SM2.

39. "Object to Living Near Respectable Negroes," *Afro-American Ledger*, 1 October 1910, p. 1.

40. "Negroes Rap West Plan," *Baltimore Sun*, 25 October 1910, p. 10; "Colored Men Protest Against Passage of West Ordinance," *Afro-American Ledger*, 8 October 1910, p. 4. For Waller's quotation, see Rev. G. R. Waller, "The Color Problem of Baltimore," Annual Conference Speeches, 2nd Session, May 1914, Papers of the NAACP, Library of Congress, Washington, DC, p. 5.

41. "Untitled," *Crisis* 1, no. 4 (February 1911): 19–20.

42. "Colored Men Protest Against Passage of West Ordinance," *Afro-American Ledger*, 8 October 1910, p. 4. For other protests, see "Monthly Meeting at Grace Presbyterian Church," *Afro-American Ledger*, 22 October 1910, p. 8; "The Segregation Act," *Afro-American Ledger*, 26 November 1910, p. 4. For other editorials critical of the law, see "Why?" *Afro-American Ledger*, 17 December 1910, p. 4; "Why Not Quit Treating Him as a 'Problem,'" *Afro-American Ledger*, 10 December 1910, p. 4.

43. Will G. McGintie to Mayor James H. Preston, James H. Preston Files, Baltimore City Archives; Mayor Joel H. Cutchin to Mayor J. Barry Mahool, 5 November 1910, J. Barry Mahool Files, Baltimore City Archives; Lorenzo G. Warfield to Mayor James H. Preston, 26 September 1913, James H. Preston Files, Baltimore City Archives. See also "St. Louis Wants Segregation Act," *Baltimore Sun*, 7 October 1913, p. 3; "Race Issue Up to Court," *Baltimore Sun*, 28 April 1917, p. 2; "Segregation," *Crisis* 15, no. 2 (December 1917): 69.

44. On the measure becoming law, see "Signs Segregation Law," *New York Times*, 20 December 1910, p. 1; W. Ashbie Hawkins, "Must Fight West Segregation Law," *Afro-American Ledger*, 24 December 1910, p. 4.

45. "West Law Defective," *Baltimore Sun*, 4 February 1911, p. 12. The judges cited a number of problems with the law, including its vaguely stated purpose and its proviso that allowed African American servants to be exempt from the law.

46. "West Segregation Law Still Causing Trouble Among Baltimore's Solons," *Afro-American Ledger*, 14 January 1911, p. 5; "Commissioners Halt the Police," *Afro-American Ledger*, 4 February 1911, p. 5; "West Test Case Saturday," *Baltimore Sun*, 25 January 1911, p. 14. See also Power, "Apartheid Baltimore Style," pp. 301–302.

47. "Negro Invasion Feared," *Baltimore Sun*, 12 May 1913, p. 14; "Eutaw Place Threatened by Negro Invasion Now," *Baltimore Sun*, 15 May 1913, p. 14.

48. Anonymous letter to Mayor James H. Preston, 1 May [year unknown], James H. Preston Files, Baltimore City Archives; C. E. Stonebraker to James H. Preston, 12 May 1913, Baltimore City Archives; Donnelly, "The Segregation Outlook," *Baltimore Sun*, 17 July 1913, p. 6; "Are the White People to Be Driven Out of Baltimore?" newspaper clipping, n.d., Baltimore City Archives.

49. J. L. Blake letter to the editor of the *Sun*, n.d., James H. Preston Files, Baltimore City Archives. This letter was eventually published in "Letters to the Editor," *Baltimore Sun*, 17 August 1913, p. 6. For another example of citizens becoming frustrated with the lack of official action, see Hannibal, "Making the Map of Baltimore Look Like a Sheet of 'Tanglefoot,'" *Baltimore Sun*, 2 September 1913, p. 6.

50. A. J. Reilly to Mayor James H. Preston, 16 June 1913, pp. 3–4, James H. Preston Files, Baltimore City Archives; Indignant, "Letter to the Editor," *Baltimore Sun*, 16 June 1913, p. 6. Reilly also wrote this letter, which she included with her communication to the mayor. See also "Baltimore Doomed!" *Baltimore Sun*, 6 September 1913, p. 6; "The Harlem Improvement Association of West Baltimore," 12 June 1913, p. 3, Baltimore City Archives.

51. On the delay in crafting a new law, see "Not to Hurry Segregation," *Baltimore Sun*, 24 August 1913, p. 12; "Negro in White Block," *Baltimore Sun*, 21 August 1913, p. 12; "More Negro Invasion," *Baltimore Sun*, 22 August 1913, p. 12; "Negro Family Moves In," *Baltimore Sun*, 7 September 1913, p. 12; "Negro Invasion Grows," *Baltimore Sun*, 14 June 1913, p. 16.

52. See, for example, "The Negro Invasion of White Neighborhoods," *Baltimore Sun*, 19 June 1913, p. 6; "While the Segregation Ordinance Waits the Negro Moves," *Baltimore Sun*, 10 June 1913, p. 8; "A Resident of the 700 Block of West Lanvale Street Shows the Character of the Section Endangered by Negro Invasion," *Baltimore Sun*, 24 September 1913, p. 6.

53. "Negro House Attacked," *Baltimore Sun*, 19 September 1913, p. 14.

54. "To Demand Quick Action," *Baltimore Sun*, 20 September 1913, p. 16. The accounts of violence were taken from "Negro Homes Stoned; Four Persons Hurt," *Baltimore Sun*, 26 September 1913, p. 14; "5 Injured in a Near-Riot," *Afro-American Ledger*, 27 September 1913, p. 8.

55. "One Shot; One Stabbed," *Baltimore Sun*, 27 September 1913, p. 16.

56. "One Shot; One Stabbed," p. 16. For Shipley, see "Along the Color Line," *Crisis*, December 1913, p. 64.

57. "Gets Jail Sentence for Defending His Home," *Afro-American Ledger*, 4 October 1913, p. 1; "4 Shot in Race War," *Washington Post*, 1 October 1913, p. 1; "Favors Segregation but Acquits Offender," *Afro-American Ledger*, 15 November 1913, p. 6. For Hawkins's quotation, see clipping found in Lucy D. Slowe, "Secretary's Report of the Baltimore Branch N.A.A.C.P. for the Year Ending May 1, 1914," Annual Conference Speeches, 2nd Session, May 1914, Papers of the NAACP, Library of Congress, Washington, DC.

58. W. Ashbie Hawkins, "Must Fight West Segregation Law," *Afro-American Ledger*, 24 December 1910, p. 4; "First Blow Against the West Ordinance," *Afro-American Ledger*, 31 December 1910, p. 4.

59. On the Gurry case, see "Attorney Hawkins to Test Segregation Law," *Afro-American*, 12 August 1911, p. 8; "Segregation Ordinance Test," *Baltimore Sun*, 11 October 1912, p. 14; "Reserves Opinion in Segregation Case," *Baltimore Sun*, 12 October 1912, p. 1. On Howe, see "Favors Segregation but Acquits Offender," *Afro-American Ledger*, 15 November 1913, p. 8.

60. "The N.A.A.C.P. and the Segregation Law," *Afro-American Ledger*, 12 October 1912, p. 4; Oswald Garrison Villard, "Segregation in Baltimore and Washington," published speech, Baltimore, October 20, 1913, copy held at Library of Congress, Washington, DC; "Reviving the Abolition Spirit," *Afro-American Ledger*, 25 October 1913, p. 1; "Against Race Segregation," *Baltimore Sun*, 21 October 1913, p. 5.

61. "A Peaceful Rebellion," *Afro-American Ledger*, 1 November 1913, p. 4. For the NAACP report, see "Minutes of the Meeting of the Board of Directors," October 7, 1913, Papers of the NAACP, Library of Congress, Washington, DC, p. 2.

62. "Baltimore Tries Drastic Plan of Race Segregation," *New York Times*, 25 December 1910, p. SM2. On Blanchard, see "Negro House Assailed," *Baltimore Sun*, 15 March 1911, p. 10. In one instance, a black family moved out after repeated incidents of violence. The family at 828 Stricker Street moved, but only after whites in the neighborhood paid their moving expenses, a month's worth of rent, and a fifty-dollar bonus. See "Negroes Move Away," *Baltimore Sun*, 28 September 1913, p. 3. On Hamer, see "Negro Homes Stoned," *Baltimore Sun*, 9 September 1910, p. 14.

63. "More Trouble with Segregation Law," *Afro-American Ledger*, 7 January 1911, p. 4.

64. "Segregation Is Roundly Scored," *Afro-American Ledger*, 17 October 1914, p. 1; "Segregation Law to Be Tested," *Afro-American Ledger*, 3 October 1914, p. 4; "Rally for Segregation Test," *Afro-American Ledger*, 31 October 1914, p. 1; "The N.A.A.C.P. and the Segregation Law," *Afro-American Ledger*, 12 October 1912, p. 4; "Local Branch of National Association Assists in Segregation Fight," *Afro-American Ledger*, 28 June 1913, p. 4; "Segregation in Appeals Court Next Week," *Afro-American Ledger*, 21 June 1913, p. 1; "Testimonial to Attorney Hawkins," *Afro-American Ledger*, 10 May 1913, p. 1. The *Crisis* reported that African Americans raised $230 but did not provide specifics. See "Along the Color Line," *Crisis* 7, no. 2 (December 1913): 64.

65. Slowe, "Secretary's Report."

66. "Dr. Young Will Expect All to Help," *Afro-American Ledger*, 6 December 1913, p. 1; "The Ghetto," *Crisis*, February 1914, p. 170.

67. "Economic Results of Baltimore's Segregation," *Afro-American Ledger*, 11 October 1913, p. 1; "Must Combat All Repressive Measures," *Afro-American Ledger*, 4 October 1913, p. 1.

68. The cartoons were published beginning with the 27 September 1913 issue of the *Afro-American Ledger*. In each instance the illustration was given top billing on the paper's first page. See, in sequential order, "Civilization as It Is Understood in America," *Afro-American Ledger*, 27 September 1913, p. 1; "They Will Want His Shirt Next," *Afro-American Ledger*, 4 October 1913, p. 1; "Advertising Baltimore by the New Ad Club—City Council and Police Department," *Afro-American Ledger*, 11 October 1913, p. 1; "He Will Eventually Break Loose and Reach the Top," *Afro-American Ledger*, 25 October 1913, p. 1.

69. The law was named for its legislative sponsor, Francis P. Curtis. "Segregation Case Argued," *Baltimore Sun*, 2 April 1915, p. 4; "Segregation Act Held Valid," *Baltimore Sun*, 8

April 1915, p. 5; "Segregation Law to Go to Court of Appeals," *Baltimore Sun*, 21 April 1915, p. 6; "Waiting on the Supreme Court," *Baltimore Sun*, 18 March 1916, p. 1.

70. "Victory," *Crisis* 15, no. 2 (December 1917): 61; W. Ashbie Hawkins, "Letter from W. Ashbie Hawkins to W. E. B. DuBois," November 30, 1917, DuBois Papers.

71. "New Segregation Bill," *Baltimore Sun*, 6 November 1917, p. 7. On the arrests, see "Segregation Case to Jury," *Baltimore Sun*, 8 November 1917, p. 5; "Resent Negro Invasion," *Baltimore Sun*, 18 November 1917, p. 9.

72. "Segregation in U.S. Court," *Baltimore Sun*, 24 November 1917, p. 1; "Rules Out Segregation," *Baltimore Sun*, 5 December 1917, p. 5. On Jackson's case, see "Segregation Act Invalid," *Baltimore Sun*, 28 February 1918, p. 5; "Segregation in Baltimore Gets Final Interment," *Afro-American Ledger*, 1 March 1918, p. 1.

73. "Letter from Alice J. Reilly to Mayor Preston," 22 June 1918, James H. Preston Files, Baltimore City Archives. Prior to this response, Preston had responded to other letter writers stating that, while in sympathy with them, he had no power to act. For a few examples, see "Letter from Mayor Preston's Office to Bertha M. Gunther," 22 April 1918, and "Letter from Mayor Preston's Office to Katherine Bald," 4 June 1918, James H. Preston Files, Baltimore City Archives. For Preston's response, see "Letter from Mayor Preston to Alice J. Reilly," 24 June 1918, James H. Preston Files, Baltimore City Archives; "Confer on Segregation," *Baltimore Sun*, 22 March 1918, p. 6.

74. The contracts were based on recently codified restrictions used in the suburbs of Roland Park and Guilford. See "Bars Against Negroes," *Baltimore Sun*, 25 November 1919, p. 22; "Home Owners Make Combine," *Afro-American*, 28 November 1919, p. A1. The Circuit Court in Baltimore upheld the contracts in 1924. See "Segregation Case Is Again in Court," *Afro-American*, 31 October 1931, p. 16; "Segregation by Contract Is Held Valid," *Afro-American*, 29 November 1924, p. A12.

75. "Judge Stanton Scores Whites," *Afro-American*, 24 September 1920, p. 12. For an analysis of the power of neighborhood protective associations in Detroit in the post–World War II years, see Thomas J. Sugrue, *The Origins of the Urban Crisis: Race and Inequality in Postwar Detroit* (Princeton, NJ: Princeton University Press, 1996).

Conclusion

1. "Name It Alexander," *Afro-American*, 18 April 1919, p. A4.

2. "Dr. H. J. Brown Buried Monday," *Afro-American*, 16 July 1920, p. 2; "Was Member of Committee of 100," *Afro-American*, 16 July 1920, p. 4. On Johnson's death, see "Dr. Johnson Buried," *Afro-American*, 19 January 1923, p. 1. On Alexander, see "Name It Alexander," *Afro-American*, 18 April 1919, p. 4. The quotation about Johnson appears in "Dr. Harvey Johnson," *Afro-American*, 19 January 1923, p. 9.

3. "Dr. Harvey Johnson," *Afro-American*, 19 January 1923, p. 9.

4. "Police Bring Peace to Union Baptist Meet," *Afro-American*, 3 March 1920, p. 10; "Union Baptist Votes Pastor Out 266–193," *Afro-American*, 17 March 1928, p. 10.

5. "Great Church, Formerly North St., Has Had Only 8 Pastors," *Afro-American*, 31 October 1931, p. 23.

6. W. Ashbie Hawkins, "Report of Attorney," Secretary's Report of the Baltimore Branch N.A.A.C.P. for the Year Ending May 1, 1914, Papers of the NAACP, Library of Congress, Washington, DC, pp. 7–8.

INDEX

Pages numbers in italics indicate illustrations. Churches are located in Baltimore unless otherwise noted.

Democratic Party: (*continued*)
  disfranchisement efforts by, 34–37, 113,
  116–19, 126, 131, 134, 137–38
Detroit Plaindealer (newspaper), 83
Digges, Walter M., 134
Digges Amendment, 114, 134–41
discrimination. *See* segregation and
  discrimination
disfranchisement efforts, 9, 114–43; black Baltimorean activism against, 114–15, 119–28,
  130–43; church activism against, 119–20,
  135–36; defeats of, 127, 134, 136–37; Democratic Party's role in, 116–19, 126, 131, 134,
  137–38; national, 116, 118; national activism
  against, 123–25; race as factor in resistance
  to, 140–41, *142*; violence associated with,
  130–31; women's activism against, 124–26,
  132–33, 136–37, 139
Dixon, Catherine, 167
Dobbin, George W., 44
Dobler, John J., 95
domestic workers, 124–25, 146. *See also*
  servants
Douglass, Frederick, 1–3, 7, 11–12, 15, 26, 114
Douglass Institute, 11–12, 16, 25, 29, 32, 37, 38,
  54, 69, 77
Dred Scott case, 48, 86
Drenford, George, 112
Driscoll, Thomas B., 73–74
Druid Hill, Lower Druid Hill, and Upper
  Druid Hill, Baltimore, 106, 146–53
DuBois, W. E. B., 7, 105, 115, 123, 140, 155, 174,
  179; *Some Notes on Negro Crime, Especially
  in Georgia*, 97
DuBois Circle, 129, 133, 139
Duffy, Edward, 44, 73–74

Eastern ME Church, 133
Ebenezer AME Church, 41, 81, 120
Eckstine, John, 58
education: of African Americans, 13–14,
  27–31; in antebellum period, 13–14; black
  activism concerning, 26–31; black opportunities in, 13, 26–27, 31, 76–80, 177;
  church-administered, 13–14, 30–31, 76;
  conditions and facilities for, 30, 31, 76, 80;
  segregation/discrimination in, 30, 79–80.
  See also public education; voter education
electoral politics, black Baltimoreans and,
  34–40, 43–46, 98. *See also* political power,
  of African Americans

Elliott, Thomas Ireland, 105, 163
employment. *See* labor and employment
Ensor, J. T., 87–88
Equal Protection Clause, 47, 54, 58, 74
Everhart, George Y., 118

Field, S. S., 174
Fields, John W., 21
Fifteenth Amendment, 1–2, 2, 6, 33, 37, 66,
  118, 134, 138
Fifth Baptist Church, Washington, DC, 84
First Baptist Church, 69, 120
First Branch City Council, 158
First Colored Baptist Church, 67–68
Fisher, Caesar, 82
Fisher, William A., 44
Foraker, Joseph B., 130
Fortune, T. Thomas, 4, 7, 40, 47, 55, 66, 90,
  153, 179
Fourteenth Amendment, 6, 16, 33, 37, 40, 47,
  53–56, 58, 60, 63, 66, 72–73, 74, 138
franchise. *See* disfranchisement efforts; vot-
  ing rights
Francis, Edmund, 81
Francis, William H., 29
Frederick Daily News (newspaper), 62
Freedman's Savings Bank, 1
Freedmen's Bureau, 27, 41
Frere, William J., 134
Fugitive Slave Act (1850), 48

Gailbraith Lyceum, 27
Gaines, A. L., 129
Gaines, Minnie L., 129
Galveston Daily News (newspaper), 83
Gans, A. L., 159
Gans, Edgar H., 72
Garey, Henry F., 44
Garnet, Henry Highland, 114
Garrison, William Lloyd, 13, 167
Gaskins, Dennis, 50
German Lutheran Church, 96
Giles, William Fells, 20, 21, 53, 187n34
Gilmor, Robert, Jr., 44
Goldsborough, Phillips Lee, 110, 137
Gorman, Arthur Pue, 34, 92, 103, 117, 118, 126,
  128
Grace Presbyterian Church, 132, 168
Graham, Robert B., 84
grandfather clause, 118, 128

Metropolitan Colored Methodist Episcopal Church, 63
MEU. *See* Maryland Educational Union
Miles, Alonzo L., 101
Milwaukee Daily Journal (newspaper), 83
Ministerial Alliance, 159
Mitchell, Clarence, 182
Mitchell, John, Jr., 66
mobility restrictions, 17–21, 40, 46–54, 122, 130, 145, 155
Morris, C. J., 52–53
Morton, Charles, 172
Moxley, Lucinda, 72
Mumford, Kevin, 203n32
Murphy, John H., 44, 136, 159
Mutual United Brotherhood of Liberty, 50, 65–91; Bastardy Act challenged by, 71–76; educational reform promoted by, 76–80; founding of, 3, 8, 65, 66, 71, 179; historical sources on, 4; impact of, 65–66, 89–90; on legal rulings, 47–48; and Navassa Island laborers, 80–89; overview of, 3–4; sociocultural context for, 66–71; women's contributions to, 3, 8, 89
Myers, Isaac, 22–26, 33–34, 39–40, 45, 67
Myers, W. E., 38
Myers, William Starr, 6

NAACP. *See* National Association for the Advancement of Colored People
Nation (journal), 146–47
National Association for the Advancement of Colored People (NAACP), 4, 7, 8, 69, 90, 115–16, 137, 140, 145, 155, 167, 168, 173–74
National Colored Labor Union (NCLU), 25–26
National Convention of Colored Men, 33
National Labor Union (NLU), 25–26
Navassa Island laborers, 4, 65, 80–89
Navassa Phosphate Company, 80–89
Naylor, H. Louis, 57
"negro disorder," 9, 93, 95, 98, 102
"negro domination," 100–101, 116–17, 127
"negro invasions," 145, 151–52, 157, 163, 164, 166
"negro menace," 157
"negro rowdyism," 9, 93, 95, 101, 102, 104, 105, 108
"negro ruffianism," 99, 101
"negro rule," 100

"negro toughs," 95
neighborhood associations, 148, 151, 155, 175–76
Neighborhood Corporation, 175
Neighborhood Improvement Association, 151
Nelson, James, 144
New England Freedman's Association, 29
New National Era (newspaper), 26, 37
New Orleans Daily Picayune (newspaper), 83
newspapers. *See* press
Newton Seminary, 69
Newton University, 11
New York Age (newspaper), 86–87
New York Evening Post (newspaper), 167
New York Freeman (newspaper), 76, 77, 90
New York Globe (newspaper), 55, 66, 67, 153, 155
New York Times (newspaper), 6, 35, 36, 80, 81, 83, 88, 153
Niagara Movement, 4, 7, 8, 66, 69, 90, 115, 123, 127, 129, 133, 140, 155
night school: for general education, 77; for voter education, 133–34, 136
Nineteenth Amendment, 138
Normal School, 28, 77, 79

Oblate Sisters of Providence, 14, 31
Old School Presbyterian, 29
Orchard Street Colored Church, 28
Order of Galilean Fishermen, 85
Order of Regulators, 43
Over, David E., 178
Ovington, Mary White, 167

Pairpoint, Alfred J., 5
Patterson Avenue Church School, 76
Payne, Charles M., 12
Payne, Daniel, 14
Pennsylvania Freedmen's Relief Association, 27
People's Advocate (newspaper), 66
Perkins Square Baptist Church, 120, 125
Perry, Calbreath B., 31
Peters, Stephen, 82
Peters, Winfield, 151–52
Phelps, Charles E., 44
Philadelphia, Wilmington, and Baltimore Railroad Company, 18
Philadelphia Inquirer (newspaper), 127
Philadelphia Press (newspaper), 17

ACKNOWLEDGMENTS

This book has been more than ten years in the making. Over that time I have incurred debts too numerous to pay. Although writing and research are most often solitary endeavors, I could not have finished this book without a remarkable community of friends, family, colleagues, and mentors.

My experience at the University of South Florida shaped my thinking in numerous ways. At USF, I was lucky to work with a number of dynamic historians who opened my eyes to the possibilities of studying the past. Robert P. Ingalls became a good friend and supporter. In addition, Fraser M. Ottanelli, Barbara Berglund, and Giovanna Benadusi offered advice and support, and they pushed me to think deeper about history. The conversations I have had with all of them, made me a much better thinker, writer, and historian. Jared G. Toney became a great friend, collaborator, and writer. The many conversations that we shared over the years have left an indelible mark on my own scholarship. I would also like to extend special thanks to the late Ward A. Stavig, to whom I am dedicating this book. Ward was a fantastic scholar and the first to encourage me to pursue a career in academia. I am certain that Ward never knew the impact that that talk had on me, yet his words meant the world to me as I was still trying to find my way.

The further away I get from my time at Rutgers, the more I appreciate my experience there. Alison Isenberg shaped this project from the outset. She continuously pushed me to rethink my assumptions and sharpen my writing. She was an expert at helping me unearth new sources and develop my ideas. Ann Fabian asked questions that I would have never thought of on my own. In answering them, my book expanded in directions I had not thought possible. Nancy Hewitt is a model academic. Not only was I fortunate enough to draw on her vast knowledge of race, gender, and activism in the nineteenth century, but she is also one of the most generous scholars I know. Donna Murch was able to see facets of my story that took me too long to figure out. I eventually got there, but I would not have been able to arrive at this moment without her keen insights. Finally, Mary P. Ryan provided invaluable advice and support and introduced me to her own talented students researching Baltimore's past. I was truly fortunate to have such wonderful scholars to guide this project. Although this book looks vastly different from its original form, their collective influence is evident on every page.

Numerous others at Rutgers contributed greatly to my professional development. Paul G. E. Clemens graciously volunteered to read portions of my manuscript and offered numerous helpful comments that have sharpened my arguments and prose. Camilla Townsend, Donald Roden, and Steven F. Lawson have shaped my teaching and scholarship. I would also like to thank Paul Israel, Louis Carlat, Rachel Weissenburger, Daniel Weeks, and Alexandra Rimer at the Thomas A. Edison Papers for their help and support. I would be remiss if I did not also thank Dawn Ruskai and Candace Walcott-Shepherd, who patiently helped me navigate the Rutgers bureaucracy.

My time at Rutgers was made all the more enjoyable by a wonderful community of friends. A special thank-you to Dina Fainberg, Zohar Manor-Abel, Tal Zalmanovich, Bridget Gurtler, Nicholas Trajano Molnar, Dora Vargha, Amir Mane, Steven D. Allen, and Kristoffer Shields for providing a crucial support network and being good friends. Tricia Hampson and Shannon D. Williams read early drafts of this project, provided sharp critiques, and helped me develop my arguments. Kara Murphy Schlichting patiently read every chapter in this book, offered helpful suggestions to refine my arguments, asked questions that I somehow missed or took for granted, and played a pivotal role in getting this book to completion.

At Virginia Tech, I have found a home with a group of supportive scholars. Thanks to Mark V. Barrow, Jr., for his assistance over the years. Paul Quigley has become a valuable collaborator, friend, and mentor. I want to extend a special note of gratitude to Peter Potter, who helped me find a home for my book and navigate the publishing world. I have also found a wonderful community of friends who have made adjusting to life in Virginia much easier. I am grateful to Carmen Gitre, Edward J. K. Gitre, Ladale Winling, Petra Rivera-Rideau, Ryan Rideau, Helen Schneider, Brett L. Shadle, Matthew Heaton, Danna Agmon, and Kathleen Jones for their friendship.

In Maryland, I have met many people passionate about Baltimore's past. In particular, I would like to thank the staff at the Enoch Pratt Free Public Library, the Maryland Historical Society, and the Maryland State Archives. Debbie Harner at the Maryland Historical Society has been especially helpful in locating sources in their vast holdings. Rev. Al Hathaway and Evelyn Chatmon at Union Baptist Church welcomed me with open arms and helped me track down sources related to their church and Harvey Johnson. My thanks as well to Rev. Raphael Koikoi at Sharp Street Methodist Church for helping me access the church's archival holdings. William Barry, Joseph W. Bennett, and George W. Liebmann provided me with opportunities to share my research. Beverly and John Carter opened their home to me at the last minute to view the DuBois Circle records and talk Baltimore history.

Numerous institutions have generously supported my research. I was able to get a head start on my research thanks to the Lord Baltimore Fellowship at the Maryland Historical Society and funding from the Andrew W. Mellon Foundation. I am appreciative as well to Virginia Tech, Rutgers University, and the Rutgers Center for Historical Analysis for funding.

I am also grateful to the anonymous readers at the University of Pennsylvania Press. Their comments and suggestions made a significant impact on the framing and arguments in this book. I would like to extend a special note of thanks to my editor, Bob Lockhart, for his help and guidance. From our first meeting, Bob understood exactly what I wanted to do with my book, and each step of the way he made it possible for me to realize that vision.

My family has been a constant source of love and support throughout these years. Thank you to my late grandparents, James and Rita Halpin. My late maternal grandmother, Elizabeth Hemsch, always encouraged me to keep up my work and push myself further. Thank you to my siblings—Jeff, Keri, Andy, and Ashley—and their families. Many thanks as well to my aunts and uncles, Jan and Jim Halpin and Renata and Tim Halpin, for their support. Finally, my parents, Ken and Dee Halpin, deserve an acknowledgment section of their own. Even when I did not want to continue my studies, they always emphasized the importance of an education. When I belatedly dove into academia with both feet, they were there to encourage and support me throughout this long journey.

Finally, Melanie A. Kiechle has been there from the start, weathering the ups and downs of writing, researching, and teaching. Even while authoring her own exceptional book, she took the time to read numerous drafts, encourage me, listen to my complaints, and reassure and push me. It is impossible to express how much all of this has meant to me, but please know that I am eternally grateful. This book would not have been possible without your love and support.